The Coming of
the First World War

The Coming of
the First World War

Edited by
R. J. W. Evans
and
Hartmut Pogge von Strandmann

CLARENDON PRESS · OXFORD

Oxford University Press, Walton Street, Oxford OX2 6DP

Oxford New York Toronto
Delhi Bombay Calcutta Madras Karachi
Petaling Jaya Singapore Hong Kong Tokyo
Nairobi Dar es Salaam Cape Town
Melbourne Auckland

and associated companies in
Berlin Ibadan

Oxford is a trade mark of Oxford University Press

Published in the United States
by Oxford University Press, New York

British Library Cataloguing in Publication Data
The Coming of the First World War.
1. World War 1. Causes
I. Evans, R. J. W. (Robert John Weston)
II. Pogge von Strandmann, H. (Hartmut)
940.3'11
ISBN 0-19-822841-4

Library of Congress Cataloging in Publication Data
The Coming of the First World War/
edited by R. J. W. Evans and Hartmut Pogge von Strandmann.
Bibliography: p.   Includes index.
1. World War. 1914–1918 — Causes.   I. Evans, Robert John Weston.
II. Pogge von Strandmann, H. (Hartmut)
D511.C623   1988   940.3'11 — dc19   88-23880
ISBN 0-19-822841-4

Printed in Great Britain by
J. W. Arrowsmith Ltd, Bristol

PREFACE

THE origins of the First World War have created a heated debate
and intensive controversy from the very beginning, in August
1914, until the present day. No other outbreak of war has
attracted the attention of so many historians, journalists, writers
of memoirs, and military authors. For decades long- and short-
term causes have been analysed, and yet no end to the debate
is in sight. New interpretations have alternated with new
evidence, but if a more profound understanding of the political,
economic, and social impact of the war on European society is
to be gained, then yet further studies of the immediate pre-war
years must be undertaken. It does not follow that great events
also have great causes, but without a wide-ranging analysis of the
origins of the war, the involvement of the powers and their
economic and ideological mobilization remain unclear. Even the
ascendancy of the United States, the Russian Revolution of 1917,
and the decline of European supremacy are linked to the pre-war
period and thus belong to the origins of the war. A strong case
could be made for connecting the fall of three empires, the
Russian, the Turkish, and the Austro-Hungarian, and the defeat
of a fourth, the German Empire, to the origins of the war. Here
it may suffice to emphasize the outbreak of the war as an
unparalleled watershed in European history.

As far as Germany is concerned, an additional factor has to be
taken into account. German society rejected the defeat and
became dominated by revanchism disguised as a bid for revising
the post-war situation in Europe. Unlike French revanchism of
the post-1871 years, German revisionism was closely associated
with the rejection of the so-called 'war guilt' clause of the Peace
Treaty. By studying the 'origins' of the conflict, the German
revisionists tried to substantiate their conviction that Germany
had not started the war. While French revanchism had aimed
primarily at regaining the two lost provinces of Alsace and
Lorraine, German revisionism aimed higher, and wanted to
restore Germany as a Great Power. Once this aim had been
achieved, it was imagined, territorial questions would fall into

place. But nothing came of it, and a largely unfulfilled revisionism, laying the foundation for the rise of National Socialism, became one of the main causes of the Second World War. The denial of any responsibility for having started the war provided many Germans with a moral legitimization for revisionism. Others were willing to accept some blame, but only if the other nations involved would admit their own share of responsibility. Essentially German historians studied the outbreak of war in order to absolve their country from guilt; the French and British—at first anyway—in order to justify the peace terms. Thus the 'origins' became an issue in national and international politics, while the debate remained hopelessly inconclusive. A constant flow of charges and counter-charges stoked up the controversy whenever a new set of documents or the memoirs of any of the participants in the decision-making process were published. After the National Socialists came to power revisionism gained a radical dimension and the bid to restore Germany's power status entered a new phase. Under the Allied response of appeasement, a willingness to modify the peace terms grew steadily and it appeared politically unwise to insist on sole German responsibility for 1914. In any case the debate about the origins of the Great War was increasingly overshadowed by the danger of yet another major conflagration.

The Second World War, far from intensifying the analysis of events in 1914, tended to exercise an opposite effect. But it did contribute to a significant shift in emphasis. After 1945 the terms of the Peace Treaty of Versailles were widely regarded on the Allied side as having been a serious mistake. It followed that the German share of responsibility for the First World War was gradually reduced. Instead of the German Empire, tsarist Russia came, under the conditions of the Cold War between East and West, to be condemned by many as the true culprit of 1914. Furthermore, if the terms of the peace insisted upon in 1919, including the 'war guilt' clause, now appeared to have been too harsh, then the moral basis for the Peace Treaty became shaky. Somehow the peacemakers of 1919 became implicated in the developments which led to 1939. In other words, if Germany was freed from sole responsibility for causing the Great War, some of the blame for the Second World War could, by pointing to the diktat of Versailles, be laid at the feet of the Allies.

These arguments were just beginning to be aired on the German side when Fritz Fischer's first book, *Griff nach der Weltmacht*, appeared in 1961. The ensuing debate focused more on the implications of the book than on its contents. The question whether Germany had started the war deliberately—as Fischer claimed—and whether her war aims in the two world wars were related, occupied the public at large. Under the disguise of a historical controversy, discussion about the book became also, by implication, a political debate about Germany's immediate past and about the foundation of two German states in 1949. This so-called Fischer Controversy has formed a crucial departure for subsequent accounts of the origins of the First World War. There had been a few scholarly treatments of the issue before his book appeared, chief among them the massive three volumes by Luigi Albertini, which appeared in English in 1952–7, but Fischer's work superseded many of the inter-war studies which had been politically biased. Once the Controversy had exploded Germany's own myths surrounding the events of 1914, the historical discussion largely lost its political character, although some political dimensions continue to exercise opinion in the Federal Republic. The debate about the 'origins' can now be put increasingly into a historical perspective, not least because of the simple passing of time. When the war began, in August 1914, the contributors were either contemporary witnesses or participants and that remained largely true for the inter-war years. The generation round Fischer—he was born in 1908—retained very few memories of 1914, but had been fully aware of the inter-war debate. More recent authors on the subject have experienced neither the First World War nor the inter-war debate.

That consideration also applies to the contributors to this book. But there is an element of continuity between the present volume and one published in Oxford shortly after the outbreak of the Great War. Immediately after the commencement of hostilities in 1914, several members of the Faculty of Modern History at Oxford University published a book in which they gave reasons why Britain had ended up fighting the war. Exactly seventy years on, in the autumn of 1984, current members of that same Faculty gave eight lectures about the origins of the conflict—although eschewing the patriotism which had inevitably attached to the earlier volume. The present book represents the fruits of their collaboration.[1] Its first purpose is to provide a concise and accessible account for the general reader of the circumstances which led directly to war: in Europe as a whole, in her Balkan crucible, and in each of the five main belligerent countries of 1914. We have therefore tried to retain the immediacy of the lecture form, as well as echoes of the particular Oxford associations of the project (audible in Chapters 1, 5, and 6); and no attempt is made to indicate the massive specialist literature, except where directly relevant to the argument. At the same time, however, we hope to have contributed something new and significant by concentrating, not upon diplomatic or military factors, whose importance has long been recognized and evaluated, or upon distant and imponderable antecedents, but upon the actual decisions of politicians and their immediate background in the public opinion and popular mood of those sultry July days. In that area, above all, much remains for future historians to accomplish.

R.J.W.E.

September 1987   H.J.O.P.v.S.

---

[1] Members of the Oxford Faculty of Modern History, *Why We Are at War: Great Britain's Case* (Oxford, 1914). Two of the lecturers, Professor Norman Stone (Russia) and Mr Denis Mack Smith (Italy), did not feel able to contribute to the volume. Dr Spring has kindly provided an essay on Russia; a chapter on Italy, which did not, of course, enter the war until spring 1915, we have judged dispensable.

We have not attempted to harmonize the different views put forward on certain issues in these chapters. Readers will have to weigh the strength of the arguments themselves to see which interpretation they find most convincing.

CONTENTS

LIST OF CONTRIBUTORS

Dr Michael Brock, formerly Warden of Nuffield College, Oxford.

Professor Richard Cobb, FBA, Emeritus Professor of Modern History and Fellow of Worcester College, Oxford.

Dr R. J. W. Evans, FBA, Fellow of Brasenose College, Oxford.

Professor Sir Michael Howard, FBA, Professor of History, Yale University.

Dr Hartmut Pogge von Strandmann, Fellow of University College, Oxford.

Dr D. W. Spring, Senior Lecturer in East European and Russian History, University of Nottingham.

Professor Z. A. B. Zeman, Research Professor in European History and Fellow of St Edmund Hall, Oxford.

1

Europe on the Eve of the First World War

MICHAEL HOWARD

IN a place of honour in the Oxford Examination Schools there hangs a portrait of the Emperor William II of Germany, wearing the robes of the Honorary Doctorate of Civil Law which was bestowed on him by the University of Oxford in November 1907. Seven years after the Kaiser received his degree, out of a total of seven Oxford honorands in June 1914, five were German. The Duke of Saxe-Coburg-Gotha, Professor Ludwig Mitteis of the University of Leipzig, and the composer Richard Strauss all received their degrees at the Encaenia on 25 June. Special sessions of Convocation were held to bestow honorary doctorates on the King of Württemberg and the German Ambassador, Prince Lichnowsky. At a banquet in the latter's honour the Professor of German reminded his audience that the Kaiser's great-grandfather, King Frederick William III of Prussia, had also received an honorary DCL exactly 100 years before. He welcomed the presence of so many German students in Oxford (fifty-eight German Rhodes Scholars had matriculated over the previous ten years) and expressed the hope that thereby the two nations would be 'drawn nearer to one another', quoting the belief of Cecil Rhodes 'that the whole of humanity would be best served if the Teutonic peoples were brought nearer together and would join hands for the purpose of spreading their civilization to distant regions'.

Three days after this Encaenia the Archduke Franz Ferdinand was assassinated at Sarajevo. When the University reconvened three months later in October 1914 many of the young Germans and Englishmen who had rubbed shoulders at those celebrations had enlisted in their respective armies and were now doing their best to kill one another. The Examination Schools had been turned into a hospital. The number of undergraduates in residence had dwindled by over half, from 3,097 to 1,387. (By 1918 it was to be down to 369.) In the vacation over a thousand of them had been recommended for commissions by a committee established under the vice-chancellor, and were already serving with the army. As yet only twelve had been killed; the slaughter of the first Battle of Ypres was still a few weeks away. Several colleges had been taken over to house troops. Organized games had virtually ceased, while the OTC, to which all able-bodied undergraduates now belonged, trained for five mornings and two afternoons a week. As if this were not enough, the Chichele Professor of Military History, Spenser Wilkinson, advertised a course of lectures 'for those who are preparing themselves to fight England's battles' which was to begin with a description of 'the nature and properties of the weapons in use—the bullet, the shell, the bayonet, the sword and the lance'.[1]

In one way it can therefore be said that the war came out of a clear sky. But the events I have described do not indicate a profoundly pacific community taken totally by surprise and adjusting itself only with difficulty to astonishing and terrible new conditions. Everyone seems to have known exactly what to do, and to have done it with great efficiency. Arrangements to take over the Examination Schools and colleges had been made by the War Office two years earlier. The OTC was already flourishing: one undergraduate in three belonged to it, and 500 were in summer camp at Aldershot when the news of the assassination came through. And, in so far as such iconographical evidence can be legitimately adduced, the group photographs of Oxford colleges and clubs show how the lolling dandies of the turn of the century, with their canes, blazers, and dogs, had given way soon after the Boer War to a new generation of muscular young men—fit, serious, short-haired, level-eyed—whose civilian clothes already seemed to sit uneasily upon them. This generation may not have expected war to break out in the summer of 1914, but it was psychologically and physically ready for it when it came. The challenge was expected, and the response full of zest.

In this respect Oxford was a microcosm, not only of Britain, but of Europe as a whole. Europe was taken by surprise by the

---

[1] The information in this paragraph comes from W. S. T. Stallybrass, 'Oxford in 1914–1918', *Oxford*, Winter 1939; H. W. B. Joseph, 'Oxford in the Last War', *Oxford Magazine*, 22 May 1941; and from the researches for the History of the University currently being carried on by Mr Mark Curthoys, to whom I owe a great debt of gratitude.

occasion for the war—so many other, comparable crises had been successfully surmounted during the past five years—but not by the fact of it. All over the continent long-matured plans were put into action. With a really remarkable absence of confusion, millions of men reported for duty, were converted or, rather, reconverted into soldiers, and loaded into the trains which were to take them to the greatest battlefields in the history of mankind. It cannot be said that during the summer weeks of 1914, while the crisis was ripening towards its bloody solution, the peoples of Europe in general were exercising any pressure on their governments to go to war, but neither did they try to restrain them. When war did come, it was accepted almost without question; in some quarters indeed with wild demonstrations of relief.

The historian is faced with two distinct questions. Why did war come? And when it did come, why was it so prolonged and destructive? In the background there is a further, unanswerable question: If the political and military leaders of Europe had been able to foresee that prolongation and that destruction, would the war have occurred at all? Everyone, naturally, went to war in the expectation of victory, but might they have felt that at such a cost even victory was not worth while? That is the kind of hypothetical question which laymen put and historians cannot answer. But we can ask another and less impossible question: What did the governments of Europe think would happen to them if they did *not* go to war? Why did war, with all its terrible uncertainties, appear to them as a preferable alternative to remaining at peace?

Clausewitz described war as being compounded of a paradoxical trinity: the governments for which it was an instrument of policy; the military for whom it was the exercise of a skill; and the people as a whole, the extent of whose involvement determined the intensity with which the war would be waged.[2] This functional distinction is of course an over-simplification. In all the major states of Europe military and political leaders shared a common attitude and cultural background, which shaped their perceptions and guided their

[2] Carl von Clausewitz, *On War*, trans. M. Howard and P. Paret, (Princeton, 1976), 89.

judgments. The same emotions which inspired peoples were likely also to affect their political and military leaders; and those emotions could be shaped by propaganda, by education, and by the socialization process to which so much of the male population of continental Europe had been subject through four decades of at least two years' compulsory military service at a highly impressionable age (though it must be noted that the British, who were not subjected to the same treatment, reacted no differently from their continental neighbours to the onset and continuation of the war). Still, the triad of government, military, and public opinion provides a useful framework for analysis, and one that I shall use for the remainder of this chapter.

First, the governments. Although none of them could foresee the full extent of the ordeal which lay before them, no responsible statesman, even in Germany, believed that they were in for 'a fresh, jolly little war'. It was perhaps only when they had taken their irrevocable decisions that the real magnitude of the risks which they were running came fully home to them, but that is a very common human experience. Bethmann Hollweg in particular saw the political dangers with gloomy clarity: a world war, he warned the Bavarian minister, 'would topple many a throne'.[3] There had indeed been a certain amount of wild writing and speaking over the past ten years, especially in Germany, about the value of war as a panacea for social ills; and the remarkable way in which social and political differences did disappear the moment war was declared has tempted some historians to assume that this effect was foreseen and therefore intended: that the opportunity was deliberately seized by the Asquith Cabinet, for example, to distract attention from the intractable Irish problem to continental adventures, or that the German imperial government saw it as a chance to settle the hash of the Social Democrats for good.[4] One can only say that minute scrutiny of the material by, now, several generations

---

[3] V. R. Berghahn, *Germany and the Approach of War in 1914* (London, 1973), 185.
[4] e.g. Arno J. Mayer, *The Persistence of the Old Regime* (London, 1981).

of historians has failed to produce any serious evidence to support this view.

Rather, the opposite was the case: governments were far from certain how their populations would react to the coming of war, and how they would stand up to its rigours. A whole generation of English publicists had been stressing the social consequences of even a temporary blockade of the British Isles: soaring insurance rates, unemployment, bread-riots, revolution.[5] The French army, for ten years past the butt of left-wing agitation, was gloomy about the prospects of anything like an enthusiastic response from conscripts recalled to the colours, and the French security services stood by to arrest left-wing leaders at the slightest sign of trouble.[6] It was only with the greatest reluctance that the German army enforced military service on the supposedly unreliable population of the industrial regions. The Russian government had within the past ten years seen one war end in revolution, and for at least some of its members this seemed good reason to keep out of another.[7] It was one thing to enhance the prestige of the government and undermine support for its domestic enemies by conducting a strong forward policy, whether in Morocco or in the Balkans. It was another to subject the fragile consensus and dubious loyalties of societies so torn by class and national conflict as were the states of Europe in 1914 to the terrible strain of a great war. Governments did so only on the assumption, spoken or unspoken, that that war, however terrible, would at least be comparatively short; no longer, probably, than the six months which had seen out the last great war in Europe in 1870. How could it be otherwise? A prolonged war of attrition, as Count Schlieffen had pointed out in a famous article in 1909, could not be conducted when it required the expenditure of milliards to sustain armies numbered in millions.[8] The only person in any position of responsibility who appears to have thought differently was Lord Kitchener: a British imperial soldier who had served outside Europe throughout his career and who had never, so far as we know, seriously studied the question at all.

---

[5] A. J. A. Morris, *The Scaremongers* (London, 1984), *passim*.
[6] Henri Contamine, *La Revanche, 1871–1914* (Paris, 1957), 195.
[7] See D. C. B. Lieven, *Russia and the Origins of the First World War* (London, 1983), 78.
[8] Alfred von Schlieffen, *Gesammelte Schriften* (Berlin, 1913), i. 17.

But whether the war was short or long, it was for all governments a leap into a terrible dark, and the penalties for defeat were likely to be far greater than the traditional ones of financial indemnities and territorial loss. So we come back to the question: What appeared to be the alternatives? And in the event of victory, what appeared the probable gains? Why, in the last resort, did the governments of Europe prefer the terrifying uncertainties of war to the prospect of no war?

Let us begin where the war itself effectively began, in Vienna. Was not the prospect which lay before the statesmen of Vienna, even if this crisis were successfully 'managed', one of continuous frustration abroad and disintegration at home? Of a Serbia, doubled in size after the Balkan Wars, ever more boldly backing the claims of the Bosnian irredentists, while the South Slavs agitated with ever greater confidence for an autonomy that the Magyars would never permit them to exercise? What serious prospect was there of the Empire hanging together once the old Emperor had gone? A final settling of accounts with Serbia while Germany held the Russians in check must have appeared the only chance of saving the Monarchy, whatever Berlin might say; and with a blank cheque from Berlin, Vienna could surely face the future with a greater confidence than had been felt there for very many years. No wonder Berchtold and his colleagues took their time in drafting their ultimatum: they must have found the process highly enjoyable. A successful war would put the Monarchy back in business again, and keep it there for many years to come.

What about the government in Berlin? Was this the moment it had been waiting for ever since the famous Council of War in December 1912?[9] I am happy to leave Dr Pogge von Strandmann, in Chapter 5 of this volume, to guide us through a controversy which has consumed so many tons of paper and gallons of ink. But if one again asks the questions, what the imperial German government had to lose by peace and gain by war, the answers seem very clear. One of the things it had to lose by peace was its Austrian ally, which would become an increasingly useless makeweight as it grew ever less capable of solving its internal problems or protecting its own (and German) interests in the Balkans against

    [9] J. C. G. Röhl, 'An der Schwelle der Weltkriege', *Militärische Mitteilungen*, 1 (1977), 100; Fritz Fischer, *War of Illusions* (London, 1975), 161.

the encroachments of Russia and Russia's protégés. Another was Germany's capacity to hold her own against a Dual Alliance in which French capital was building up a Russian army whose future size and mobility appeared far beyond the capacity of any German force to contain. It would not be too anachronistic to suggest that the shadow of Russia's future status as a superpower was already rendering out of date all calculations based on the traditional concept of a European balance. If war was to come at all—and few people in the imperial government doubted that it would—then it was self-evidently better to have it now, while there was still a fair chance of victory. By 1917, when the Russians had completed the Great Programme of rearmament and railway building which they had begun, with French funding, in 1912, it might be too late.

And, for Germany, there was a lot to be gained by war. The domination of the Balkans and perhaps the Middle East; the final reduction of France to a position from which she could never again, even with allies, pose a military threat to German power; the establishment of a position on the Continent that would enable her to compete on equal terms with England and attain the grandiose if ill-defined status of a world power: all this, in July 1914, must have appeared perfectly feasible. In September, when the Programme of her war aims was drafted, it looked as if it had almost been achieved. Even in a less bellicose and more self-confident society than Wilhelmine Germany, the opportunity might have appeared too good to miss.[10]

In Vienna and Berlin then, there seemed much to be lost by peace and gained by war. In St Petersburg, the ambitions for Balkan expansion and the 'recovery' of Constantinople, checked in 1878 and 1885, were far from dead, but they can hardly be counted a major element in Russian political calculations in July 1914. More serious were the costs of remaining at peace: abandoning Serbia and all the gains of the past five years; facing the wrath of the pan-Slavs in the Duma and their French allies; and watching the Central Powers establish and consolidate an unchallengeable dominance in south-east Europe. Even so, these costs were hardly irredeemable. Russia had been humiliated before in the Balkans and been able to restore her authority. She

---

[10] This is the thesis expanded and documented by Fritz Fischer in *Germany's Aims in the First World War* (London, 1967).

had no vital interests there which, once lost, could never be recovered. Above all, she had nothing to lose, in terms of military power, by waiting, and a great deal to gain. Of all the major powers, Russia's entry into the war can be categorized as the least calculated, the most unwise, and ultimately of course the most disastrous.[11]

As for Paris and London, a successful war would certainly remove—as it ultimately did—a major threat to their security. But the advantages to be gained by war did not enter into their calculations, whereas the perils of remaining at peace quite evidently did. The French government took little comfort from the long-term advantages to be gained from the growth of Russian military power and the consequent advisability of postponing the issue until 1917. It was more conscious of its immediate weakness confronted by the growing numbers of the German army. In 1914, after the increase of the past two years, the German peacetime strength had reached 800,000 men, the wartime strength 3.8 million. Thanks to their new and controversial Three-Year Law, the French could match this with 700,000 men in peace, 3.5 million in war. But with a population only 60 per cent of the German, that was almost literally their final throw. Completion of the Russian reforms was three long years away. In the long run Russian strength might redress the balance, but in the long run a large number of Frenchmen could be dead and their nation reduced to the status of Italy or Spain. So the French government saw no reason to urge caution on St Petersburg, and even less reason to refrain from supporting its ally when Germany declared war on her on 1 August.[12]

For the British government, composed as it was very largely (though by no means entirely) of men to whom the whole idea of war was antipathetic and who were responsible to a parliamentary party deeply suspicious of militarism and of continental involvement, there appeared nothing to be gained by war, and perhaps more than any of its continental equivalents it was conscious of the possible costs. But it was equally conscious of the cost of remaining at peace. Britain would not be the *tertius*

[11] Lieven, op. cit (above, n. 7), 139–57.
[12] John F. Keiger, *France and the Origins of the First World War* (London, 1983), 153 ff.; Douglas Porch, *The March to the Marne* (Cambridge, 1981), 227.

gaudens in a continental war. She had no demands to make on any of the belligerents, no territorial aspirations, no expectation of economic gain. So far as the British government was concerned, Norman Angell's famous book *The Great Illusion* was preaching to the converted. But if the Dual Alliance defeated Germany unaided Britain would be, for the two victors, an object of hostility and contempt. All the perils of imperial rivalry temporarily dispersed by the Entente with France of 1904 and the accords with Russia of 1907 would reappear. If, on the other hand, Germany won and established a continental hegemony, Britain would face a threat to her security unknown since the days of Napoleon. Leaving any consideration of honour, sentiment, or respect for treaties on one side—and let us remember that that generation of Englishmen did *not* leave them on one side but regarded them as quite central—every consideration of *realpolitik* dictated that Britain, having done her best to avert the war, should enter it on the side of France and Russia once it began.[13]

When the statesmen of Europe declared war in 1914, they all shared one common assumption: that they had a better-than-evens chance of winning it. In making this assumption they relied on their military advisers; so it is now time to look at the second element in our triad: the soldiers.

The first thing to note about the soldiers, certainly those of western Europe, is that they were professionals; most of them professionals of a very high order. Those of them who were well-born or aspired to that status certainly shared all the feudal value-system so excoriated by Professor Arno Mayer in his work on *The Persistence of the Old Regime*. Those who were not probably had more than their fair share of the prevalent philosophy of Social Darwinism and regarded war, not as an unpleasant necessity, but as a test of manhood and of national fitness for survival. In all armies, then as now, there were incompetents who through good luck or good connections reached unsuitably high rank; but a study of the military literature of the period strongly indicates

[13] Zara S. Steiner, *Britain and the Origins of the First World War* (London, 1977), 242 ff.

that the military, especially those responsible for the armament, training, organization, and deployment of armies, were no fools, worked hard, and took their professions very seriously indeed. And they, also, shared certain common assumptions.

The first was that war was inevitable. The now much-quoted statement made by General von Moltke at the so-called Council of War in December 1912, 'I hold war to be inevitable, and the sooner the better',[14] can be paralleled with comparable expressions by responsible figures in every army in Europe. They may have differed over the second part of the sentence—whether it was better to get it over with quickly or wait for a more favourable moment—but from 1911 onward it is hard to find any military leader suggesting that war could or should any longer be avoided. The change of mood in the summer of that year, provoked by the Agadir crisis, was very marked. In France a new political leadership appointed new military chiefs, who belatedly and desperately began to prepare their ramshackle army for the test of war. The Dual Alliance was reactivated, Russian mobilization schedules were speeded up, and the Great Programme of Russian military modernization was set on foot. In Germany the agitation began which contributed so powerfully to the massive increase in the military strength of the German army. In Britain the government gave its blessing to the army's plans for sending the British Expeditionary Force to France, and Winston Churchill was sent to the Admiralty to bring the navy into line. The extent to which war was generally regarded as inevitable or desirable by the public as a whole is still difficult to gauge—though if the 'distant drummer' penetrated into the summer idylls of A. E. Housman it is reasonable to suppose that less remote figures found the sound pretty deafening. But certainly for the military the evidence is overwhelming that the question in their mind was not 'whether' but 'when'. They saw their job as being, not to deter war, but to fight it.

The second assumption, which they shared with the statesmen they served, was that the war would be short. It required quite exceptional perspicacity to visualize anything else. Ivan Bloch in his work *La Guerre future*, published in 1898, had forecast with amazing accuracy how the power of modern weapons would

---

[14] See Röhl, op. cit. (above, n. 9).

produce deadlock on the battlefield and how the resulting attrition would destroy the fabric of the belligerent societies.[15] Bloch's thesis was widely known and much discussed in military periodicals. But since he was in effect saying that the military were now faced with a problem which they could not solve, it was not to be expected that many soldiers would agree with him. As for his conclusion, that war in future would be, if not impossible, then certainly suicidal, it had already been shown not to be true.

In 1904–5 Russia and Japan had fought a war with all the weapons whose lethal effects were so gruesomely described by Bloch, and Japan had won a clear-cut victory which established her in the ranks of the major powers. The effect on Russia had been much as Bloch had described, but revolution and defeat always stalked hand in hand. The war had indeed lasted for well over a year, but it had been fought by both belligerents at the end of long and difficult supply lines. In Europe, where communications were plentiful and short, and armies at hair-trigger readiness, the pattern of the German wars of unification seemed much more relevant: rapid mobilization and deployment of all available forces, a few gigantic battles—battles, indeed, which might be prolonged for days if not weeks as the protagonists probed for a flank or a weak point in the enemy defences—and a decision within a matter of months. Because that decision would be reached so quickly, it was important that all forces should be committed to action. There was no point in bringing up reserves after the battle had been lost. There was even less point—if indeed it occurred to anyone to do so—to prepare an industrial base to sustain a war of *matériel* which might last for years. The idea that any national economy could endure such an ordeal was self-evidently absurd.

This shared assumption—that the war would inevitably be short—led on to another: that the best chances of victory lay in immediately taking the offensive. With the wisdom of hindsight it is easy for subsequent generations to condemn the suicidal unreality of this idea, but in the circumstances of the time it appeared reasonable enough. An offensive gave the best hope of

---

[15] I. de Bloch, *La Guerre future aux points de vue technique, économique et politique* (6 vols., Paris, 1898), trans. and summarized as *Is War Now Impossible? The Future of War in its Technical, Economic and Political Relations* (London and Boston, 1899).

disrupting or pre-empting the mobilization of the opponent and bringing him to battle under favourable conditions. As in a wrestling-match which had to be settled in a matter of minutes, to yield the initiative was to court defeat. The French had stood on the defensive in 1870 and been defeated. The Russians had stood on the defensive in 1904–5 and been defeated. Those who had studied the history of the American Civil War, who included all students of the British Army Staff College at Camberley, knew that the only hope of a Confederate victory had lain in a successful offensive, and that once Lee passed over to the defensive after the Battle of Gettysburg his defeat was only a matter of time. The lessons of history seemed to reinforce the strategic imperatives of 1914.

And let us not forget what those strategic imperatives were. The Germans had to destroy the French power of resistance before the full force of Russian strength could be developed. The Russians had to attack sufficiently early, and in sufficient strength, to take the weight off the French. The Austrians had to attack the Russians in order to take the weight off the Germans. For the French alone a defensive strategy was in theory feasible, but the precedent of 1870 made it understandably unpopular, and the national mood made it inconceivable. The doctrine of the offensive was certainly carried, in the pre-1914 French army, to quite unreasonable lengths, but that does not in itself mean that a posture of defence would necessarily have been any more effective in checking the German advance in 1914 than it was in 1940.

Finally we must remember that the stalemate on the western front did not develop for six months, and that on the eastern front it never developed at all. The open warfare of manœuvre for which the armies of Europe had prepared was precisely what, in the autumn of 1914, they got. It resulted in eastern Europe in a succession of spectacular German victories, and given bolder and more flexible leadership it might very well have done the same in the West. The terrible losses suffered by the French in Alsace in August and by the British and Germans in Flanders in November came in encounter battles, not in set-piece assaults against prepared defensive positions; and they were losses which, to the military leadership at least, came as no great surprise.

For this was the final assumption shared by soldiers throughout Europe: in any future war, armies would have to endure very heavy losses indeed. The German army, for one, had never forgotten the price it paid for its victories in 1870, when the French had been armed with breech-loading rifles which in comparison with the weapons now available were primitive. Since then the effects of every new weapon had been studied with meticulous care, and no professional soldier was under any illusions about the damage that would be caused; not simply by machine-guns (which were in fact seen as ideal weapons of a mobile offensive), but by magazine-loading rifles and by quick-firing artillery firing shrapnel at infantry in the open and high explosives against trenches. Their effects had been studied not only through controlled experiment, but in action, in the South African and Russo-Japanese Wars. The conclusion generally drawn was that in future infantry would be able to advance only in open formations, making use of all available cover, under the protection of concentrated artillery fire.

But whatever precautions they took, sooner or later troops would have to assault across open ground with the bayonet, and they must then be prepared to take very heavy losses. This had happened in Manchuria, where the Japanese were generally seen as having owed their success not simply to their professional skills, but to their contempt for death. European Social Darwinians gravely propounded the terrible paradox, that a nation's fitness to survive depended on the readiness of its individual members to die. Avoidance of casualties was seen as no part of the general's trade, and willingness to accept them was regarded as a necessity for commander and commanded alike. Into the literature of pre-war Europe there crept the word which was to become the terrible leitmotiv of the coming conflict: 'sacrifice'; more particularly, 'the supreme sacrifice'.

That may have been all very well for professional soldiers whose job it is, after all, to die for their country if they cannot arrange matters any less wastefully. But the people who were going to die in the next war were not going to be just the professional soldiers. They would be the People: men recalled to the colours from civilian life or, in the case of England, volunteering to 'do their bit'. Would these young men, enervated by urban living, rotted by socialist propaganda, show the same Bushido spirit as the Japanese? This question was constantly propounded in military and right-wing literature during the ten

years before the war. Kipling for one, surveying the civilians of
Edwardian England in the aftermath of the Boer War, very much
doubted it, and taunted his fellow countrymen in a series of
scornful philippics:

> Fenced by your careful fathers, ringed by your leaden seas,
> Long did ye wake in quiet and long lie down at ease;
> Till ye said of Strife, 'What is it?' of the Sword,
>   'It is far from our ken';
> Till ye made a sport of your shrunken hosts and a toy
>   of your armèd men.[16]

In Germany Heinrich Class and Friedrich von Bernhardi, in France
Charles Maurras and Charles Péguy expressed the same doubts
about the capacity of their peoples to rise to the level of the
forthcoming test. But the astonishing thing was that, when the
time came, they did so rise. Why?

This brings us belatedly to the third element in the triad, the
People. Without the support, or at least the acquiescence of the
peoples of Europe, there would have been no war. This is the
most interesting and most complex area for historians to
investigate. We know a lot—almost to excess—about the mood
of the intellectuals and the élites in 1914[17], but what about the
rest? There are now some excellent studies of local and popular
reactions in Britain, largely based on the superb sources at the
Imperial War Museum. M. Jean-Jacques Becker had done path-
breaking work for France in his study *1914: Comment les Français
sont entrés dans la guerre* (Paris, 1977) but elsewhere there remains
much research to be done or, where done, brought together.
My own ignorance forces me to treat this vast subject briefly
and impressionistically, and I hope that others will be able
to correct some of my misconceptions and fill some of the
yawning gaps.

What does appear self-evident is that the doubts which
European leaders felt about the morale of their peoples proved
in 1914 to be ill-founded. Those who welcomed war with

---

[16] Rudyard Kipling, 'The Islanders', in *Rudyard Kipling's Verse* (London,
1982), 301.
[17] e.g. R. Wohl, *The Generation of 1914* (London, 1980).

enthusiasm may have been a minority concentrated in the big cities, but those who opposed it were probably a smaller minority still. The vast majority were willing to do what their governments expected of them. Nationalistically oriented public education; military service which, however unwelcome and tedious, bred a sense of cohesion and national identity; continuing habits of social deference: all this helps explain, at a deeper level than does the strident propaganda of the popular press, why the populations of Europe responded so readily to the call when it came. For the 'city-bred populations' so mistrusted by right-wing politicians the war came as an adventure, an escape from humdrum or intolerable lives into a world of adventure and comradeship. Among the peasants of France, as M. Becker has shown us, there was little enthusiasm, but rather glum acceptance of yet another unavoidable hardship in lives which were and always had been unavoidably hard; but the hardship fell as much on those who were left behind as on those who went away. The same can no doubt be said of the peasants of central and eastern Europe as well.

There was probably only a tiny minority, also, which considered the idea of war in itself repellent. Few military historians, and no popular historians, had ever depicted the realities of the battlefield in their full horror, and only a few alarmist prophets could begin to conceive what the realities of future battlefields would be like. Their nations, so the peoples of Europe had learned at school, had achieved their present greatness through successful wars — the centenaries of the battles of Trafalgar and of Leipzig had recently been celebrated with great enthusiasm in Britain and Germany — and there was no reason to think that they would not one day have to fight again. Military leaders were everywhere respected and popular figures (Kitchener and Roberts more so, probably, than Balfour and Asquith); military music was an intrinsic part of popular culture. In the popular mind, as in the military mind, wars were seen not as terrible evils to be deterred, but as necessary struggles to be fought and won.

I have touched on the Social Darwinism of the period: the view, so widespread among intellectuals and publicists as well as among soldiers, that struggle was a natural process of development in the social as in the natural order of the world, and war a necessary procedure for ensuring survival of the fittest, among nations as among species. It is hard to know how seriously to take this. Its manifestations catch the eye of a contemporary historian if only because they are, to our generation, so very shocking. But how widely were such views really held, and how far were people like F. N. Maude, Sidney Low, or Benjamin Kidd generally regarded as cranks? The same applies to the much-touted influence of Nietzsche and of Bergson among intellectuals—the creed of liberation from old social norms, of heroic egotism, of action as a value transcending all others. How widespread was their influence? Did it make the idea of war more generally acceptable than it otherwise would have been? Intellectuals, I am afraid, tend to overrate the importance of other intellectuals, or at best attribute to them an influence which becomes important only among later generations. Webern and Schoenberg may have been composing in pre-war Vienna, but the tunes which rang in the ears of the 1914 generation were those of Franz Lehár and Richard Strauss.

And if there was a 'War Movement', there was also, far more evident and purposeful, a Peace Movement, derived from older liberal-rationalist roots. It was stronger in some countries than in others; then as now, it flourished more successfully in Protestant than in Catholic cultures, at its strongest in Scandinavia, the Netherlands, and Britain (not to mention the United States), weakest in Italy and Spain.[18] It was indeed the apparent strength and influence of the Peace Movement, especially at the time of The Hague Conferences, that provoked so much of the polemical writings of the Social Darwinians and caused so much concern to nationalistic politicians. In imperial Germany the Peace Movement had an uphill struggle; but if Heinrich Class and the Pan-German League were thundering out the dogmas of the War Movement, the far larger and more important Social Democratic Party rejected them[19]—as did the overwhelmingly dominant Liberal–Labour coalition in England and the left wing led by Jean Jaurès which triumphed at the polls in France in the spring of 1914. Social Darwinism may have been

---

[18] A. C. F. Beales, *A History of Peace* (London, 1931).
[19] See the contrasting studies by Roger Chickering, *Imperial Germany and a World without War* (Princeton, 1975) and *We Men Who Feel Most German: A Cultural Study of the Pan-German League 1886–1914* (London, 1984).

not so much the prevailing *Zeitgeist* as a sharp minority reaction against a much stronger and deeply rooted liberal, rational, and progressive creed whose growing influence seemed to some to be undermining the continuing capacity of nations to defend themselves.

But the events of 1914 showed these right-wing fears to be misplaced. Everywhere the leaders of the Peace Movement found themselves isolated: small and increasingly unpopular minorities of idealists, intellectuals, and religious zealots. Events made it clear that, whatever their influence among intellectuals and élites, both the Peace and the War Movements were marginal to the attitudes of the peoples of Europe. Those peoples did *not* reject war. Nor did they regard it as the highest good, the fulfilment of human destiny. They accepted it as a fact of life. They trusted their rulers and marched when they were told. Many did so with real enthusiasm; perhaps the more highly educated they were, the greater the enthusiasm they felt. None knew what they were marching towards, and any romantic notions they had about war shredded to pieces the moment they came under artillery fire. But they adjusted to the ordeal with astonishing speed and stoicism. It was indeed because they adjusted so well that the ordeal lasted for as long as it did.

2

The Balkans and the Coming of War

Z. A. B. ZEMAN

Two years after the Sarajevo assassination, in the summer of 1916, Gavrilo Princip, the assassin of Archduke Ferdinand, was interviewed by Dr Pappenheim, the psychiatrist at the Terezín fortress prison. Dr Pappenheim made a shorthand record of their conversations, which was published in Vienna in 1926, under the title *Gavrilo Princips Bekenntnisse*, the Confessions of Gavrilo Princip. In a large library of books on the outbreak of the First World War, the short pamphlet still stands out as a unique document. In that pamphlet, Princip recreated convincingly the atmosphere in which he and his friends felt compelled to act against the representatives of the Habsburg state.

When he talked to Dr Pappenheim, Princip was in very poor shape. He had been badly beaten up immediately after the assassination and some of his wounds had not yet healed. He had attempted suicide on one occasion; he was seriously ill with tuberculosis. He had been in solitary confinement, in chains, until Dr Pappenheim visited him. They talked in German, a language in which Princip was not entirely at home, and he talked with a lucidity born of despair. His short staccato sentences, his habit of often referring to himself in the third person, add a stark, haunting quality to the document.

In their talks, Princip and Pappenheim were concerned mainly with three subjects: Princip's personal and intellectual reasons for rebellion against the Habsburg Empire; the revolt itself and the general circumstances which gave rise to it; and, finally, Princip's own responsibility for the outbreak of the war. He had murdered Franz Ferdinand and his wife when he was still under twenty and, under Austrian legislation, he could not be tried on a capital charge. Princip belonged to the first literate generation in his family: he told Dr Pappenheim that books were his life, and that the most difficult part of his prison existence was to be without them. Earlier, during his interrogation in Sarajevo, he said he had been regarded by his friends as 'a man who would be completely ruined by the immoderate study of literature'. So detached was Princip from everyday life.

Princip was well acquainted with Russian revolutionary writing, especially with the writing of Kropotkin and Herzen; among the few local Balkan sources of rebellion Princip had been especially impressed by a poem entitled *The Death of a Hero*, written to celebrate an earlier attempt to assassinate a Habsburg official. The intellectual origins, therefore, of Princip's rebellion against authority—and the same was true of his friends, the other young Bosnian rebels—were east European, and especially Russian. In addition to the literature of Russian radicalism, the example of the terrorist wing of the Russian revolutionary movement was decisive for the growth of rebellion in Bosnia.

About the turn of the century, there existed a contrast between the main sources of Balkan revolutionary radicalism on the one hand, and, on the other, the models for the government institutions used by the Balkan élites. Historians of the Balkans are on the whole agreed that Balkan élites and the states they created were highly imitative.[1] Their models came from western Europe: constitutional government, political parties, a parliament of sorts; and capital towns were built and extended on the pattern of Paris. The reason, I think, why the Balkans were at one time so popular with Western writers and travellers of every kind— from, say, Arthur Evans to Olivia Manning—was that they saw there an unusual reflection of their own society. The reflection was sometimes distorted, but it was also starker and simpler, and revealed the hard structure, the bare bones of a capitalist society in the making. The attempt to modernize and westernize the new states of the Balkans gave the Balkans a bad name: Balkanization, popular early in this century, was a term of political disapproval.

Recently, I came across a leader in the *New York Times*, which commented on the savage coup in Belgrade in June 1903. I shall return to this incident later: the coup replaced one dynasty with another. The leader is, I think, an excellent, though perhaps

---

[1] Cf. for instance Barbara Jelavich, *History of the Balkans* (Cambridge, 1983), ii. 45 ff.

extreme, example of the way Balkan politics were seen at that time in the West. It also contains some remarkable stereotypes. It was entitled: 'Out of the Window!'

The character of different races shows most clearly when the moment is one of excitement and inborn nature comes to the surface. The rest of the world was not spared a typical last horror in the tragedy of Belgrade, when the brutal assassins threw the bodies of their victims out of the window; but the rest of the world was surprised. Not so that part of the world which is Slavic. The opening of a window and throwing people out is a racial characteristic.

Patriotic inhabitants of Prague will show you with certainty of eliciting your interest and pride scarce concealed the windows in the old Rathaus from which the followers of one faction precipitated those of another. As the bold Briton knocks his enemy down with his fists, as the southern Frenchman lays his foe prostrate with a scientific kick of the savate, as the Italian uses his knife and the German the handy beermug, so the Bohemian and Servian 'chucks' his enemy out of the window . . .

The reason must be sought in the ancestral habits of Russians, Poles, Servians, Sorbs, Polabians, Croats, Cassubes, Wends, Lusatians, and other stripes and variations of the type. They were forest-dwelling tribes living in square-built log houses generally provided with a door, a fireplace of some kind, and a chimney or smokehole. In the event of an unpleasantness in the log cabin the stronger party held the door while the weaker was being pounded. The only exit was the smokehole or, in finer habitations, a window. Ages of indulgences in vodka, brandy, and other fire waters with the concomitant excitement of thrusting an opponent through the window or up the smokehole have made the Slav a slave to the window habit.[2]

The Balkans, then, acquired, on the whole, a bad name in the West. While Balkan élites looked to western Europe for guidance, contemporary western European radicalism made little impact there. Balkan rebels tended to find Russian examples more attractive.

Princip told Pappenheim that he was convinced that unity of the South Slavs could not be achieved under Austria. He said:

In 1878 many Serbs begged the Emperor and the generals to free them from the Turks. The older generation spoke of a freedom which would be granted by Austria in the legal way. We don't believe in such a freedom. Our compatriots are not well off in Austria. I believe that neither

[2] *New York Times*, 24 June 1903.

are the Czechs nor the Poles. I have heard that the Slav peoples are not well off in Austria; they are persecuted in Bosnia with treason trials and martial law.

Princip believed that when Austria ran into difficulties there would be a revolution. But the ground for such a revolution had to be prepared. 'The assassination would create the mood. There had been assassinations before, the assassins were the heroes of our youth. He [Princip was referring to himself here] did not think that he wanted to be a hero. He only wanted to die for his ideals.' Princip added that he believed that every people had to go through a nation-building phase. When Pappenheim said that Austria could create a kind of bridge, Princip replied that the time was not suitable for that, in the capitalist period. Earlier, Princip hinted at a change of mind about assassination and the national phase of development. He told Pappenheim that he now thought that a 'social revolution everywhere in Europe is possible, to change things . . .'. He told the psychiatrist that he had always been an idealistic person, who 'wanted to avenge the nation. The motives: revenge and love. The whole youth is in such a revolutionary mood.' Princip gave Dr Pappenheim a close-up view of a primitive peasant society and of several of its young sons who could come to terms neither with that society nor with its new Austro-Hungarian masters.

Historians too tend to be restrained in their admiration for the Habsburgs' development policies in their Balkan possessions. Under the provisions of the imperial order of 22 February 1880, the united province of Bosnia-Hercegovina came under the sole authority of the joint Minister of Finance. It remained outside both the Austrian and the Hungarian parts of the Monarchy. The Hungarians did not wish for any increase in the number of Slavs on their territory; nevertheless, Bosnia-Hercegovina became a Hungarian rather than an Austrian colony. For the best part of the four decades while the province remained under Habsburg rule the Ministers of Finance were members of the Magyar gentry. Benjamin Kállay was the Minister of Finance from 1882 to 1903, and his successor, István Burián, came from a similar background.

For twenty-one years, Kállay ruled the province single-handed, in a secretive, dictatorial way. He concentrated on industrial development and transport, and left agriculture alone. Nothing was done in the way of land reform; the main purpose of the developing industries was to process local agricultural produce. According to Burián, Kállay's priorities were: first to raise the living standards of the province; then to concentrate on the development of education; and finally to turn to political self-government.

It seems that even with regard to the purely economic aims, the administration of the province achieved only limited success. The local population benefited little from the development policies of their rulers: they picked up unskilled jobs in factories, casual jobs in connection with the construction and maintenance of the railways, or minor posts in the administration. Perhaps the greatest obstacle to the economic development of Bosnia-Hercegovina was that the Magyar Minister of Finance bound it closely to the Hungarian economy. The railways which were built made the province dependent on the trade and transport policies of the Hungarian government, with few links to the more developed part of the Habsburg Monarchy. Until 1914, there was no direct connection between Bosnia-Hercegovina and the Austrian half of the Empire.[3] Bosnia-Hercegovina remained cut off from the more prosperous, industrial territories of Austria; and it became a province of a province, run by men who were quite inflexible in the belief in their own civilizing mission.

A network of military garrisons, fortresses, and gendarmerie posts underpinned the network of railways and factories. Many Bosnians were rather surrounded by growing prosperity than touched by it. Though education started to reach the sons of the local peasants, schools were more a way of dealing with the growing population pressure on the countryside than the preparation for a specific role in society. After the occupation of Bosnia-Hercegovina, Austrian administration neglected the highlands of western Bosnia as much as the Turks had done. It was here that Princip's family lived, in a village called Grahovo, in the poorest part of a poor province. The bare slopes of the

---

[3] Cf. Peter F. Sugar, *Industrialization of Bosnia-Hercegovina 1878–1918*, (Seattle, 1963), 80.

mountains reminded the local population of Turkish raids against the local peasant rebels, when the Turks set fire to the mountain forests. The routes into Bosnia-Hercegovina taken by Habsburg civilization—along the Drina, Bosna, and Vrbas rivers—bypassed Princip's birthplace. Apart from the few new high schools in the province[4] there was nowhere else for the sons of the peasants to go. Gavrilo Princip and most of the other Sarajevo conspirators came from peasant families, and they were alienated both from their own society and from its temporary masters. In his talks with Dr Pappenheim as he lay dying in the Terezín fortress prison in the summer of 1916, Princip not only re-created the pre-war atmosphere of rebellion against the Habsburg state; he also set down the lines on which some of the post-war controversy about the origins of the First World War was to move. He told Dr Pappenheim that the war would have broken out in any case, even without the Sarajevo assassination. He added that the assassination of Franz Ferdinand was his own idea, and that he was fully responsible for involving his friends in it. He was talking to Dr Pappenheim, we should bear in mind, at a time when independent Serbia no longer existed: it had been occupied by enemy armies in the summer of 1916.

The war, it seemed, would not help to advance Serbia's cause, and Princip perhaps felt inclined to say that it would have broken out in any case. Otherwise, he took full responsibility for the assassination in Sarajevo. At this point, we enter a shadowy world, the world of conspiracy: I should like to indicate Princip's place in that world. He was a reserved, withdrawn person, a loner at the centre of a conspiracy. In Sarajevo, he told his interrogators that 'I had little to do with people at all. Wherever I went, people took me for a weakling . . . and I pretended that I was a weak person, which I was not.'[5] Love and revenge for his people, action and sacrifice were closely linked in his mind. It seems that the idea of 'his people' was, for Princip, much less sharply defined

---

[4] Princip told Dr Pappenheim that in Belgrade alone there were six high schools, whereas only four high schools existed in the whole of Bosnia. There were in fact twelve high schools in the province in 1908. Nevertheless, the level of illiteracy was still high, running at about 90 per cent at the turn of the century: in 1902, only thirty Bosnians had received higher education. An act of educational chicanery barred them from attending those universities in Austria-Hungary where instruction was given in a Slav language.

[5] V. Dedijer, *The Road to Sarajevo* (London, 1966), 197.

than the figure of his enemy, the Habsburg authorities in Bosnia-Hércegovina. For Princip and his friends, their people were the South Slavs. They believed in a vague union of the Serbs, the Croats, and the Slovenes, under the leadership of the kingdom of Serbia. At the outset of the Balkan Wars in 1912, Princip volunteered in Belgrade to serve in a partisan unit. He was turned down because he was too small. The person who had refused Princip's offer was Major Tankosić, who was to become one of the central figures in the Belgrade military conspiracy to assassinate Franz Ferdinand. On his visit to Belgrade, when the assassination was being prepared, Princip refused to see Tankosić: he never forgave Tankosić for his earlier humiliation. Again referring to himself in the third person, Princip told Dr Pappenheim that 'Čabrinović and Grabež [the other two young Bosnians who went to Sarajevo to carry out the assassination] were with him [i.e. Princip] in Serbia. The three had resolved to carry out the assassination. It was his [i.e. Princip's] idea. . . . Major Tankosić knew only at the last moment, when they were spiritually ready.' At his Sarajevo trial, Princip described Tankosić as a 'naïve man'.

In the summer of 1916, there was no need for Princip to defend either his friends or Serbia. The latter no longer existed, and his friends were either in prison or dead. He probably genuinely believed that the assassination was his idea; and apart from saying that the idea of assassinating Franz Ferdinand was very much in the air, and that other people conceived it at the same time as Princip, it is difficult to contradict him. There may have been another reason why Princip believed that the final decision to go ahead with the plans for the assassination was his. According to one version of the preparations to assassinate Archduke Franz Ferdinand, soon after 15 June a message was sent to Sarajevo by the military conspirators united in the secret society called Unity or Death (Ujedinjenje ili smrt), through Major Tankosić, that the assassination plan should be aborted. Apparently, Princip refused to obey.[6]

For several years before the summer of 1914, parts of the Austrian establishment were obsessed with the threat of a South Slav conspiracy against them, involving Serbia and, at one remove,

---

[6] Cf. Dedijer, op. cit. (above, n. 5), 393.

Russia. The origins of that fear must be sought in developments which were set in motion just a hundred years earlier. The history of the modern kingdom of Serbia reaches back to the first two decades of the nineteenth century, and the early phase of the national revolutions against Ottoman rule in the Balkans. In December 1806, Belgrade was occupied by a Serbian peasant army, which took control of the whole pashalik. The first revolt against the Turks was led by Karadjordje; Miloš Obrenović led the second uprising, in 1814. From then on, the two families of Serb pig-breeders contested the leadership of Serbia into the twentieth century. After the second revolt, the pasha was removed from Belgrade, and Miloš Obrenović replaced him, administering the country and collecting tribute for the Turks. Autocratic, corrupt, and illiterate, he was close to the peasants he led, and became a popular prince. He ran the pashalik as his private property, and his success rested on his shrewd dealings with the declining Ottoman power. The pashalik was poor, primitive, and remote, and was crossed by only two roads which were thought suitable for carriages. The uprisings had delivered the land into the hands of Serbian peasants. They grew maize, and the breeding of, and commerce in, swine created little enclaves of prosperity in their country.

In October 1830, the Ottomans granted Serbia autonomous status; three years later, a long strip of territory was added to the pashalik on its southern border. The first political organization—the Constitutionalist Party—was founded during the reign of Miloš, and a constitution was agreed on. The Constitutionalist Party disapproved of the Prince's singular ways, and supported the election in 1842 of Alexander Karadjordjević, the son of the revolutionary leader. The new prince lost much of the power possessed by his predecessor to a council representing the emergent groups, including servants of the state and business men. In the 1860s, the Obrenović dynasty was back in power: Michael Obrenović distinguished himself by making the army stronger, and by laying down a network of agreements—with Montenegro, Greece, and Roumania—which were based on the assumption that the Balkan peoples had a common interest in getting rid of the Ottoman impositions.

Under King Milan however, renewed military conflicts with the Ottomans after 1875 exhausted the Serbs, and then the

Congress of Berlin provided another shock for the remaining optimists in Belgrade. Austria was awarded control of the areas which the Serb nationalists coveted, and regarded as their own: Bosnia, Hercegovina, and the Sanjak of Novi Pazar. The Russians showed as yet little interest in the Serbian cause. Reluctantly, the Serbs had to deal with Vienna rather than with St Petersburg over the future of their country. Commercial agreements were made between Vienna and Belgrade, and Serbia's agricultural produce was dispatched to Austria, a large market, and one close at hand. In 1882, Vienna supported Belgrade's endeavour to endow Serbia with the status of a kingdom. New political parties emerged, and an old constitution was employed for the time being to regulate a more vigorous political life. Nikola Pašić began organizing the peasantry for the first time in his Radical Party. King Milan's private life scandalized those who knew about it; then his divorce from Queen Natalija divided the country. In 1887 the Queen left Serbia, taking with her their son Alexander, the heir to the throne. The Obrenović dynasty was coming under growing pressure, and Milan had to resign. From the end of the year 1888, Alexander, the new king, did his best to resist. He had inherited his father's natural predilections, and proved, if anything, even more prone to personal as well as political accident.

The turning-point in the relations between Austria and Serbia was not so much the annexation of Bosnia-Hercegovina in 1908, as the brutal military coup in Belgrade five years earlier, which has already been mentioned. The King, his Queen, her two brothers, and the Minister of War were assassinated and thrown out of the window by a group of military conspirators, ambitious for their country, who installed Peter Karadjordjević, from the rival dynasty, as ruler. The coup was on the whole approved of in Serbia; we have noted that it was abroad where distaste for the deed was strongly expressed. Immediately after the change of dynasty in Belgrade, there was unpleasantness between Austria and Serbia concerning credits, railways, and the sale of military equipment. The Austrians then placed an embargo on the import of Serbian livestock in 1906, and this 'pig war' dragged on for five years. Shortly before the outbreak of the pig war, in 1905, the Serbs had concluded a pact with the Bulgarians which provided for improved economic relations and an eventual economic union between the two countries. Austria's effort to prise them apart drove Serbia closer to Russia and to her ally, France.

In 1908, Vienna decided formally to annex Bosnia and Hercegovina. Soon, several societies aimed at weakening and dislodging Habsburg power in the Balkans began to be formed, both on Habsburg territory and in Belgrade. Unity or Death, also known as the Black Hand, was run in Belgrade by Col. Dimitrijević, one of the 1903 conspirators and the head of the Serb army intelligence. It had links with Bosnia, and perhaps some Russian support. The Austro-Hungarian government was, it should be said, highly suspicious of Russian intentions in the Balkans, suspicions which were deepened by reports concerning pan-Slav agitation in eastern Galicia, close to the Russian–Austrian border. And when they came to deal with the so-called South Slav conspiracy, the authorities in Vienna blundered easily. In 1909 and 1910, at the Agram (Zagreb) and Friedjung treason trials the evidence produced to substantiate the alleged connections between Belgrade and the South Slav rebels was shown to have been forged. Yet the Austrians did not give up in their pursuit of the South Slav conspiracy. Their moment came in the summer of 1914. The Austrian ultimatum to Serbia has been described as 'tardy, incompetent, designed to be rejected'.[7] It contained a reference to the 'existence of a subversive movement in Serbia, the aim of which is to detach certain territories from Austria-Hungary'.[8] The ultimatum also included a demand that Austrian officials should join an investigation concerning the Sarajevo murders, an investigation which was to be conducted in Serbia itself.[9]

The question of Serbia's complicity in the Sarajevo murders was central to the Austrian declaration of war on Serbia on 28 July. Little need be added to the fact that Col. Dimitrijević was involved, together with his secret society, in preparing the assassination.

[7] J. Remak, '1914: The Third Balkan War — Origins Reconsidered', *Journal of Modern History*, 43 (1971), 353–66.

[8] Z. A. B. Zeman, *The Break-up of the Habsburg Empire* (London, 1961), 38.

[9] The links between the Sarajevo assassins and Belgrade continued to haunt the Austrians. When Emperor Charles's brother-in-law, Prince Sixtus of Bourbon-Parma, approached Clemenceau in the matter of a separate peace treaty in February 1917, the proposal contained the request that all those responsible for the Sarajevo assassination should be punished and that all secret societies which had been active against the Habsburg Empire should be dissolved.

Equally, it is known that the Prime Minister, Pašić, was hostile to the army conspirators, that he knew of the preparations for the Sarajevo assassinations, but that he took no effective steps to stop them in the late spring and early summer of 1914.[10] The war between Austria and Serbia which broke out on 28 July was a war which both sides wanted, and the First World War was in the first place a war between them. The initial belligerence of Austria and Serbia was first submerged by a general war, and then largely disappeared from historical memory. Serbia emerged among the victors in 1918, and was rewarded by the peacemakers for its suffering during the war. Allied publicity during the war created the image of Serbia as a small, noble, and brave country. The Habsburg Empire, though it no longer existed at the end of 1918 (or perhaps because it did not) also acquired a pacific reputation. The Austro-Hungarian army came to be remembered as a comic operetta army; the late Emperor Francis Joseph emerged, first in biographical literature written in German, as a benevolent bureaucrat, who loved his many peoples, rather than as a petulant old man, with a preference for military uniforms and military solutions.

The militarization of western European societies before 1914, when the requirements of the armies and the navies defeated financial and budgetary prudence, extended to eastern Europe and the Balkans. In Serbia, civil government was unable to control military spending or military conspiracy. The last act of the feud between the civil government and the military clique was played out at the Saloniki trial during the war, when Col. Dimitrijević was sentenced to death. Historians who have described the First World War as the Third Balkan War have had, I think, a valid point to make. Professor Fritz Fischer made at one time a gallant attempt to annex war guilt as a German historical province.[11] United Germany was a young state, its ambition not yet tempered by experience; it nevertheless played the international game according to recognized rules. In the case of the Balkan conundrum, it seems to me, there were other, longer-term and less perceptible factors in play. They operated beyond the

---

[10] Dedijer, op. cit. (above, n. 5), 390. Cf. also L. Albertini; *The Origins of the War of 1914* (Oxford, 1953) ii. 97; and Borivoje Nešković, *Istina o Solunskom procesu* (Belgrade, 1953), *passim*.

[11] Cf. Preface, above.

political considerations and diplomatic moves which took Austria and Serbia first, and then Austria and Russia, into the war.

The Balkans possess a certain geographical ambiguity: they are linked to the centre of Europe and the Pannonian plain of the Eurasian steppe. The Balkan peninsula is not protected by mountain ranges as are the Italian and the Iberian peninsulas: the river valleys run from the coastal plain deep inland. The peninsula is open to the north and to the east. For centuries the Austrians and the Russians fought the Turks and the Tartars on the periphery of the Ottoman Empire. Austria and Russia used similar strategy: the Habsburgs established their military border in the northern territory of the Balkans and peopled it with Slavs. The Russians had their steppe Cossacks: they fulfilled a similar function to that of the *granichari*, the Slav frontiersmen of the Habsburg Empire. These military borders came to form a virtually continuous zone on the northern periphery of the Ottoman dominions, and by the end of the eighteenth century the Russians and the Austrians had fought and advanced— sometimes in alliance—against different parts of those dominions. In 1812 the Russians completed the move, which had taken them into Crimea, with the acquisition of Bessarabia. About the same time, in the north, the Polish state disappeared. The Habsburg and the Russian spheres of interest began to move closer together. It was only a matter of time and of political circumstance before their interests in the Balkans would start to overlap closely.

In addition, the demographic situation in the Balkans was sharply different from that of the rest of Europe. Until about 1880, the rate of population growth for the whole of the Balkans was below the European average. In the 1880s, the Balkans started to move well ahead of the rest of Europe: a sudden leap in population took place here in the two or three decades before the outbreak of the war.[12] Among the newly independent Balkan countries, Roumania and Bulgaria showed a large increase first

[12] Cf. D. V. Glass and E. Grebenik, 'World Population 1800–1950', *The Cambridge Economic History of Europe*, vol. 6 (Cambridge, 1965) pt. 1, p. 62; I. T. Berend and G. Ránki, *Economic Development in East-Central Europe in the 19th and 20th Centuries* (New York, 1974), 19.

(more than forty births for 1,000 people); after 1900, death-rates in those two countries, as well as in Serbia, began to decline. In the last pre-war decade, population growth in all three countries moved ahead in virtual uniformity, at the high rate of about 1½ per cent a year. It amounted then to about double the average annual population growth in Austria-Hungary.[13]

The usual outlets for population pressure seem not to have been readily available in the Balkans during these three or so decades before the First World War. There was, it is true, some displacement of religious and ethnic minorities, consequent on the decline of the Ottoman Empire. But such displacement resulted in refugees rather than migrants. The habit of long-distance emigration, on the other hand, was not well established in the Balkans, and the opportunities for internal emigration were also severely curtailed. The growth of industries and of towns was delayed or stunted. Perhaps more than anywhere else in Europe, population pressure in the Balkans remained, in the first and the last instance, on the land.

Land reform, together with nationalism, has been recognized by historians of central and south-eastern Europe as the main problem of the area in the century after 1848. Beyond land reform, there lay the even less tractable problem of growing population pressure in the countryside. Nevertheless, it seems that the newly independent Balkan states devised one way of dealing with their difficulties. They acquired huge peasant armies, and they learned to use them in an aggressive and impatient way. The First and the Second Balkan Wars occupied the years 1912 and 1913, and resulted in severe losses of population. In this sense as well, the First World War, which grew out of the Balkan seed-plot, was indeed the Third Balkan War.

In Bosnia-Hercegovina, the high Balkan rate of population growth seems likewise to have been sustained. In the years between 1880 and 1910, the population of the united province increased by some 64 per cent.[14] Bearing in mind the unreliability of population statistics and the understandable reluctance of political historians to address themselves to

---

[13] J. Lampe and M. Jackson, *Balkan Economic History, 1550–1950* (Bloomington, Ind., 1982), 164.

[14] From 1,158,440 to 1,898,055 in 1910. Cf. Sugar, op. cit. (above, n. 3), 5.

demographic problems, I should nevertheless like to suggest that the drastic demographic changes in the Balkans lay closer to the surface of Balkan politics than we have hitherto assumed.[15] In the states of Western Europe, where national identities were sharply defined and where there existed well-functioning outlets for the growing population, the demographic ebb and flow—and its political implications—were perhaps less obvious. In the Balkans, neither of those two conditions obtained. There, national identities were much less firmly fixed; and nascent ethnic and political groups were about to clash over their share of a place in the sun. Population pressure added an extra dimension to political and military conflicts. It was much less easy to relieve such pressure there than it was in western Europe.

Gavrilo Princip wanted to be a soldier, and he bore a lasting grudge against the man who turned him down for service in the Serb army. He became a conspirator instead. On 28 June 1914, seven potential assassins stalked their victims through the streets of Sarajevo. Five of the seven were not yet twenty years old. They were the sons and brothers of peasants, village schoolmasters, innkeepers, priests. All their families lived in the poor, increasingly over-populated countryside. They grew up in an area where one imperial power had recently been replaced by another. They were convinced that there was no future for them and for their people in Austria-Hungary. They gladly allowed their youth and their idealism to be used in a daring act of violence. Their frustration was a symbol of the tensions in the Balkans which came to a head early in the twentieth century. In an area with a strenuously military past, it is hard to see how those tensions could have had any other than a military solution.

[15] It seems that, in Russia as well, in the most densely populated area of the Empire, the north-east to south-west axis running across European Russia, there also occurred a striking shift of balance. Until about half-way through the nineteenth century, it was the north-eastern part of the axis where population was increasing most quickly. By 1914, the balance had moved to the south-west of that axis, especially to the Ukrainian provinces of Kiev, Podolia, and Poltava, the very territories which adjoined the Habsburg Empire and the Balkans.

3

The Habsburg Monarchy and the Coming of War*

R. J. W. EVANS

ONE notable Austrian historian, Friedrich Engel-Janosi, recounts in his memoirs how in 1914 he discussed with a student colleague which regiment they should volunteer for. 'I suggest the howitzers,' said the other. 'But what is a howitzer?' asked Engel-Janosi. 'Well, if we enlist there we should find out.'[1] I am in the same boat with them; I know nothing of the technicalities of warfare. Yet I do know one thing about the howitzer. It belongs among the handful of English words which derive from one of the (non-German) vernaculars of the Habsburg lands, from Czech in fact. It may therefore serve me as the introductory symbol for an Austro-Hungarian dimension to the events of 1914 which is nowadays too often forgotten.

Responsibility for the decisions taken in the exact calendar month between Sarajevo and the bombardment of Belgrade has, of course, been richly and minutely documented. There are upwards of 1,500 separate items for the month of July 1914 in the authoritative series of official volumes entitled *Österreich-Ungarns Außenpolitik* and related documents. Ever more detailed exercises in the apportionment of blame culminated in the monumental and superb examination by Luigi Albertini— himself engaged against Austria in the public life of Italy on the eve of the war, but in his later years a scrupulous scholar none the less—which appeared in English during the 1950s.[2] The

---

*This text stands more or less as it was delivered in 1984. S. R. Williamson, in S. R. Williamson and P. Pastor (eds.), *Essays on World War One: Origins and Prisoners of War* (New York, 1983), 9–36, has likewise sought a reassessment of Austria-Hungary's role in the outbreak of war.

[1] F. Engel-Janosi, . . . *aber ein stolzer Bettler* (Graz, 1974), 43.

[2] *Österreich-Ungarns Außenpolitik 1908–1914*, ed. L. Bittner and H. Uebersberger, i–viii (Vienna, 1930), vol. viii; L. Albertini, *The Origins of the War of 1914*, i–iii (Oxford, 1952–7). The earlier bibliography is very fully recorded in K. and M. Uhlirz, *Handbuch der Geschichte Österreichs und seiner Nachbarländer Böhmen und Ungarn*, i–iv (Vienna, 1927–44, vol. iii. 7–78.

problems of the Dual Monarchy formed the starting-point and the continuing focus for Albertini's analysis; and yet received opinion here is now inclined to pass lightly over them. On the one hand (outside a small band of specialists) the 'antique', 'obsolete' social and political system of Austria-Hungary and her unregenerate procedures appear a sufficient condemnation in themselves. On the other hand, since Fritz Fischer, Germany bears a sufficient weight of opprobrium for her ally to be quietly dropped from consideration. There is no need to penetrate her Byzantine corridors for they are not the corridors of power. The American historian Barbara Tuchman, in her otherwise very perceptive and spirited popular account of August 1914 and its antecedents, accords to Austrian actions a grand total of five words: she describes them as exemplifying the 'bellicose frivolity of senile empires'.[3]

Something has gone wrong here. We are, after all, not dealing with *a* European war widely thought inevitable, but with *the* European war engaged as the direct consequence of the assassination of the heir to the throne of the Habsburgs, a war which no one else would have precipitated at just that time or in just those conditions. The first important point for me to make is that the high policy-makers of the Monarchy actively provoked that war, because they saw the circumstances of the assassination as themselves a fateful provocation to Austria-Hungary. They were able to do so because of a remarkable unanimity among those who directed the cumbrous machinery of government that the death of the Archduke must be avenged, some who moved most swiftly being among those who had most disliked him. 'A higher power has restored that order which I alas could not sustain.' Thus runs one of the more plausible quotations widely attributed to the old Emperor, Francis Joseph, on hearing the news from Sarajevo. But it soon appeared that

---

[3] F. Fischer, *Germany's Aims in the First World War* (Eng. trans. London, 1967), 29 ff.; id., *War of Illusions* (Eng. trans. London, 1975), 470 ff. J. Remak's explicit riposte to Fischer, in *Journal of Modern History*, 43 (1971), 353–66, is too lightweight to convince. B. Tuchman, *The Guns of August* (New York, 1962), 91. Several contributions in *Österreich-Ungarn in der Weltpolitik, 1900–1918*, ed. Fritz Klein (Berlin, 1965), deserved more international resonance than they appear to have found. The author of one of them, Leo Valiani, concentrates in his *The End of Austria-Hungary* (Eng. trans. London, 1973) mainly on relations with Italy.

the higher power still needed a further nudge in the right direction.[4]

I do not need to dwell on Franz Ferdinand, about whose gifted but authoritarian and at times well-nigh paranoid character, and whose superficially radical, yet in essence profoundly Catholic-conservative schemes, there is now much belated historiographical agreement. It was typical of the Archduke that he planned to rule as Francis II, thus wilfully reviving memories of the most obscurantist period in Austrian history.[5] But we should note a further double irony. Though breathing fire against domestic insubordination and slaughtering Bohemia's wildlife with reckless abandon, Franz Ferdinand had actually been peaceable towards the Balkans, apparently because he feared a conflagration with Russia which, subverted by Freemasons and the like, might bring down both empires. His death therefore not merely gave the pretext for war, but removed a major obstacle to it; and by cutting off the heir's own headquarters in the Belvedere palace in Vienna it also simplified the machinery for implementing it. Most important of all, though, it changed the mind of an exact contemporary of the Archduke's, who had shared his Balkan caution. Berchtold was persuaded into belligerence.

Leopold, Count Berchtold, career diplomat and Foreign Minister of Austria-Hungary since the death of Aehrenthal in 1912, has often been depicted as a fainéant, even a cipher. Some contemporaries viewed him thus too, but at least since the publication of his letters, diaries, and other testimonies to his

[4] For the Emperor's remark: V. Bibl, *Die Tragödie Österreichs* (Leipzig and Vienna, 1937), 502; *Ein General im Zwielicht: Die Erinnerungen Edmund Glaises von Horstenau*, ed. P. Broucek, i (Vienna, Cologne, and Graz, 1980), 276–7 and n. The question of how far the Austro-Hungarian leadership actually willed a *general* war is surely unanswerable. Clearly there was a preparedness to risk it, especially among military chiefs. A later comment by the Minister of War, Krobatin (printed in *Protokolle des Gemeinsamen Ministerrates der Österreichisch-Ungarischen Monarchie (1914–1918)*, ed. M. Komjáthy [Budapest, 1966], 370), has been adduced as evidence that they had already discounted the risk involved, though I fancy the passage cannot bear so much weight.

[5] R. A. Kann, *Erzherzog Franz Ferdinand Studien* (Munich, 1976), is very authoritative. Cf. M. von Auffenberg-Komarów, *Aus Österreichs Höhe und Niedergang, eine Lebensschilderung* (Munich, 1921), 226 ff.; R. Sieghart, *Die letzten Jahrzehnte einer Großmacht* (Berlin, 1932), 234–43 and *passim*; F. Funder, *Vom Gestern ins Heute* (2nd edn. Vienna and Munich, 1953), 486–517, for some contemporary testimonies.

commitment and sense of duty by Hantsch twenty-five years ago, that seems an unfair and misleading opinion.[6] Berchtold, brought unwillingly back out of retirement merely out of loyalty to Francis Joseph, was a mirror of his diplomatic service perhaps: firmness had paid off in 1908 over the Annexation, and twice in 1913 when the Serbs had been on the point of occupying the Albanian coast. But Berchtold did not share the general hawkishness of men like Forgách (tarred with the brush of the Zagreb trial forgeries), Giesl, Musulin, Hoyos, and Burián;[7] he had previously been accommodating almost to a fault, which was why some belittled him. Now, however, he personally modified the existing *aide-mémoire* on Austro-Hungarian foreign policy into that document of immediate militancy which, known to history as the Hoyos memorandum, was sent to Berlin on 5 July.[8] We may surmise that, in the light of Serbian actions and attitudes on both sides of the frontier, he henceforth perceived little difference between peace and war anyway. And we can hardly blame him for believing that, at some point, prestige was worth fighting for—one great commonplace of his or any age.

Of course, Austria-Hungary needed to ensure German support: the 'blank cheque' in response to Count Hoyos's mission; she also needed, as an explosive corollary, to show herself worthy of the alliance—the soft underbelly, as it were, of the need for prestige. But so did Germany *vis-à-vis* Austria-Hungary: the literature on the Dual Alliance illustrates that clearly, at all events since Agadir.[9] We may compare the simultaneous, equal but opposite,

[6] H. Hantsch, *Leopold Graf Berchtold: Grandseigneur und Staatsmann*, i–ii (Graz, 1963).

[7] W. Giesl, *Zwei Jahrzehnte im Nahen Orient* (Berlin, 1927); A. von Musulin, *Das Haus am Ballplatz: Erinnerungen eines österreichisch-ungarischen Diplomaten* (Munich, 1924), scrappy; A. Hoyos, *Der deutsch-englische Gegensatz und sein Einfluß auf die Balkanpolitik Österreich-Ungarns* (Berlin and Leipzig, 1922), an impersonal little tract. In general see Hantsch, op. cit. (above, n. 6), i, chs. 5–7; ii, chs. 8–9.

[8] H. B. A. Petersson in *Scandia*, 30 (1964), 138–90, an important article.

[9] Albertini, op. cit. (above, n. 2), ii. 120 ff., 254 ff., is very thorough on this aspect of the July Crisis: 'Berlin could encourage and spur on to attack, but the initiative was taken by Austria' (ibid. 148). See Fischer, op. cit. (above, n. 3), 147, 205 ff., 291 ff., and F. R. Bridge, *From Sadowa to Sarajevo: The Foreign Policy of Austria-Hungary, 1866–1914* (London, 1972), 310 ff., for developments in the years before 1914, the latter adding a firmly un-Fischerite view of the aftermath of Sarajevo.

hesitations of the two powers in the last moments of peace, at the end of July. Vienna was certainly not waiting for instructions; indeed, the Habsburg capital exhibited a rare harmony of its military and civil leadership.

The military were notoriously spoiling for a fight: a limited engagement presumably, no worse than the Boer War, which represented a plausible scenario for a campaign in the Balkans on several grounds (is it significant that Berchtold had served in London around 1900 and sympathized with the British?). They even sought a cleansing *démarche* against the Italians, a posture commonly reckoned the height of Chief of Staff Conrad's hubris, though the planning for it before 1914 and its later execution suggest that the Italian front, not the Serbian, was best suited to the joint army's talents.[10] Yet the military carried no great weight with the twin governments, Austrian and Hungarian, of the Monarchy. Indeed the unpreparedness of the army, thanks to politicians, is a leitmotif of the public utterances and memoirs of service chiefs — awkwardly yoked, it must be said, to the same men's advocacy of preventive war. And despite the sophistication of some Škoda armaments, even by German standards (witness their use on the western front in August 1914), that was true.[11]

Why were governments now ready to place their fate in the army's hands? It was a turbulent business, as any textbook tells us, to rule Austria. Freud (of whom more later) cited as an example of parapraxis — i.e. a 'Freudian slip' — the case of a president of the lower house of the parliament (Reichsrat) in Vienna, who

[10] F. Conrad von Hoetzendorf, *Aus meiner Dienstzeit*, i–v (Vienna, 1921–5), *passim*. War against Italy is clearly calculated into the combat instructions provided for the Austro-Hungarian army before 1914, e.g. *Mobilisierungsinstruktion für das k.u.k. Heer. Allgemeiner Teil* (2nd edn. Vienna, 1910), 22 (interpreters), 147 ff. ('Kriegsfall J'), etc.; *Detailbeschreibung des österreichisch-italienischen Grenzgebietes Plöcken-Isonzo* (Vienna, 1905; Nachtrag, 1909). There is an interesting argument by M. Palumbo in Williamson and Pastor (eds.), op. cit. (above, asterisked n.) 37–53, that Austria-Hungary actually reached some kind of *rapprochement* with Italy on the eve of Sarajevo, thanks to the pro-*Triplice* views of the Italian chief of staff, Pollio, who died on — 28 June 1914. Cf. now the early chapters of H. J. Pantenius's massive *Der Angriffsgedanke gegen Italien bei Conrad von Hötzendorf* (Cologne and Vienna, 1984).

[11] *Die Vorgeschichte von 1866 und 19??* (Vienna and Leipzig, 1909) is an example of pamphleteering 'von einem alten kaiserlichen Soldaten' [in fact Hugo Kerchnawe?]; Auffenberg-Komarów, op. cit. (above, n. 5), 154 ff. an example from the memoir literature.

opened a session by declaring it closed.[12] In March 1914 the Premier, Stürgkh, was forced, not altogether unwillingly, to prorogue the unruly Reichsrat. Was this Austria's 'Kiel canal', the green light for an active policy, precisely in mid-1914, which might bind the squabbling nationalities together in a more coherent bond of loyalty? Maybe. The diarist Joseph Redlich records the Emperor as confiding: 'In meinem Reich kann man nicht parlamentarisch regieren.' But Redlich, maverick politician and bitter enemy of Stürgkh, is himself good evidence that bellicose noises were widespread in ruling circles in Austria.[13]

The Hungarian regime was less amenable still to army demands. In fact the military question lay at the root of Hungary's constitutional struggle with the Emperor and the rest of the Monarchy. (Since the Magyars have so often been excoriated for this by historians, often by historians not otherwise conspicuous for their sympathy to the Habsburg cause, it is worth observing, parenthetically, that they had a case: at the beginning of 1914 a mere 7 per cent of officials in the War Office were Hungarian.)[14] At a ministerial council on 7 July the Hungarian Premier, István Tisza, alone resisted the preparations to crush Serbia; a week later he fell in with them, provided there should be no annexations. His shifting position has engendered much debate. Was he persuaded by the evidence of Serbian guilt, as he himself claimed? Hardly, since little more was forthcoming during the week when he changed his mind. Was he persuaded by German pressure, as most commentators have assumed? Hardly, since German backing was known about on the 7th, and Tisza, who had just fortified himself with extra domestic powers, albeit not on the scale of Stürgkh's, was no man to be browbeaten. Perhaps — so Hungarian historians have recently argued (one of

[12] E. R. Tannenbaum, *1900: The Generation before the Great War* (New York, 1976), 251.

[13] 'My Empire cannot be ruled by a parliament': *Schicksalsjahre Österreichs. Das politische Tagebuch Joseph Redlichs 1908-1919*, ed. F. Fellner, i-ii (Graz and Cologne, 1953-4), i. 94. Cf., for Redlich's own view, ibid. 24: 'The State and the Empire have both become so weak that only an energetic recovery of full monarchical power will be able to help'; and 164-5 on the need for a 'policy of the bold offensive', a 'ruthless offensive in concert with the German Reich'.

[14] J. Galántai, *Magyarország az első világháborúban 1914-1918* (Budapest, 1974), 18-19. The subject is too large to be broached here. N. Stone, in *Past and Present*, 33 (1966), 95-111, surely exaggerates.

very few recent contributions to the themes of this section of the present chapter)—he rather reconsidered the larger international situation, came to doubt the advantages of delaying an inevitable Balkan adventure, and accepted the urgings of the Emperor.[15] At all events his qualms, never entirely assuaged, but soon overlaid by furious activity, were revealed to the world at large only in 1918.

Thus action could be agreed and co-ordinated. But the form action would take, and its implications for the rest of Europe, were fatally influenced by the labyrinthine workings of the Austro-Hungarian state apparatus: especially slow-moving, indeed, where Bosnia was concerned, since Bosnia-Hercegovina was administered as a joint territory of the Monarchy and yielded peculiarly sharp squabbles between military and various civil authorities.[16] Hence, in part, the inadequate security preparations for Franz Ferdinand's visit which have often been remarked upon, and which I cannot go into here. After Sarajevo the clumsiness of the decision-making process meant a time-span neither short enough nor long enough to defuse the situation. Why was there no immediate retaliation against the Serbs, when a shocked and condolatory Europe might have remained on the sidelines? Why, on the other hand, a whole month later was the Monarchy so desperate to avoid international attempts at mediation that a border incident had to be invoked (even faked?) to justify invasion? Again the questions raised here, familiar to specialists, are not suited to be dwelt on in a general survey.

Undoubtedly the authorities felt it necessary first to measure and demonstrate the complicity of the Serbian kingdom. The need for moral and legal sanction, which led to a fact-finding

---

[15] Galántai, op. cit. (above, n. 14), 100–18; id., in *Századok*, 98 (1964), 687–709; I. Diószegi, *A magyar külpolitika útjai: tanulmányok* (Budapest, 1984), 278–87. Cf. N. Stone in *Journal of Contemporary History*, 1 (1966), 153–70, for received views; and contrast earlier Magyar attempts to mitigate his—and Hungary's—responsibilities, finding some leverage in documents released to the West by H. Marczali in *American Historical Review*, 29 (1924), 301–15, and in Tisza's letter to his daughter in *Gróf Tisza István összes munkái*, ser. 4, vol. v (Budapest, 1933), pp. xxxv–xl.

[16] Auffenberg-Komarów, op. cit. (above, n. 5), 128 ff.; L. Biliński, *Wspomnienia i dokumenty, 1846–1922*, i–ii (Warsaw, 1924–5), i. esp. 231 ff., 272 ff.; J. M. Baernreither, *Fragmente eines politischen Tagebuchs*, ed. J. Redlich (Berlin, 1928), *passim*. See now especially L. Thallóczy, *Tagebücher 23. VI. 1914–31. XII. 1914*, ed. F. Hauptmann and A. Prasch (Graz, 1981); Thallóczy was a bureaucrat, a senior adviser on the Balkans, and a historian.

mission by the diplomat Friedrich von Wiesner in mid-July, between the two crucial ministerial councils, was not just a pretext. Otherwise the Austrians would hardly have allowed the Serbian army commander Putnik, who happened to be drinking the waters in Styria, to return home unmolested on the eve of the conflict.[17] Undoubtedly the authorities then felt the need for a firm hand, leaving no loopholes for the shameless cunning of Pašić: hence the presentation of watertight demands, which would most probably be rejected. (Even so they were not watertight enough.) Undoubtedly, large logistical issues were involved in putting the main and subsidiary Habsburg armies on a war footing: the mobilization instructions, general and particular, cover hundreds of closely printed pages and tables.[18]

Yet the events of July, equally undoubtedly, compromised the Monarchy's integrity. First the sordid circumstances of the exequies of Franz Ferdinand and his morganatic wife were aggravated by an unwillingness to invite foreign heads of state to them; thus was lost a chance for fruitful diplomatic exchanges. Then Wiesner—to his credit, in a way, and foreshadowing the fair trial later accorded to Princip and his fellow conspirators—actually minimized Serbian involvement in the assassination. He was, of course, wrong. So the subsequent Austrian decision to inculpate the blanket organization called the Narodna Odbrana rather than the 'Black Hand' must appear either incompetence (since others at the Ballhausplatz were not ignorant of Dimitrijević and his henchmen, who led the clandestine activities of the latter) or a machiavellian ploy to name an official organ in Belgrade rather than a secret one. Finally we have the incontinent haste both about delivery of what was an ultimatum in all but name and about rejection of the submissively prevaricating Serb response. The bizarre consequence of the precipitate decamping of the Austro-Hungarian ambassador from Belgrade was that the declaration of war had to be sent by wire, with the result that

---

[17] On Wiesner: Hantsch, op. cit. (above, n. 6), ii. 589 ff. On Putnik: H. Haselsteiner in *Österreichische Osthefte*, 16 (1974), 238–44.
[18] The *Mobilisierungsinstruktionen* were divided into an 'Allgemeiner Teil' (cf. above, n. 10), and twenty-seven 'Anhänge', all with a complicated apparatus of appendices.

Pašić at first suspected it to be a hoax.[19] Mobilization, delayed by considerations of harvest-time and desire to avoid needless expense, was shot through with confusion about how much of the army could actually be deployed against Serbia, how much was required to bolster German forces resisting a putative Russian offensive on the eastern front.[20] But in one area, at least, things moved swiftly: the parliament building in Vienna was promptly converted into a military hospital.

If her rulers succeeded in presenting the Monarchy to many in the world at large as a culpable amalgam of aggressiveness and irresolution, how did Francis Joseph's own subjects react? That is well-nigh impossible to reconstruct: there has been an understandable industry of obfuscation since the shipwreck of old Austria-Hungary spoiled the market in imperial loyalist stocks. The official response which I have outlined so far operated at a high level of secrecy and within a very restricted circle. The wider response was clearly not altogether in phase. We know that people felt emotion when they first heard of the assassination: whether shock, anger, foreboding, or relief—for the unpopularity of the Archduke was admitted, even by his admirers.[21] Not least we know it since so many could later recall exactly what they were doing at the time on that glorious summer Sunday: whether listening to a spa band which suddenly fell silent and left the podium, like Stefan Zweig; or on their knees in a church of the Vienna Woods, like the Christian Social publicist, Funder; or stalking roebuck on the Bohemian veldt, like Prince Clary, till the cook on a bicycle brought the message; or even sitting in a private archive studying the constitutional

---

[19] Albertini, op. cit. (above, n. 2), ii. 1–119, 346 ff., 453 ff., is very balanced on all this, though some puzzles remain. Cf. V. Dedijer, *Sarajevo 1914* (2nd edn. Belgrade, 1978), for fascinating details of the plot, set in a rather contrived framework of explanation. For the ambassador's view: Giesl, op. cit. (above, n. 7), 263 ff. The ultimatum was drafted by Musulin, the Serbian expert in the Austro-Hungarian Foreign Ministry being *on holiday* (Musulin, op. cit. (above, n. 7), 219 ff.). Cf. above, pp. 25, 28, for Dimitrijević and the Black Hand.

[20] N. Stone in *Historical Journal*, 9 (1966), 201–28; id., *The Eastern Front 1914–1917* (London, 1975), 70 ff.

[21] O. Czernin, *Im Weltkriege* (Berlin and Vienna, 1919), 45 ff.; O. von Bardolff, *Soldat im alten Österreich: Erinnerungen aus meinem Leben* (Jena, 1938), 129 ff.; Hantsch, op. cit. (above, n. 6), 551 ff.

history of the South Slavs, like the Balkan specialist Thallóczy (whose recently published diaries represent an important new source).[22] Equally we know that the excitement soon died back. The subdued crowds on the streets rapidly ebbed away. The introspective Arthur Schnitzler already found himself considerably more relaxed by dinner-time on the same day. Even the hypersensitive Redlich, while perceiving an 'hour of destiny for the Monarchy', could detect little immediate sign of a *démarche*. High-ranking soldiers like Auffenberg were baffled at the apparent inaction.[23]

The lull lasted right through the next four weeks, despite a continuing press campaign and flag-waving by the middle-class political parties. All the recent political clichés about the Balkans, which littered the writings of public and not-so-public figures: the need to 'make order' ('endlich Ordnung/Ruhe/reinen Tisch/klare Verhältnisse zu schaffen'), the language of tidy-minded bourgeois and colonialists *manqué*; these clichés now came home to roost. Most striking, perhaps, is the pugnacity of the Hungarian opposition, one section of which had so recently been posturing with pointed, quasi-diplomatic overtures to France, America, even Russia. But then some of those who called most vociferously for a separate Magyar-spirited army had looked thereby to *improve* the country's (and the Monarchy's) fighting potential. It has been argued that it was precisely the strength of feeling in his own and rival parties which reduced Tisza's room for manœuvre and forced him to heed the Viennese position on the ultimatum.[24]

When the wider sentiments of the population were once more engaged, after publication of the demands on Belgrade, they do

[22] S. Zweig, *Die Welt von Gestern* (Vienna, 1948), 290 ff.; Funder, op. cit. (above, n. 5), 481–2; A. Clary, *A European Past* (Eng. trans. London, 1978), 153 ff.; Thallóczy, op. cit. (above, n. 16), 5 ff.
[23] A. Schnitzler, *Tagebuch 1913–1916*, ed. W. Welzig *et al.* (Vienna, 1983), 123. Redlich, *Schicksalsjahre*, i. 233 ff.; cf. Thallóczy, loc. cit. (above, n. 16); Auffenberg-Komarów, op. cit. (above, n. 5), 256 ff.
[24] I. Dolmányos in *Annales Universitatis Scientiarum Budapestinensis, Sect. Hist.* v (1963), 147–84; Galántai, op. cit. (above, n. 14), 129 ff.; Diószegi, op. cit. (above, n. 15), 219–67; and on Tisza cf. above, n. 15. A contemporary spokesman: L. Windischgraetz, *Vom roten zum schwarzen Prinzen* (Berlin and Vienna, 1920), 16–17 and *passim*.

not seem to have been very different, either towards an offensive strike against the Serbs, or towards a European conflict conceived—with the help of Sazonov's Russian mobilization— as entered into in self-defence. The Socialist press indeed remained quite fiercely critical of the 'imperialist' attitudes of government during most of July, but by the end of the month it rallied, partly no doubt for fear of the censor, partly in hope of rewards for loyalty, but mostly because the rank and file were swept up in a fervour which their leaders could or would do little to check. We have plenty of testimony to wild enthusiasm in the first August days, with Hungarians singing the Austrian imperial hymn and so forth.[25] I would suggest that this was not an abdication of national commitment; rather a temporary heightening of it, as true patriotism suddenly embraced *ethnicum* and Monarchy at the same time, and people felt a fleeting need to express solidarity with both. The more sectional interest fuelled and complemented the larger one (rather as it had, on a more limited scale and in a different emotional register, a hundred and more years earlier), especially perhaps since the dynastic focus now rested squarely once again on Francis Joseph alone, whom most people, foremost among them the Emperor himself, reckoned to be scrupulously obeying the call of duty.

On the other hand, as is well known, certain leaders of those same nationalities, having betaken themselves into the security of exile, spoke out from the beginning of the war for the total destruction of the Dual Monarchy. Were not these calls for self-determination a kind of Austrian mirror-image of the Fischerite 'September Memorandum': in other words a true statement of what her peoples, at least her Slav peoples, really wanted when the war broke out? Hardly. Besides a number of Yugoslav propagandists confirming the point which Princip had already made more dramatically; besides the evidence, mostly at a level of mild public disorder (severely repressed) from Serb and

---

[25] Most memoirists, if they record anything at all for late July and early August 1914, record this. A good example is Hans Loewenfeld-Russ, *Im Kampf gegen den Hunger. Aus den Erinnerungen des Staatssekretärs für Volksernährung* (Munich, 1986), 1 ff. On the Socialists: L. Brügel, *Geschichte der österreichischen Sozialdemokratie*, i–v (Vienna, 1922–5), v. 152 ff.; Galántai, op. cit. (above, n. 14), 139 ff. On the mood of the army, including recruits, at the outbreak of war: *Österreich-Ungarns letzter Krieg*, i (2nd edn. Vienna, 1930), 3–38; *General im Zwielicht* (above, n. 4), 274 ff.

Ruthene areas, where some disaffection at the prospect of fighting
blood-brothers seems hardly surprising; the major case is that of
the Czechs, and they are very difficult to assess. Masaryk, more
honourable in his memoirs than most heads of state, admits to
uncertainties. He says he had hoped and expected that war would
be avoided, and hesitated to take up his moral crusade for
liberation until he encountered Kitchener's opinion that the
struggle would be a very protracted one.[26] Other nationalist
reminiscences are much more forthright, tasteless, and
implausible. The Social Democrat leader, Gustav Habrman (a
Czech, despite his name), tells us how he heard of the
assassination from a crowd leaving an open-air workers' concert
in Pilsen, none of whom expressed any sorrow. Perhaps; but when
he goes on to say that no one thereafter talked of anything but
war, a hateful war for an alien cause, he surely falsifies the record,
not least since a powerful group in his own party looked
ideologically to Vienna, centre of a multinational polity, as they
would later look to Moscow after 1918.[27]

Have we not, nevertheless, been vouchsafed a special revelation
about the mood of Bohemia in 1914? I cite the very first page
of the most famous novel by any Czech:

'So they've killed our Ferdinand,' said the charwoman to Mr Švejk,
who had left military service years before, having been finally certified
as an imbecile by an army medical board, and who now lived by selling
dogs — monstrous, ugly mongrels — whose pedigrees he forged. Apart
from that he suffered from rheumatism, and was at this moment rubbing
his knees with embrocation.

'Which Ferdinand, Mrs Müller?' he asked. 'I know two Ferdinands.
One is a messenger at Průša's the chemist; once by mistake he drank
a bottle of hair oil. The other is Ferdinand Kokoška, who collects dog
manure. Neither of them is any loss.'

'Oh no sir, it's his Imperial Highness Archduke Ferdinand . . . the fat
pious one.'

'Good Lord,' exclaimed Švejk. 'That's a fine thing. Where did it
happen?'

[26] T. G. Masaryk, *Die Weltrevolution: Erinnerungen und Betrachtungen*
(Berlin, 1925), 2–3, 6, and *passim*; *Masaryk erzählt sein Leben: Gespräche mit
Karel Čapek* (Berlin, n. d.), 138 ff.

[27] G. Habrman, *Mé vzpomínky z války* (Prague, 1928), 11 ff.; C. W. Chrislock,
'Reluctant Radicals: Czech Social Democracy and the Nationality Question' (diss.,
Indiana Univ., 1972).

'They bumped him off at Sarajevo, sir. . . . He drove there in a car. . . .'
'Well, there you are, Mrs Müller: in a car. Yes of course a gent like
him can afford it, but he never imagines how a drive like that might finish
up. And at Sarajevo into the bargain! That's in Bosnia, Mrs Müller. I expect
the Turks are at the bottom of this. You know, we ought never to have
taken Bosnia and Hercegovina from them.'[28]

The Good Soldier Švejk, of course, is not history. Yet its view of
society is not quite as burlesque as its hero's view of international
relations in the Balkans. That notorious real-life rheumatic forger
of dog pedigrees, Jaroslav Hašek, may tell us something of Czech
attitudes. Czech regiments fought rather less well, with statistically
rather fewer losses, than average; in a few cases they were a
shambles from the very beginning.[29] And if Hašek does offer
insights, it is worth noting that his creation, Josef Švejk, whether
out of cunning or idiocy, *did* volunteer; and that the author
allows himself regular satirical asides about how many of his
compatriots feathered their nests just as well in Habsburg
officialdom on the threshold of the war as later under the
Czechoslovak Republic.

The private reactions of ordinary folk (of the Mrs Müllers, as
it were) to Sarajevo and its aftermath, are still, so far as I am aware,
largely unknown. Perhaps they are largely unknowable, in that
we cannot put the right questions. If those questions be crude,
then they are inadequate to the situation; if sophisticated, then
they are not in a form which contemporaries could have
understood. We are restricted to rare glimpses, like that of Béla
Bartók who, writing a little later, describes the peasants who
supply him with folk-songs, not so far from the firing-line, as 'so
merry and light-hearted one might think they don't care a hang
about the war'.[30]

Yet there is another area—already suggested by the names of
Hašek and Bartók—where we have learned much more about

[28] My translation from J. Hašek, *Osudy dobrého vojáka Švejka*, i–iii (Prague,
1966), is based on that by C. Parrott (London, 1973), with some modifications
and abridgement.
[29] Cf. R. Plaschka in *Österreich und Europa: Festgabe für H. Hantsch* (Graz,
Vienna, and Cologne, 1965), 455–64; id., *Nationalismus, Staatsgewalt,
Widerstand* (Munich, 1985), 210–61.
[30] J. Ujfalussy, *Béla Bartók* (Budapest, 1971), 129.

Austria-Hungary in recent years. I mean the remarkable surge of international scholarly interest in the intellectual culture of Vienna and its hinterland on the eve of war, which contrasts so strongly with the neglect of the Monarchy's political contribution I pointed to earlier. I take Mrs Tuchman as target again (with respect for her achievement in other ways): her decision in *The Proud Tower*, a study published in 1966, to confine her 'portrait of the world before the war' to that 'Anglo-American and West European world from which our experience and culture most directly derive' now looks not only wrong, but dated.[31] What of Schnitzler, Kafka, Rilke, Musil, Hofmannsthal, Kraus, and Trakl? What of Klimt, Schiele, Kokoschka, and Loos? What of Mahler, Schoenberg, Berg, Webern, Janáček, Bartók, and Kodály? What of Freud and Adler, of Herzl and Buber, of Kelsen and Schumpeter, of Wittgenstein, Lukács, and Mannheim? What of more shadowy figures like Julius von Wiesner, father of our diplomat-investigator, Jewish founder of the world's first institute of plant physiology, to whom a British pupil, Houston Stewart Chamberlain, dedicated his notorious *Grundlagen des neunzehnten Jahrhunderts*?[32]

The ideas of these and other creative writers, artists, scientists, and scholars, so formative for the world of today, so forward-looking that many needed decades to take root, are now commonly reckoned to have stood in radical tension with the society which generated them. We hear much talk of intellectual revolution bred by the inertia of a moribund Monarchy, of *fin-de-siècle* withdrawal, of 'alienation', of a 'gay apocalypse', of a 'laboratory for world destruction', which brought to birth modernity out of decadence.

Does this dichotomy help us to grasp the underlying assumptions of Austria-Hungary's seemingly desperate push for war in 1914, assumptions perhaps not so much 'unspoken' as ultimately—in the language of Ludwig Wittgenstein—unspeakable? It is worth a brief look at a few of these individuals, outstandingly articulate, yet somehow characteristic of at least the elevated cultural milieu which nurtured them, in the

[31] B. Tuchman, *The Proud Tower* (New York, 1966), p. xvii.
[32] On Julius von Wiesner (1838–1916), Professor, later Rector, at the University of Vienna, cf. W. M. Johnston, *The Austrian Mind: An Intellectual and Social History, 1848–1938* (Berkeley, Calif., 1972), 70, 329.

immediate context of the weeks after the assassination. I do not propose to focus primarily on the creative achievements themselves, which raise many problems of interpretation. Though a beating of the drums may sometimes be heard—Schnitzler found indications in his own recent work, once they were pointed out to him by a patriotic newspaper article in September 1914[33]—political echoes are usually, as in Švejk, muffled, even so inaudible as to confirm critics in their view of a total divorce between intellectuals and the Habsburg state. (Besides which we may recall that the most devastating premonition of war came from a very mild music-teacher in London with a penchant for astrology: Gustav Holst composed his music for the planet Mars during the careless weeks immediately before Sarajevo.) Rather, many of those intellectuals kept diaries and wrote copious letters; and much of this material has been published. Besides the mass of personal preoccupations we shall find some larger hints.

One advanced opinion which exercised a not insignificant role within the Habsburg lands before 1914 was certainly pacifism. The pacifist movement was instigated by the redoubtable Bertha von Suttner, authoress of the best-selling novel *Lay down Your Arms* (*Die Waffen nieder*), which passed through thirty-seven editions between 1889 and 1905. She had persuaded Alfred Nobel to endow his Peace prize in the first place, and she duly won it herself, as did her fellow-Austrian collaborator, Alfred Fried (*nomen est omen!*). Maybe that does not mean too much: the prize was actually offered to Foreign Minister Aehrenthal in 1907, one year before his Bosnian adventure. But Baroness von Suttner foresaw the enormities of total war. When she died, seven days before Sarajevo, she was busy with plans for a peace congress to meet, in Vienna, in August 1914.[34]

Her ideas were taken up by other intellectuals of markedly diverse backgrounds: by Friedrich Adler, son of the Austrian Socialist leader, himself leader of a radical socialist grouping, who was then to be so goaded by war and the conduct of it that he

[33] Schnitzler, op. cit. (above, n. 23), 135.
[34] In general: R. Chickering, *Imperial Germany and a World without War: The Peace Movement and German Society, 1892–1914* (Princeton, 1975), 77 ff. and *passim*, who, while neglecting the Habsburg lands as such, shows how the German movement was dominated by these two cantankerous Austrians. Bridge, op. cit. (above, n. 9), 291 (Aehrenthal).

assassinated the Austrian premier Stürgkh in 1916; by the anarcho-syndicalist Ervin Szabó in Hungary; by the distinguished academic lawyer, Heinrich Lammasch, whom only the personal intervention of Francis Joseph kept from imprisonment in 1914, and who was to function four years later as the last premier of Habsburg Austria; by students like the Galician Jew, Joseph Roth, subsequently a nostalgic literary chronicler of the Austrian military tradition.[35] Literary manifestations of anti-militarism would be a subject in themselves, from Schnitzler's stream-of-consciousness monologue *Leutnant Gustl* (1900), for which he was cashiered as a reserve officer, to Hašek, who began writing stories about Švejk in 1911: but not, perhaps, a large subject. Its most famous representative was the virulent satirist Karl Kraus. Yet Kraus, for all his forebodings before 1914: 'We're complicated enough to build machines, too primitive to be served by them . . . we're propelling the world onward with narrow-gauge minds'; for all his one-man campaign after 1914 to lacerate the Central Powers as the chief perpetrators of the 'Last Days of Mankind', Kraus appears as an unpredictable, in some ways a conservative, even a reactionary figure. In July 1914 he published an extraordinary vindication of the ideals of the dead Archduke, condemning the disruptive forces of progress and nationalism.[36]

Centrifugal nationalism indeed found some support among creative modernists. Leoš Janáček's violin sonata, written in the summer of 1914, contains a passage (a nervous high tremolo in the piano part) supposed to herald the march of the Russian armies into the Monarchy. During July Janáček ordered the secretary of the local Moravian-Russian friendship circle to destroy any incriminating minutes, while his wife disposed of some of his own foreign correspondence. Perhaps Hašek belongs

[35] Adler's views represent an extremer version of those of his father Victor, who said at an international Social Democratic gathering at Basle in 1912: 'It is certain that even a successful war, besides the mass misery which it must surely bring, would mean the beginning of the end for the structure of the Austrian state' (Brügel, op. cit. (above, n. 25), v. 121). Gy. Litván, *Szabó Ervin* (2nd edn. Budapest, 1978). For Roth: D. Bronsen, *Joseph Roth, eine Biographie* (Cologne, 1974), 154 ff.; E. Williams, *The Broken Eagle: The Politics of Austrian Literature from Empire to Anschluss* (London, 1974), 91–112.

[36] F. Field, *The Last Days of Mankind: Karl Kraus and his Vienna* (London, 1967), 74 ff. and *passim*; quoted from the German in Johnston, op. cit. (above, n. 32), 471.

here too, if anywhere at all: that anarchic individualist who, just after war was declared, booked into a Prague hotel under the name of Ivan Fedorovich Kuznetsov of Moscow and stated he had come to investigate the activities of the Austrian General Staff.[37]

Commoner was the kind of aesthetic neutrality which Bartók, after an early burst of Magyar jingoism, seems to have reached by 1914. Franz Kafka's diary on the visit to Berlin in July, when his engagement to Felice Bauer was broken off, appears entirely absorbed in a world of private sensibility: observing people in trams and restaurants, agonizing about how to eat pears with a knife in public. On 2 August he noted merely: 'Germany has declared war on Russia; p.m.: swimming lesson.' Four days earlier—for what that may be worth—we encounter the very first mention of his literary *alter ego*, Joseph K.[38] Schnitzler, who in a dream on 1 June had turned down an instruction from the Jesuits to murder Franz Ferdinand, confided little about politics in his diary thereafter. On 3 August he was absorbed with a lengthy missive to a Scandinavian friend, soliciting support for his own claims to the Nobel prize for Literature; though two days later he already saw deeper: 'We are experiencing the ruin of the world, a monstrous (*ungeheuer*) moment in world history.'[39]

Kafka, Schnitzler, and others who reacted like them: Zweig, Werfel, Broch, Lukács, and Jászi, were Jews. Should we ascribe the cool response to that fact? Scarcely. Just before he left the country, Masaryk made a special (quixotic?) plea to the governor of Bohemia to curb, in their own interests, the provocative Austrophilia of Jews in Prague.[40] Besides, the powerful Jewish component in the Monarchy's cultural life provides other evidence too. Sigmund Freud may have resented some of his

[37] J. Vogel, *Leoš Janáček, život a dílo* (Prague, 1963), 203–4. C. Parrott, *The Bad Bohemian: The Life of Jaroslav Hašek* (London, 1978), 140–1.

[38] Ujfalussy, op. cit. (above, n. 30), 127–8. F. Kafka, *Tagebücher, 1910–1923* (Berlin, 1951), 407 ff.

[39] Schnitzler, op. cit. (above n. 23), 117 ff., 129; *Georg Brandes und Arthur Schnitzler, ein Briefwechsel*, ed. K. Bergel (Berne, 1956), 107–11; cf. R. Wagner, *Arthur Schnitzler, eine Biographie* (Vienna, 1981), 275 ff.

[40] Masaryk, op. cit. (above, n. 26), 26. Oszkár Jászi, though he opposed the war from the outset, became a convert in the following year to the ideal of *Mitteleuropa*: P. Hanák, *Jászi Oszkár dunai patriotizmusa* (Budapest, 1985), 59–60.

experiences in Vienna, but he was fiercely unwilling to move anywhere else. In the summer of 1914 he had just suffered the defection of Jung, which followed quickly on that of Alfred Adler, and the war perhaps offered him some kind of release. 'For the first time in thirty years', he wrote, 'I feel myself to be an Austrian and feel like giving this not very hopeful Empire another chance.' Indeed, Freud went further, first speaking of the ultimatum as a 'deliverance through a bold-spirited deed', and then announcing: 'All my libido is given to Austria-Hungary.'[41] What Francis Joseph, not to say Jung or Adler, might have made of this potent donation, is not recorded.

Arnold Schoenberg, leading the shock-troops of the new music, had still greater difficulty than Freud with Austrian audiences, and he spent much time in Berlin on the eve of the war. His immediate response to the outbreak of it does not seem to be known. Yet Schoenberg was evidently a patriot; later he volunteered for the army, to the despair of his friends, who struggled to have the asthmatic composer released again.[42] Hugo von Hofmannsthal, that ultra-refined scion of successful Jewish entrepreneurship, spent July 1914 in close correspondence with Richard Strauss over their opera *Die Frau ohne Schatten*, apparently oblivious of the real shadows which were gathering; but when the issue was joined he had no doubts. 'Believe me', as he wrote to another friend on 28 July, having just enlisted, 'all of us here, down to the last man, are entering into this business and all its possible consequences, with a resolution, even a joy, which I have never before experienced and would never have thought credible.'[43]

Hofmannsthal's reaction shades into the wider sentiments of Austrian intellectuals. Robert Musil, apostle of the disjunction

[41] E. Jones, *The Life and Works of Sigmund Freud*, i–iii (London, 1953–7), i, 192; R. W. Clark, *Freud: The Man and the Cause* (London, 1980), 364. This was no momentary impulse; at the end of the war Freud declared: 'Austria-Hungary is no more. I do not want to live anywhere else. Emigration is out of the question. I will continue to live with this torso and will imagine that it is the whole' (ibid. 39–40).

[42] H. H. Stuckenschmidt, *Arnold Schoenberg: His Life, World and Work* (Eng. trans. London, 1977), 190 ff.

[43] *Richard Strauss: Hugo von Hofmannsthal, Briefwechsel*, ed. W. Schuh (5th edn. Zurich, 1978), 274 ff.; *Hugo von Hofmannsthal: Ottonie Degenfeld, Briefwechsel*, ed. M. T. Miller-Degenfeld (Frankfurt on Main, 1974), 304–5 (quoted). Williams, op. cit. (above, n. 35) is good on the behaviour of Hofmannsthal and other writers once war was under way.

between *Kultur* and *Zivilisation*, whose epic uncompleted novel *Der Mann ohne Eigenschaften* (*The Man without Qualities*) seems to cut off its hero spiritually, bit by bit, from the sinking ship of the Habsburg Empire, and whose diaries reveal nothing of the political tensions of mid-1914, nevertheless volunteered as an infantry officer, served later as military journalist, and never forswore the initial comradeship of arms. The poet Georg Trakl, already half-stupefied by his addiction to drink and drugs, immediately offered himself for service at the front, as a medical orderly. Within four months he was dead.[44]

Alban Berg, though frustrated by Vienna, where his 'Altenberg Songs' had provoked a full-dress riot the previous year, asserted in August 1914 that it was 'downright wicked to be thinking of other things but the war. . . . The urge to take active part in it [doesn't] let me work.' Later he served briefly as officer cadet, until his health, like that of his mentor Schoenberg, collapsed. So did his colleague, Anton Webern, for whom the conflict may have seemed preferable to conducting overblown operetta in the round of provincial Austrian and German opera-houses, but whose patriotism was equally securely anchored by a stake in the brittle, bracing culture of pre-war Vienna.[45] And Berg and Webern were no revolutionaries at all when it came to the comfortable certitudes of Austrian bourgeois life. The young Oskar Kokoschka, a genuine *bohémien*, whose Expressionist art had recently provoked from Franz Ferdinand himself the comment: 'That fellow ought to have every bone in his body broken', nevertheless hastened to play his part in avenging the Archduke's murder, and fought with reckless bravery.[46]

The philosopher Ludwig Wittgenstein, just returned from lonely contemplation in Norway, promptly offered himself, despite a severe stomach complaint, for training as an artillery officer. (Wittgenstein, for one, knew exactly how to handle a

[44] R. Musil, *Tagebücher*, ed. A. Frisé, i–ii (Reinbek, 1978), fragmentary for mid-1914; H. Hickman, *Robert Musil and the Culture of Vienna* (London, 1984); Williams, op. cit. (above, n. 35) 148–86. H. Lindenberger, *Georg Trakl* (New York, 1971).
[45] M. Carner, *Alban Berg: The Man and the Work* (2nd edn. London, 1983); F. Wildgans, *Anton Webern* (Eng. trans. London, 1966), 69–70, and *passim*.
[46] E. Hoffmann, *Kokoschka: Life and Work* (London, 1947), 86 (quoted), 128 ff.

howitzer.) Even the supreme aesthete, Rainer Maria Rilke, that compulsive letter-writer, who gave no hint in the epistles of July 1914 to his aristocratic lady-friends that the world extended beyond Hölderlin and his own psychiatrist in Munich, exhibited a brief spiritual exultation in the 'Fünf Gesänge' written at the beginning of August. Admittedly Rilke later proved a hopeless recruit, and he had to be seconded to a haven in the Imperial War Archives, alongside his friends Zweig and Werfel.[47]

I have presented a very small sample, largely of German-speakers. But I suspect they are fairly representative. Those intellectuals who loathed the business of war often, like Zweig, even Schnitzler, covered up a certain amount of initial equivocation, or were nevertheless deeply attached to the order it defended, like the economist Joseph Schumpeter, whose stepfather had been General Commandant of the Vienna garrison, and who attended meetings of his university faculty in riding-boots.[48] In Hungary the visionary pacifism of Ady or Babits seems outweighed by the patriotic instincts of such novelists as Zsigmond Móricz, that merciless social critic, or such poets as Gyula Juhász and Géza Gyóni. Historians and social scientists: Heinrich Friedjung, say, whose involvement in South Slav affairs before the war had contributed, via the scandal of the Zagreb libel trial, to harming the Monarchy's credit abroad; or Redlich, pronounced Anglophile, expert on British government, visiting lecturer at Harvard; even the Socialist theorists Karl Renner and

---

[47] Biographical sketch by G. H. von Wright in N. Malcolm, *Ludwig Wittgenstein, a Memoir* (Oxford, 1958), 4 ff. Despite Wittgenstein's notorious secretiveness, there must be more to be learned about this aspect of his career than has yet emerged from the numerous books devoted to him. R. M. Rilke, *Gesammelte Briefe*, iii–iv (*1907–21*) (Leipzig, 1938–9); W. Leppmann, *Rilkes Leben, seine Welt, sein Werk* (2nd edn. Berne and Munich, 1981), 350 ff.

[48] Zweig's account in *Die Welt von Gestern* contains a certain amount of self-justification. At the time he displayed some signs of enthusiasm: D. A. Prater, *European of Yesterday: A Biography of Stefan Zweig* (Oxford, 1972), 64 ff.; *Stefan Zweig, Leben und Werk im Bild*, ed. D. Prater and V. Michels (Frankfurt am Main, 1981), 105 ff.; Williams, op cit. (above, n. 35), 113–31. For Schnitzler see above. The case of Hermann Broch, later a fierce critic of Austrian decadence, is likewise not perfectly clear; cf. E. Schlant, *Hermann Broch* (Boston, 1978). *Schumpeter: Social Scientist*, ed. S. E. Harris (Cambridge, Mass., 1951), 1–47; and see now E. März, *Joseph Alois Schumpeter: Forscher, Lehrer, und Politiker* (Munich, 1983).

Otto Bauer (an early volunteer), behaved in a positively hawkish fashion for the most part once war was in the offing.[49]

Intellectual radicals, then, widely unpolitical in their general stance, nevertheless proved widely loyal in the aftermath of Sarajevo to the crisis of a Monarchy with which many felt, perhaps a sudden, perhaps a surprising, emotional identification. Of course many, if not most, were soon repelled by protracted war. And many soon realized that the Monarchy as they had known it was beyond recall. By 1915 it was becoming clear that Austria-Hungary could not survive the war in the same form, if at all. Even a victory, which could manifestly only be achieved by force of German arms, would decisively alter the internal balance, with the nationalities finally alienated and many German-Austrians willingly embracing new opportunities (it is striking how the intellectual reaction of the latter in late July 1914 was already usually a defence of German rather than Austrian culture).

Larger judgments on the fate of the Monarchy anyway lie outside the terms of my conclusions here. Naturally the descent into her last war can be explained in part by the ever more serious dislocations of an over-extended, deeply fractured, and seriously disorganized polity. Elements of feudal survival entered into inflammatory combination with nascent imperialist assertiveness. Both generals and bankers could play a role, sometimes an unseemly role, in ways which it still remains for historians to investigate: the influential Joint Finance Minister, Leon Biliński, for example, richly deserves our attention.[50] Yet in the end structural factors can only establish the general terms for an

---

[49] On Friedjung and other historians see G. Ramhardter, *Geschichts-wissenschaft und Patriotismus: Österreichische Historiker im Weltkrieg 1914–1918* (Munich, 1973). For Redlich see above. Major Socialist biographies like J. Hannak, *Karl Renner und seine Zeit* (Vienna, 1965), and *Otto Bauer: Auswahl aus seinem Lebenswerk* (Vienna, 1961), 9–101 (by J. Braunthal), slide over this question.

[50] B. Michel, *Banques et banquiers en Autriche au début du 20ᵉ siècle* (Paris, 1976), is excellent, and surely right to stress the general lack of direct linkage between finance and politics (except for the special case of oppositional politics in Bohemia). But he may neglect more indirect channels (cf. the comment by Gy. Ránki in *Acta Historica Academiae Scientiarum Hungaricae*, 23 [1977], 174–5) and he says little about individuals like Biliński, Popovics, Sieghart, and Spitzmüller, who played a dual role.

analysis. Military and financial interests were conspicuous in the
Dual Monarchy by their comparative impotence. Thus Biliński,
one of the half-dozen men who attended the key ministerial
council on 7 July may have voted for war (potentially a war
against Russia) in part because he was a Polish patriot, certainly
not because he was an economist and financier.[51]

Austria-Hungary's war—hence to a considerable extent
Europe's war—of August 1914 was the product of a mood acting
upon individuals. Some larger logic lies in the fact that many
forces in the Monarchy willed that first strike, beyond which no
one could see: not indeed on the surface of things, as the muted
reaction to the assassination itself demonstrates, but at a deeper
level. 'We had to die. But we could choose the means of our
death, and we chose the most terrible.' Thus the famous remark,
in 1919, of Count Czernin, that aristocratic arch-frondeur, later
Foreign Minister, who had done nothing to make the task of his
diplomatic and political colleagues easier five years before.[52]
Then the choice had fallen to two men above all: to the
inscrutable Emperor, grimly embattled and resolute;[53] and to
another aristocrat from the Bohemian lands, much less
belligerent, much less waspish, than Czernin, one who, I suspect,
as I have here summarily indicated, embodied the semi-articulate
strivings of the Monarchy in July 1914 far more than casual
observers have supposed.

It was Leopold Berchtold, cosmopolitan and polyglot, a true
'Austro-Hungarian' (he actually possessed citizenship in both
countries), connoisseur and amateur of art as of politics, who
chose then to forsake his characteristic hesitation and to steel
himself for the inevitable. Historians at least owe it to Berchtold

---

[51] Biliński, op. cit. (above, n. 16), i. 289–90. This seems to have been a
common assumption at the time; cf. the entry on Biliński in *Ottův slovník
naučný nové doby*, i (Prague, 1930), 617.
    [52] Czernin, op. cit. (above, n. 21), 41; cf. Kann, op. cit. (above, n. 5),
157–205.
    [53] There are few pointers to Francis Joseph's inner convictions during the July
crisis. But R. A. Kann, *Kaiser Franz Joseph und der Ausbruch des Weltkrieges*
(Österreichische Akademie der Wissenschaften, Phil. Hist. Klasse, Sitzungsberichte
274, Vienna and Cologne, 1969), argues convincingly, on the basis of reported
conversations of Biliński, that he had moved by 1914 towards positive approval
for a military solution. Cf. his suggested influence on Tisza above. 'If the Monarchy
must go to ruin', he said to Conrad, 'let it at least go to ruin decently (*anständig
zugrunde gehen*)': Conrad von Hoetzendorf, op. cit. (above, n. 10), iv. 162.

to respect the seriousness of his motivations, and to contemplate with dispassion the society and culture which engendered them. After all, Berchtold's devoted biographer, the notable Austrian historian Hugo Hantsch, with whom I now end, like his exact contemporary and close friend Engel-Janosi, with whom I began, was anything but a warmonger. When Franz Ferdinand was assassinated at Sarajevo, Hantsch had just entered a Benedictine monastery.

4

Russia and the Coming
of War

D. W. SPRING

THE critical point for Russia in the July crisis of 1914 was the Council of Ministers of 24 July. Here it was decided to advise Serbia to attempt to avoid a conflict by conceding to the Austrian ultimatum in so far as it would not infringe her sovereignty. But in contrast to previous comparable crises a request was made for the Tsar to order the armed forces to carry out those measures decreed for 'the period preparatory to war', with a view to a partial mobilization against Austria if it became necessary. A. V. Krivoshein, the leading voice in the Council concluded: 'All factors tended to prove that the most judicious policy Russia could follow in present circumstances was a return to a firmer and more energetic attitude towards the unreasonable claims of the Central Powers.'[1]

Given the way the crisis developed—Austrian rejection of the Serbian reply, abrupt withdrawal of the Austrian Minister in Belgrade, declaration of war and bombardment of Belgrade— the subsequent Russian measures of mobilization flowed naturally from the decisions made by the full Council of Ministers on 24 July and confirmed by the Tsar on 25 July. These decisions cannot be understood within the narrow confines of the July crisis or the workings of international relations, but only by examination of the Russian context in which they were made and of the Russians' view of their position and recent developments which determined it. There was a consciousness in the Russian

---

[1] P. L. Bark, 'Iyul' 1914', *Vozrozhdenie* (1959), 22. Also see D. C. B. Lieven *Russia and the Origins of the First World War* (London, 1983). Lieven has used the manuscript of Bark's memoirs in the Columbia University Bakhmetev archive which may be fuller than the published version. See also K. A. Krivoshein, *A. V. Krivoshein, yego znachenie v istorii Rossii nachala XX veka* (Paris, 1973), 199–200.

government of there being 'no alternative' to the stand it took
on the ultimatum to Serbia, which was shared by the major press
organs. What perception of Russia's position in international
relations and of its historical development underlay the
conviction that this was the time to make a stand?

It is noteworthy that the decisions of 24 July were not made
by the Tsar and Foreign Minister Sazonov in isolation, but
unanimously by the full Council of Ministers with their varying
responsibilities, knowledge, and perspectives on Russia's situation
and needs. Several of them by the nature of their responsibilities
were necessarily closer than the Foreign Ministry to the mood
and feelings of sections of society outside the bureaucracy. The
government's decisions were no longer made in isolation from
'society'. The existence of the Duma and the development of the
press since 1905 ensured this, and it was the case even in foreign
affairs.[2] In referring to public opinion and its influence we
cannot here mean the largely silent majority of the peasantry
whose views on Russia's international position are very much a
matter of guesswork. By public opinion we mean a more
restricted phenomenon: the views of the non-governmental,
largely propertied, educated, and semi-educated elements of
society articulated through the public press, through their Duma
representatives, and through public organizations. The radical and
socialist wing of that opinion was of course of considerable
significance in general. But for our purposes the more moderate
and conservative elements of the political spectrum are more
relevant as representing those social groups on which the
government sought to rely and which, by the nature of their
various views, were more accessible to the decision-makers, more
likely to be taken account of, and not to be dismissed out of hand.
But even if some of the governing authorities listened to them,
did they take account? And which 'public' and which 'opinion'?

The force of the most vociferous elements of opinion was
certainly not compelling. In October 1912, early in the First

---

[2] See I. V. Bestuzhev, *Bor'ba v Rossii po voprosam vneshnei politiki,
1906–10* (Moscow, 1961); I. V. Bestuzhev, 'Bor'ba v Rossii po voprosam vneshnei
politiki nakanune pervoi mirovoi voiny (1910–14 ff.), *Istoricheskie Zapiski*, 75
(1965), 44–85; C. Ferenczi, 'Funktion und Bedeutung der Presse in Rußland vor
1914', *Jahrbücher für Geschichte Osteuropas*, 30 (1982), 362–98; C. Ferenczi,
Außenpolitik und Öffentlichkeit in Rußland 1906–1912 (Husum, 1982).

Balkan War, Sazonov had advised his European ambassadors that it was to Russia's advantage that public opinion should be seen to be a more pressing and restrictive force on the Russian government's decision-making than it actually was.[3] In his failure to support Serbian demands for a territorial outlet to the Adriatic and the cession of Scutari to Montenegro, Sazonov was able to resist a fairly broad, though not all-embracing, consensus in press and Duma. And when a campaign of banquets in support of the Slavs began to get out of hand in April 1913 with demonstrations of up to 50,000 people in the capitals, he was able to obtain a ban or postponement of them. This was not, he said, a situation comparable to that of 1876.[4]

Sazonov was thus not simply a slavish follower of public opinion. Yet there was a broad recognition in government that the views expressed by that 'public', even on international affairs, were relevant, perhaps influential, after 1905. Sazonov's advice to his ambassadors in October 1912 was probably as much for the benefit of his autocratically minded sovereign. Nicholas might declare on his travels abroad: 'I am completely indifferent to the views of Mr Guchkov' [Leader of the Octobrist party]; but many of his own officials appreciated the significance of Guchkov, and even held a sympathetic respect for his views.[5] Izvol'skii understood the impact of public opinion and warned Sazonov that it would make it as difficult simply to conduct a policy of cool calculation in the Balkan wars as it had been in the Bosnian crisis when, he considered, the public's obsession with Bosnia had prevented him fulfilling a deal with Austria.[6]

The establishment of a Press Department in the Foreign Ministry in 1906; consultations with Duma leaders in the Bosnian crisis;

[3] Sazonov to Izvol'skii etc., confidential letter no. 678, 18/31 Oct. 1912, *Krasnyi Arkhiv*, 16 (1926), no. 45, p. 15.

[4]*Novoe Vremya*, 25 Mar./7 Apr. 1913, p. 3, col. 2; Margarete Wolters, *Außenpolitische Fragen vor der vierten Duma* (Hamburg, 1969), 85–8.

[5] See, for instance, on Guchkov's Balkan tour: Shtrandtman (Belgrade) to Sazonov, 15/28 July 1912 with Tsar's comment (27 July/9 Aug.); Neklyudov (Sofia) to Sazonov, 13/26 July 1912, *Mezhdunarodnye otnosheniya v epokhu imperializma . . .* [MOEI], ser. II, vol. 20, pt. i, nos 365 and 378. Also the favourable reports on Guchkov from the military attachés in Vienna and Berlin: MOEI, ser. II, vol. 20, pt. ii, nos. 480, 573.

[6] For instance Izvol'skii to Sazonov, 10/23 Oct. 1912, in René Marchand (ed.), *Un Livre noir* (Paris, n.d. [1922?]), i. 333–4.

Sazonov's annual explanations of his policy in the Duma in the debate on the budget of the Foreign Ministry; his discussions over cups of tea with press editors and Duma representatives: all reflect the changed context of the making of Russia's foreign policy. The publication in March 1914 of the 'Orange Book' of correspondence during the Balkan wars revealed Sazonov's references to the pressures of Russian public opinion in the negotiations and strengthened the confidence of the press in their influence. And in the Duma in May he was hailed as the only minister who took the public's representatives seriously.[7] The lines between Foreign Ministry and 'society' even began to be blurred with the appointment of the influential G. N. Trubetskoi, who had a non-governmental career behind him, as head of the Near Eastern Department of the Ministry in 1912. References were now more frequently made in the Council of Ministers to public opinion, even in discussion of foreign affairs. In his critical speech at the Council on 24 July Krivoshein emphasized that 'public and parliamentary opinion would fail to understand why, at the critical moment involving Russia's vital interests, the Imperial Government was reluctant to act boldly'.[8] In convincing the Tsar of the need for general mobilization, where the arguments of the military had failed on 30 July, Sazonov insisted that 'Russia would never forgive the Tsar' if he capitulated to the Central Powers, a point specifically made to him only a few hours before by none other than Rodzyanko, chairman of the Duma.[9]

In previous comparable crises the Russian government had not committed itself to any kind of mobilization at the outset. In March 1909 it had submitted to the German diplomatic

---

[7] *Novoe Vremya*, 15/28 Feb. 1914, first leader; Milyukov in *Rech'*, 12/25 and 15/28 Apr. 1914 and 10/23 May 1914, first leader; *Stenograficheskii otchet: Gosudarstvennaya Duma* (4th Convocation) [SOGD], pt. 3, sess. 2, cols. 348-9.

[8] Bark, op. cit. (above, n. 1), 22. For G. N. Trubetskoi see Lieven, op. cit. (above, n. 1), 92-102; Council of Ministers example: Kokovtsov, 'an annexation of north Manchuria would be foreign to the public opinion of Russia . . .'. 19 Nov./2 Dec. 1910, in B. Siebert (ed.), *Graf Benckendorffs diplomatischer Schriftwechsel* (Berlin, 1928), i, no. 302, pp. 392-8.

[9] S. D. Sazonov, *Fateful Years* (London, 1928), 203; M. V. Rodzyanko, *The Reign of Rasputin* (London, 1927), 106-8.

ultimatum; in November 1912 it had warned Serbia that it could not go to war for a port on the Adriatic and decided against measures of mobilization; in April 1913 it refused to concede to the insistent demands of Montenegro for Scutari. Even in January 1914 in the crisis over the appointment of the German general Liman von Sanders to command the Turkish First Army Corps at Constantinople, no decision was made for military preparations. The Special Conference of ministers, aware of the potential for a conflict with Germany, in essence decided against forceful military measures against Turkey, except in circumstances which were not likely to materialize in that particular case—the assurance of British as well as French support. Sazonov and the Tsar grasped with relief at the modest concession offered of the promotion of Liman von Sanders to marshal, so that he was too senior to command the First Corps, and they declared the crisis over in spite of the dissatisfaction of the press.[10] We must therefore ask what change of opinion and circumstances, what particular characteristics of the July Crisis, what view of Russia's international position, and what atmosphere of public opinion determined the more robust response of 24 July. It must be emphasized that these decisions were still aimed at a peaceful conclusion; they were not made in a spirit of enthusiasm or confidence at the prospect of war. But they set a limit to concessions, beyond which Russia would resort to asserting her readiness to use her military power to ensure that her voice was heard: 'Russia could not be indifferent.'[11]

These decisions coincided with the views of major organs of the press on the limits of concession in July. The influential conservative-nationalist *Novoe Vremya* recognized before the ultimatum that Austria-Hungary had a right to expect that 'the Serbs must help as far as possible in finding the roots of the assassination, but not more'. The moderate liberal *Birzhevyye Vedomosti*, which in March had published the 'Russia is ready'

[10] Report of the Special Conference 31 Dec. 1913/13 Jan. 1914, *Vestnik Narodnogo Komissariata Inostrannykh Del* (1919), no. 1, pp. 26–32. Tsar's reaction 9/22 Jan. 1914: 'For the moment we must hold back from further pressure and give the Germans a breather': MOEI, ser. III. vol. i, no. 69.

[11] Government statement in *Russkii Invalid*, see *Novoe Vremya*, 12/25 July 1914, p. 1.

article inspired by War Minister V. A. Sukhomlinov, now, before
the ultimatum, recognized that 'nobody will object to demands
on Serbia to take measures against political clubs. . . . In Belgrade
they know Russia will sympathize with as much concession as
possible to justifiable Austrian demands.' But 'Russia can never
under any circumstance be reconciled with' the infringement of
Serbian independence. Even the Kadet *Rech'* of P. N. Milyukov,
anxious to avoid a clash and advising that absolutely no
encouragement should be given to Serbia, found the ground taken
from beneath its arguments by the conciliatory Serbian reply and
concluded: 'Fuller satisfaction [for Austria-Hungary] could not
have been imagined.'[12]

That war did break out was a result of Austria-Hungary's
unequivocal commitment to dealing with Serbia without any
distraction. The crisis was different from previous ones in the
uncompromising bluntness and directness of the actions of
Austria-Hungary, which Sazonov rightly concluded must have the
support of Germany. Without this, Russian ministers would not
have felt that they had been pushed 'with their backs to the wall'.
But why was this particular issue at this particular time taken to
be the one for which Russia should make a stand?

There remained in July 1914 very sound reasons for the Russian
government to avoid taking the initial steps of military
preparation for a possible partial mobilization, which it was
understood could precipitate a European conflict. The urban
social problem was particularly acute in 1914. A new wave of
strike activity stemmed from the Lena goldfields massacre in April
1912. There were more strikes in the first half of 1914 than at
any time since 1905. In the middle of July, in the capital itself,
180,000 industrial workers out of a total of 242,000 were on
strike; barricades were erected and there were clashes with the
police and troops. The urban workers' movement had moved
distinctly to the left, as was evident from the increasing appeal
of Bolshevism, and it even showed signs of escaping the control
of its leaders. The example of the Russo-Japanese War made
evident the connection between war and revolution. The most
perceptive and direct analysis and warning of this was made to

[12] *Novoe Vremya*, 1/14 July 1914, leader; *Birzhevyye Vedomosti*, 10/23 July
1914, leader: *Rech'*, 15/28 July 1914, p. 1, leader.

the Tsar himself in the well-known memorandum of former Interior Minister P. N. Durnovo as late as February 1914. Meanwhile the sharp internal political crisis, essentially over whether and how the role of the Duma and principles of the October Manifesto should be developed, remained unresolved. By the summer it reached the point where significant parts of the budget were rejected by the Duma. And the general tension between government and propertied, educated 'society' remained evident there and in much of the press, not simply its liberal and oppositional wing.[13]

If this evidence of political and social crisis—the danger of revolution—ought to have been enough to convince the decision-makers of the vital necessity of avoiding war, the state of Russia's military forces could be adduced to consolidate the argument. The four years after defeat in the Russo-Japanese War had been ones of stagnation for the army. In March 1909 War Minister A. F. Rödiger had admitted that it was not even ready for defence. Much had been done under his successor Sukhomlinov, but not until March 1913, under pressure from the deteriorating international situation, increases in the German military budget and over-extension of Russia's own military responsibilities, was a decision made to undertake the 'Great Programme' of development and expansion of the army. Its central feature was an increase in the yearly contingent of recruits, which would ultimately mean 460,000 more men in Russia's peacetime army. But while progress was meanwhile made on the further modernization of the army, the major military bill was not passed by the Duma until the end of June 1914. The improvements in strategic railways agreed with the French, who thought them so urgent, were also only to be undertaken from 1914.

The preparations of the navy were equally incomplete. The excessive expenditure on this branch of the armed forces to the detriment of the army after 1905 showed (apart from a good dose of Mahanism) that a great land conflict in Europe was for long not foremost in the minds of the decision-makers. As late as 1914

[13] L. Haimson, 'The problem of social stability in urban Russia, 1905–17', *Slavic Review*, 23 (1964), 619–42; Hans Rogger, 'Russia in 1914', *Journal of Contemporary History*, 1/4 (1966), 95–120; for Durnovo's memorandum in translation see F. A. Golder, *Documents of Russian History, 1914–17* (New York, 1927), 3–23.

the commitment to Dreadnought fleets on both Baltic and Black Seas was maintained with a new navy bill for the latter location, where the navy recognized that it would be significantly weaker than Turkey for at least two years because of the slowness of its building programme.[14] No more were Russia's overall finances in a satisfactory condition to face war. In March 1914 the Committee of Finance, reviewing the financial position of Russia and particularly the condition of the State Bank in the event of war with the Central Powers, considered that 'at the present time in the financial field we are much less ready for war than ten years ago'. The gold reserve of the Bank may have increased from 903 to 1,068 million roubles as a result of foreign loans, but notes in circulation had increased by three times and were barely covered even by the nominal reserve.[15]

Nor was the ground prepared diplomatically, according to the Foreign Ministry's judgment of what was required to enable Russia to prevent or meet a conflict. Izvol'skii's attempt to pursue an independent policy with some balance between Britain and Germany had eventually been abandoned by Sazonov. As late as 1912 he had told Bethmann Hollweg that he would never hear him use the term 'Triple Entente'.[16] But following his disappointment with the outcome of the Balkan Wars and the breakdown of the Balkan alliance and strengthening of the Central Powers in Albania, Bulgaria, and Turkey, he came to the conviction that their opponents' successes were a result of the lack of cohesion of the Triple Entente. In January 1914, debating Russia's policy towards the appointment of Liman von Sanders, Sazonov recognized that if it came to a conflict, France and Russia were not enough to weigh in the balance. They had to be certain of Britain, whose participation 'would be fatal for Germany, which is conscious of the danger of being brought to complete internal social catastrophe within six weeks by English action'.[17] He was puzzled by the fact that though the Triple Entente appeared stronger on paper, it did not seem able to make its rivals

[14] I. I. Rostunov, *Russkii front pervoi mirovoi voiny* (Moscow, 1976), 57–9, 96–104; K. F. Shatsillo, *Russkii imperializm i razvitie flota* (Moscow, 1968).

[15] Committee of Finance Protocol, 14/27 Mar. 1914, MOEI, ser. III, vol. ii, no. 99.

[16] *Große Politik . . .*, 31 (1927), nos. 11558, 11592.

[17] *Vestnik NKID* (1919), no. 1, pp. 28–30.

take that power fully into account in their calculations. Sazonov's activity in early 1914 concentrated therefore on attempting to consolidate the Entente.

One must recognize [he wrote] that the peace of the world will only be assured when the Triple Entente, whose real existence is no more proved than that of the sea serpent, is transformed into a defensive alliance. . . . On that day the danger of a German hegemony will be definitely removed and we will each of us be able to peacefully occupy ourselves with our own affairs, the English to find a solution to the social problems with which they are absorbed, the French to enrich themselves free from the danger of any external threat, and we to consolidate and work on our economic reorganization.[18]

But neither Sazonov nor the French were able to bring the British to contemplate an alliance. The proposed Anglo-Russian naval agreement was not going to have much substance in it, as the British would not enter the Baltic; and the disputes over Russian policy in Persia, which was the central feature of the 1907 convention, reached a particular intensity in the summer of 1914, underlining the absence of a common view on that problem. Given the importance which Sazonov in January had attributed to British participation in a conflict, he had little reason to contemplate complications in July with more confidence. Why then did these factors not weigh more fully in the balance in July? Did Russia move towards a more robust line in foreign policy because of, or in spite of, the crises she faced?

It must first be recognized that the Council of Ministers of 24 July had undergone a significant change in its composition and balance since the Liman von Sanders crisis and the Balkan Wars. V. N. Kokovtsov had been dismissed as Chairman of the Council and Finance Minister in February 1914. Like Stolypin, he had been a firm opponent of any adventurous tendencies and of the impatient nationalistic ethos which had built up in a section of the Council. He had been an essential and powerful supporter of Sazonov's much criticized policy of compromise and conciliation through the Balkan Wars. He had been decisive in

[18] Sazonov to Benckendorff, letter, 6/19 Feb. 1914, MOEI, ser. III, vol. i, no. 289.

preventing measures of mobilization in November 1912, and again in January 1914 in bringing the Special Conference of ministers to the unanimous conclusion that war was undesirable and 'would be a disaster for Russia'.[19]

Kokovtsov's successor, I. L. Goremykin, gave no comparable lead at the Council of 24 July; and the new Minister of Finance, P. L. Bark, simply bowed to the superior authority of his colleagues. The key role was played by A. V. Krivoshein, the Minister of Agriculture, generally recognized as the leading voice in the government after February. Krivoshein was not an adventurer. He was gloomy about the prospects for Russia in the event of a conflict. He did not seek war. But he was not the man to take over Kokovtsov's role of warning that a war would be 'disastrous' whatever the circumstances and motivation, or to advise his colleagues to accept a further humiliation in the interests of peace. In 1912 Krivoshein's usual line had been, Kokovtsov recalled, that 'it was necessary to believe more in the Russian people and its age-old love for the motherland which was higher than any chance preparedness or unpreparedness for war'.[20] His view, shared by colleagues and a wider public outside, was that the recent history of Russia in international relations had been one of retreat, humiliation, and withdrawal, and that they must set a limit to it. His speech in the Council of 24 July was, however, moderate in tone. He argued that Russia's opponents had taken advantage of her desire for peace in previous crises, and it was with regret rather than bellicosity that he came to the conclusion that on this occasion they must try a different and more robust tactic.[21]

Kokovtsov's pacifying role at the end of 1912 and in the Liman von Sanders crisis is undoubted. Had he been present on 24 July he would certainly have played a more outspoken role than either of his successors, Goremykin and Bark. There must, however, remain some uncertainty as to whether he would have been able to come to a different conclusion. The characteristics of the crisis of July 1914 were different from those of November 1912 and January 1914. The range of options open to Russia had become

---

[19] V. N. Kokovtsov, *Iz moego proshlago* (Paris, 1933), ii. 122–9, 153–4, 157–62; *Vestnik NKID* (1919), no. 1, pp. 30–2.

[20] Kokovtsov, op. cit. (above, n. 19), ii. 128.   [21] See n. 1.

narrower. In particular the directness of the challenge to a major Russian interest and the commitment of her opponents to finally 'dealing' with Serbia were starkly evident in a way they had not been in the earlier crises. And Kokovtsov admitted that even in 1912 his sympathies had been 'wholly with Serbia'.[22]

The dismissal of Kokovtsov did nevertheless reflect a deeper underlying change, a dissatisfaction with what was seen as passive leadership particularly in foreign affairs, which was evident in the conflicts within the Council. The dissatisfaction was symptomatic of Russia's failures and supposed failures in international relations and the absence of any exhibition of Russia's power on the international scene. Even in governmental circles it was becoming increasingly difficult to argue the case for continuing a policy of 'recuperation': of gathering strength, doing nothing for fear of creating a crisis while Russia was still unprepared. Krivoshein's judgment that they needed to 'return' to a more energetic attitude was a comment on the character of recent policy experiments and their effectiveness. In so far as Russia's lack of will was evident to her opponents, they would take advantage. The Bosnian crisis had been the most obvious and painful recent example, and the Liman von Sanders affair provided decisive corroborating evidence undermining Sazonov's own conviction of the possibility of managing the relationship with Germany. Not a word had been said to him about the appointment of the German general in Constantinople, even though he had held friendly conversations in Berlin in October 1913, only ten days before the matter became public.

The Russian press exhibited a deep-seated irritation at these failures in international relations. They were attributed to that cautious tradition of *recueillement* stemming from Gorchakov, who after the Crimean War first had to adjust foreign policy to the perceived relative decline of Russia in relation to the other Great Powers. While the *Novoe Vremya*, for instance, was convinced that Russia needed peace, it had for long considered that the historical lessons from Gorchakov's time as well as more recently indicated that this 'disinterestedness' of Russian diplomacy would be used by opponents to the detriment of Russia. There were alternatives if the diplomats were willing to

---

[22] Kokovtsov, op. cit. (above, n. 19), ii. 122.

assert themselves—such was the essence of the criticism.[23] And it was no coincidence that the memoirs of N. P. Ignat'ev, exponent of the 'nationalist' school of diplomacy and a bitter critic of Gorchakov, were posthumously serialized in 1913–14 in *Istoricheskii Vestnik* with pertinent editorial footnotes highlighting the historical lessons of Gorchakov's failure in relation to Germany and Austria.

Though Krivoshein did not recall this historical baggage, it is in the context of the perceptions of Russia's past policies and the lessons of recent events that his words should be seen. At the same time the stand he took at the Council of 24 July was symptomatic of the decline of the pro-German lobby amongst the landowning interests. Their conservatism had long been a link with the Prussian Junkers. But by 1914 an awareness was growing of the conflict of agrarian interests with those of Germany. The debate over the coming revision of the Russo-German commercial treaty of 1904 was taken up by the landed interests and reached particular intensity in the spring of 1914. And again the attacks at the congress of exporters at Kiev in February 1914, for instance, were directed as much at their own government for its pusillanimity as at Germany. The government, it was claimed, had been sacrificing agrarian interests to those of industry. Now even substantial quantities of German rye were being imported into Finland as well as into the western provinces of the Russian Empire, and the Scandinavian markets had been lost.

Krivoshein sympathized with the campaign against the existing terms of trade in commerce with Germany and had been involved in the rather haphazard preparations for review at least since 1912. Kokovtsov had believed that an amicable compromise settlement was possible between the two powers. But quite apart from the industrial interests involved (which had tended to be more hostile towards German rivals), Krivoshein considered that a robust stand should be taken for the protection of agriculture. The first sign of this was the tariff on imported rye passed by the Duma in April 1914, which created a furore in Germany. Even at its right-wing fringes the community of outlook and common interests between Prussian Junkers and Russian landowners was being undermined. And even P. N. Durnovo, who warned so

---

[23] *Novoe Vremya*, 14/27 Jan. 1914, leader.

prophetically of the social catastrophe to come and the need to avoid conflict with the Central Powers, was brought into contradiction. As a supporter of agrarian interests he would have taken up a more uncompromising line against high German grain tariffs than Kokovtsov in the forthcoming negotiations with Germany. These attacks, further intensified in 1914 by the revelation of the 1913 trade statistics, fuelled the debate and the conviction in governing circles and a wider public that both in political and economic terms Germany's interests represented a strait-jacket which restricted and demeaned Russia.[24]

By the time of the 24 July Council the views of Sazonov on how Russia could best cope with her international problems had undergone a change as compared with previous crises. How much this resulted from continually critical public opinion is a matter of dispute. However that may be, by 1914 there was a coincidence between his views (if not his actions) and those of a broad spectrum of opinion on the root cause of the instability of the international situation and what was necessary to end it. Yet Sazonov had resisted the pressure of opinion during the Balkan Wars, and again by his settlement of the Liman von Sanders crisis had run the inevitable gauntlet of the press, which accused him of failing to defend Russian interests. Why did he then appear vulnerable to the idea of a more robust policy precisely in July 1914?

Sazonov shared many of the preconceptions of the public press about the trends evident in the Balkan problem, the legitimacy of the claims of the Slav states and their inevitable consolidation as national units. To this were added in 1914 similar expectations for Roumania. With his impatient critics he differed essentially on the timetable and methods. In attempting to control the Balkan states in the first nine months of 1912, he had emphasized that they should remain passive for the time being, as Russia was not 'ready'. He did not separate Russia from their aspirations; yet nor did he give any indication of when Russia might consider the

[24] B. Bonwetsch, *Kriegsallianz und Wirtschaftsinteressen in den Wirtschaftsplänen Englands und Frankreichs, 1914–17* (Düsseldorf, 1973), 18–33.

moment appropriate. Although the military campaign of the Balkan allies was unexpectedly successful, Sazonov still called on them to limit their aspirations. The implication of this line was that the Russian army was 'unready', not necessarily for war, but to enable Russia's full weight to be felt in the international disputes. Such an implication was resented by the War Ministry, since it placed the responsibility for Russia's failures in international relations, not on inept diplomacy, but on disorganized military still smarting from the humiliations of the Russo-Japanese War and the admission of impotence in 1909.

Sukhomlinov at the War Ministry did not wish to be saddled with such responsibility. He was adept at avoiding responsibility. Therefore he increasingly emphasized that the army was ready if called upon. It was the responsibility of the Foreign Ministry to determine when the time was appropriate to reveal Russia's military power in some form. Thus he urged Sazonov in October 1912 to meet to discuss the role of the military in the existing crisis. He then sought to provide independent support for Russian policy by a partial-mobilization proposal to the Tsar in November, without the knowledge of Sazonov and Kokovtsov. If the army lacked anything, it was a consequence of the parsimonious policy of Kokovtsov; if Russian diplomacy failed to achieve national objectives, it was the result of the incompetence of the diplomats. In the Liman von Sanders crisis he told the Special Conference: 'The army is ready for single combat against Germany, let alone Austria.' He was responsible for the articles in the *Birzhevyye Vedomosti* in March and June 1914 claiming that Russia's military forces were 'ready'. It was not that Sukhomlinov was particularly bellicose. But like his sovereign he probably thought that war with Germany would not come easily, and that a strong gesture and display of Russia's power would be enough to ensure a peaceful and successful outcome for Russia in international crises. It must be remembered that there was no collective responsibility in the Russian Council of Ministers. It remained a body of feuding, competing, and conflicting individuals and factions.[25]

So gradually one pin of the Kokovtsov–Sazonov policy of restraint was removed. The undoubted progress in the

[25] Sazonov to Kokovtsov. 10/23 Oct. 1912; Siebert, op. cit. (above, n. 8), ii. no. 696, p. 459; Kokovtsov, op. cit. (above, n. 19), ii. 122–9; *Vestnik NKID* (1919), no. 1, p. 30; V. A. Sukhomlinov, *Vospominaniya* (Berlin, 1924), 218–19, 296–302.

development and reform of the army, together with the insistent assurances of the military that they were ready, encouraged Sazonov to contemplate the use of the military arm, even to court war rather than to keep firmly to Kokovtsov's line that the risk was too great to take. In January 1914 he contemplated the use of force against Turkey in the Liman von Sanders crisis. In spite of his own recognition that in a struggle with Germany Russia could only be sure of the outcome if she had the support of England, one detects a certain willingness to risk complications, sure in the support of France alone. Kokovtsov's leadership at that ministerial conference and the modest German concession ensured that the crisis ended. But Sazonov knew it was not a very creditable performance, and it strengthened his conviction that some consolidation of the Triple Entente should be achieved to ensure that they should not suffer such defeats in the future. He shared the frustrations expressed in the public press about the unachieved potential of the Entente. His experience indicated that support of Russia's friend and ally could only be maintained if Russia was clear about what was wanted and ready to take responsibility. The prelude to the Russian reaction in July was therefore not only the changes in the Council, but also changes in Sazonov's attitude.

There was a further necessary component which enabled Russia to take a firmer line over this crisis than on previous occasions: the attitude of France. In 1908 France had not favoured taking the matter to the point of conflict. In fact she had adopted quite a sympathetic line towards the Austrians. Without the certainty of French support in July 1914 the arguments in favour of taking military measures to back Russian diplomacy and thus to court war would have been decisively weakened. Even with the knowledge of French support, Sazonov's advice to the Serbs was to go to the limit of concession in their reply to the ultimatum. Poincaré had only just left St Petersburg on 23 July. Strong rumours were already circulating in the press about a forthcoming ultimatum from Austria, and it is inconceivable in these circumstances that Poincaré and Sazonov in their final discussions did not come to some degree of understanding on what their response should be.

It was not simply that Sazonov could be sure of French support to the limit on this issue; there were also the consequences of any failure to take a firm line on an issue so close to Russia's interests as the independence of Serbia in a situation in which Bulgaria had already been lost (France and Russia had failed to secure the Bulgarian loan at the beginning of July) and German influence in Turkey had visibly strengthened. Russia had no significant commercial presence in the Balkans to fall back on in case her political influence failed. Poincaré had in 1912 accepted that the obligations of the alliance could be activated by a change of balance in the Balkans. He and his military leaders had been disturbed at the limited degree of military activity in Russia at the end of 1912. They emphasized that it was not France's fault if Russia chose to take a soft line over the Scutari issue. And in January 1914 Sazonov told his colleagues that France was ready to go to 'extreme measures' in supporting Russia. The French military were equally insistent that they knew what preparations were necessary for Russia: they had better get on with them urgently. All this is not to say that the French actively encouraged Russia to war, but they did not want to be associated with another humiliating climb-down by Russia.[26]

The members of the Council of 24 July were made fully aware of the limited options open to Russia. Concessions now, Sazonov argued, would simply mean that they would face similar forceful challenges by Germany in the future. It was time to show that such methods could no longer be effective. On 24 July it was the civilian-dominated Council of Ministers which made the decisions, including the request to the War Minister to propose to the Tsar the execution of the measures agreed for the 'period preparatory to war', with a view specifically to partial mobilization if the development of the situation required it. It was the civilian ministers Sazonov and Krivoshein who took the lead in proposing to bolster the diplomatic posture with military preparations. Sukhomlinov agreed that there was 'no objection to a greater display of firmness in our diplomatic negotiations',

[26] On Franco-Russian relations see in particular V. I. Bovykin, *Iz istorii vozniknoveniya pervoi mirovoi voiny (Otnosheniya Rossii i Frantsii 1912–14)* (Moscow, 1960).

but he admitted that the Great Programme for strengthening the army had only just begun to get under way.

The increased numbers and equipment foreseen by the Programme had not yet been fulfilled. The army would have to be mobilized and concentrated on the basis of the highly cautious plan of 1910, with some bolder modifications from 1912. A new timetable for mobilization (Programme no. 20) was due to be completed in December 1914. But even this would only achieve a speeding-up of concentration at the expense of numbers. The plan for the first campaign foresaw offensives in Galicia and East Prussia, the latter at the insistence of the French. But this latter, even if successful, was hardly going to bring about the collapse of Germany. The Russian army no longer had the pre-1905 confidence to propose a concentration in the west of Russian Poland and an offensive towards Berlin. The new element in the plans from 1910 was that going over to the offensive in the first stages of the campaign was foreseen as a necessity even before the completion of concentration.[27]

The Russian military who were closest to the decision-making circles on 24 July were therefore not notably bellicose. So little did the military expect to exploit the July Crisis that the experienced and authoritative Quartermaster-General Danilov, a key figure in possible mobilization measures, was sent off on his normal inspection of the Caucasian troops in mid-July, and the chief of the western sector of the mobilization department was sent on vacation. The fact that only partial mobilization was foreseen by the meetings of 24–5 July confirms the prevalence of a cautious attitude. Partial mobilization against Austria alone could only be a means of supporting diplomacy, as even the supporters of partial mobilization knew that if war broke out it would be a war against both Germany and Austria. Partial mobilization was not effective even for a war against Austria alone as the Warsaw Military District was not to be mobilized, in order not to direct pressure against Germany. But this district covered both the German and Austrian front, and would have left Poland open to an Austrian attack. What degree of mobilization should be contemplated was not a matter for the civilian ministers. The

Chief of Staff, Yanushkevich, had been warned just before the Council meeting of 24 July that a partial mobilization would create chaos with army timetables if a general war did ensue. He does not appear to have raised this problem at the meeting which foresaw only a partial mobilization. The only other military authority present was Sukhomlinov, and in spite of his denials he must be seen as responsible for letting the matter rest. He held the view that military measures were a good way to give conviction to Russia's diplomacy in conditions in which her opponents could well doubt the seriousness of her commitments. But he did not think these would lead to war if they were only directed against Austria. Indeed, in November 1912, when Sukhomlinov had proposed a similar partial mobilization, he was so sure of the consequences that he proposed to go abroad on vacation as soon as the matter had been decided![28]

Nicholas II was no keener to precipitate a conflict. At a meeting on the morning of 25 July he accepted the measures for the 'period preparatory to war', with a view to partial mobilization. Once Austria had declared war on Serbia the Tsar felt compelled to take military action, and he signed a decree for general mobilization which conceded to the arguments of Sazonov and the General Staff, the latter being convinced that partial mobilization was 'madness'. Yet at the first opportunity Nicholas returned to his original inclination, and it seems that without further consultation and on his own initiative he withdrew the decree before it had been issued in favour of one for partial mobilization. The following day (30 July) he stubbornly resisted all the arguments of the military, led by Yanushkevich, in the conviction that general mobilization *would* mean war. Only the intervention of the civilian Sazonov brought the reluctant final decision for general mobilization. In November 1912 the Tsar had argued strongly the case for partial mobilization, to put pressure on Austria, while reassuring his ministers that Germany would not intervene. His acceptance of the idea in July 1914 shows that he had not been entirely convinced by Kokovtsov's counter-arguments.

Nicholas had a taste for a nationalistic, authoritarian tone in Russia's foreign relations, particularly where such a position could

---

[28] Danilov, op. cit. (above, n. 27), 11–21; Sukhomlinov, op. cit. (above, n. 25), 296–301; Kokovtsov, op. cit. (above, n. 19), ii. 122–7; S. Dobrorol'skii, *Die Mobilmachung der russischen Armee 1914* (Berlin, 1922), 10–29.

be taken with impunity—in Persia, northern Manchuria, Mongolia 'we are the boss'. He was sensitive to Russia's recent failings in foreign affairs and inclined to feel that a display of power would be enough to convince her opponents that they could not count on her passivity. Consequently he sympathized with the nationalist group amongst his ministers. As Kokovtsov wrote later:

This was not because the sovereign was aggressive; in his essence he was deeply peace-loving. But he liked the raised tone of the nationalistically minded ministers. He was more satisfied with their panegyrics on the theme of unlimited loyalty of the people to him, of its invincible power, of the colossal upsurge of its well-being, requiring only more extensive supply of money on its productive requirements. He also liked assurances that Germany was only frightening by her preparations and would never decide on an armed conflict with us and would therefore be the more conciliatory, the more clearly we gave her to understand that we were not afraid of her and would bravely go along our national road.[29]

The Tsar's conviction that partial mobilization would be a support to diplomacy and effective warning to Austria not to go too far, allowed him to pass over the opportunity of sorting out at his Council on 25 July the problems of possible mobilizations and where they were heading, thus avoiding the confusion of 29–30 July. The only alternative, however, would have been no mobilization at all. This might have given Austria time to get bogged down in Serbia and made her more vulnerable. But there was no guarantee that Serbia, given her exhaustion, would not be defeated by her powerful neighbour within ten days if Russia remained passive as her opponents hoped.

The consciousness of having conceded too far and too much in the past, and of the need to take a more robust stand, evident in the Council on 24 July, had been publicly aired for some time in the press. In response to the German press debate about

[29] Dobrorol'skii, op. cit. (above, n. 28), 23–9; Sazonov, op. cit. (above, n. 9), 193–205; Kokovtsov, op. cit. (above, n. 19), ii. 129; Tsar's comment (referring specifically to north Persia) 28 Sept./11 Oct. 1911 on Neratov to Poklewski (Teheran), tel. 1407, 23 Sept./6 Oct. 1911: MOEI, ser. II, vol. 18, pt. ii, no. 537, p. 84.

preventive war against Russia in March the *Novoe Vremya*'s influential columnist M. O. Men'shikov replied in one of his more serious and controlled articles: 'The Germans have no idea of Russia if they think we are preparing to fight them . . . Russia is ready to fight if she is pushed to the wall and there is nothing else to do, but she will take the challenge to war extremely unwillingly.' And the leader echoed the same theme: 'The foreign policy of Germany for forty years has consisted in a systematic frightening of her opponents with the prospect of war. . . . She plays on the fact that others do not want it. . . . She threatens and will threaten only so far as others give way to her.'[30]

That Russia's opponents were only aware of her potential strength is evident from the German side of the press campaign and in Bethmann Hollweg's correspondence. And even Russia's friends were impressed. Verneuil, chief stockbroker on the French stock exchange, predicted in mid-1913 after a visit to Russia: 'There is something truly formidable being prepared in Russia, the symptoms of which must strike even the most cautious spirits.' In the next thirty years there would be 'un prodigieux essor économique'. Arthur Nicolson at the Foreign Office emphasized Russia's strength and the need to be friendly to her: 'Russia is continually progressing in every possible way and is already, I think, one of the most formidable factors in Europe. She can moreover, were she unfriendly, cause us great annoyance and embarrassment in Central Asia and we should be unable to meet her on anything like equal terms.' And Buchanan, ambassador in St Petersburg, commented: 'Russia is rapidly becoming so powerful that we must retain her friendship at almost any cost.'[31] In Asia Russia's position seemed particularly strong: to security in north Manchuria as a result of agreement with the Japanese were added a new near-protectorate in Mongolia, a more dominant role in north Persia, and a settlement with Turkey which gave Russia a role in reforms for Armenia.

---

[30] *Novoe Vremya*, 1/14 Mar. 1914.
[31] Verneuil to Pichon, 7 July 1913, *Documents diplomatiques français 1871–1914*, ser. III, vol. 7 (Paris, 1934), no. 309. Nicolson to Hardinge, 22 Apr. 1913, Carnock MSS, vol. 4 of 1913; Buchanan to Nicolson, 16 Apr. 1914, G. P. Gooch and H. W. V. Temperley, *British Documents on the Origins of the War, 1898–1914*, vol. x, pt. ii (London, 1938), no. 538, pp. 784–5.

While her opponents thus concentrated on Russia's potential strength (and on their own weaknesses), this was not how the Russian government and public saw their position in the world in 1913–14. They did not feel that they could base their policy on a consciousness of strength and an aggressive *élan*. For much of Russian opinion the threats from the outside world continually distracted from her own development. Again Men'shikov made the point in the *Novoe Vremya*: 'Russia really does desire peace because she is concentrating on great internal tasks', and she will still have those in 25, 50, and 100 years' time.[32] The assertions of Russia's military preparedness made in the press at Sukhomlinov's initiative in March were the product, not of aggressiveness, but of a desire to reassure the public which doubted if Russia was prepared, and to warn opponents that Russia could not be expected to simply concede to a further diplomatic ultimatum. After all, serious press organs in Germany were discussing the possibility of preventive war! The *Rech'*, from its liberal point of view, apprehensive about excessive chauvinism, understood Russia's own nationalists. Their outbursts were not based on aggression from strength, but on 'a psychology of fear—the same which had led to too great concessions last year'.[33] And at the very Council of 24 July, Krivoshein outlined Russia's dilemma: if they acted too strongly they might bring about a war; if they acted too weakly, as experience showed in the past, they would suffer diplomatic defeat and encourage further demands and 'the public would not understand it'. Yet in the long run 'it seemed doubtful whether our army and our fleet would ever be able to compete with those of Germany or Austro-Hungary as regards modern technical efficiency' because of Russia's cultural and industrial backwardness.[34]

The consciousness of having her 'back to the wall' was a vitally important ingredient in the outlook of the influential Russian public and government in 1914. It seemed that critical historical problems were coming to a denouement with Russia unable to project her power and assert her interests. The problem of the future of the Slav populations in Austria-Hungary might force that

---

[32] *Novoe Vremya*, 1/14 Mar. 1914.

[33] *Russkie Vedomosti*, 15/28 May 1914; *Rech'*, 16/29 May 1914, p. 1.

[34] Bark, op. cit. (above, n. 1), 22.

government to reverse the trend and counter pressures from outside by asserting a protective role over a wider Slav world. This would have implications for Poland and even perhaps the Ukraine, since there were already irritating Ukrainian national movements in Galicia. Similarly it seemed that the Straits issue was coming to a conclusion at a time when, as a result of the development of south Russia, it was acquiring even greater economic and strategic significance, yet at the same time Russia still lacked the capacity to bring her power to bear. The weak ending of the Liman von Sanders crisis showed the dangers, even though through their military attaché Bazarov in Berlin the Russians had precise knowledge of the bombastic aspirations of the Kaiser for the mission. Russia was still not in a position to 'solve' the Straits problem, even when it seemed that they might be dominated by another great power. In November 1912, as the Bulgarians approached Constantinople, there were not enough ships available to mount an expedition. And in the Special Conference on the Straits issue in February 1914 it was recognized that the situation had not improved. Nothing could be done but to set a deadline of three years. Yet the chances of being in a better position in three years were slim because, apart from the paralysing dispute amongst the strategists over whether an expedition was the best way to secure Russia's interests at the Straits, the difficulty in providing ships related to a fundamental weakness in the transport of Russia's foreign trade and in its merchant shipping companies.[35]

At the same time the uncertain course and results of Russia's economic development fed a consciousness of Russian weakness and vulnerability. The sluggish development of the country's resources put it always on its guard in relation to its economically more dynamic neighbours in the West. In the new century, while her development was not without success, the evidence was that Russia was still running hard to stand still, if not to fall further behind.[36] And this was increasingly a problem not only in the west, but along the whole border through Asia. Russia was

---

[35] A. S. Avetyan, *Germanskii imperializm na Blizhnem Vostoke* . . . (Moscow, 1966), 81–2, citing the archives of the Russian General Staff; Special Conference, 8/21 Feb. 1914, *Vestnik NKID* (1919), no. 1, pp. 37–9.

[36] D. Geyer, *Der russische Imperialismus* (Göttingen, 1977), 205. Geyer argues that the gap was growing between Germany and Russia.

necessarily an opponent of the development of her Asiatic neighbours as it would put unbearable strains on her own economy and finances. The development of Japan showed the potential. Communications improvements in north China, in Persia, in eastern Anatolia would bring more effective military threats to which the overburdened Russian military budget would have to attempt to respond. Likewise the successful economic development of the bordering countries, with the intermediary role of Chinese and other traders, would bring the goods as well as the economic influence of the more industrialized powers to her unprotected borders. Yet after 1910 it was no longer possible simply to veto railway-building in eastern Anatolia, Persia, and north China. Time was running out for the benefits which geographical isolation had given the Russian borders in Asia. When the influence of economically more dynamic powers appeared in the bordering areas, would Russia's periphery be adequately integrated to withstand the pull from outside?[37]

The Petersburg and Moscow press in late 1913 and 1914 was consumed by a consciousness of Russia's international failure, by the incompetence and lack of will of the governing authorities. It was obsessed with the failure to maintain the Balkan alliance and bruised by the consolidation of German military influence at Constantinople. To such opinion it seemed that other powers had achieved startling recent successes — Austria in Bosnia, Italy in Libya, Japan in Korea, France in Morocco, Germany at Constantinople — while Russia's international policy remained weak and dilatory, unable to turn situations to its advantage. And Russia's own apparent recent success in Mongolia was already, in the view of the press of all political persuasions, turning distinctly sour by the early months of 1914. This mood of impotent frustration at Russia's humiliations brought back to memory of the nationalist press the long mythology of the country's betrayals from the Crimean War through the Congress

---

[37] D. W. Spring, 'Russian Imperialism in Asia in 1914', *Cahiers du monde russe et soviétique*, 20 (3-4) (1979), 305-22, and paper presented at Third World Congress of Slavists, Washington, Oct. 1985: 'The Dilemmas of Expansion: Russia and Mongolian Autonomy, 1911-13'.

of Berlin, the Russo-German commercial treaty of 1904, and the Bosnian crisis. The cup of humiliation was overflowing and responsibility was laid at the door of diplomacy, always the scapegoat of frustrated nationalists since the 1870s. A broad consensus of opinion in the press and the Duma concluded that in international relations Russia needed to take up a firmer stand and show her opponents her real power.

Russian diplomacy's tactic, wrote the *Novoe Vremya*, had been 'peace at any price', and their opponents had 'misused our love of peace and dealt us a series of painful blows which will for long reflect on our position in Europe. . . . We have wasted much of what has been achieved by several generations'. They had 'no gifted diplomats'; the Germans did not need to take any account of Russia and 'we seem only to be used to retreating'.[38] The *Rech'* agreed that 'for the Triple Entente there remain only defeats and disappointments . . . in the Balkans, Austria and Italy, make rain or fine weather'.[39] Following the Liman von Sanders affair, which neither liberals nor nationalists thought had been satisfactorily dealt with, the *Novoe Vremya* ran a series of articles and leaders on German activity in Asia Minor, Persia, and China, concluding that Russia was threatened with encirclement. It was in this mood that Russian commentators met the German press campaign at the beginning of March, and were clearly somewhat perplexed that Germany should actually fear them so much for the press to debate the need for a preventive war! It was not Russia, Men'shikov pointed out, which had been in the forefront of the arms race for forty years. In the meantime other powers had grown in Russia's rear. They were bordered by ten states with half the world's population and three or four of them were Great Powers directly hostile. The German attacks were taken to be preparation for a new military bill or to soften Russia up for the Russo-German commercial treaty negotiations, and the columnists advised that Russia should 'recognize immediately the significance of the approaching danger from Germany and take a whole series of necessary internal and external measures to maintain the

---

[38] *Novoe Vremya*, 1/14 Jan. 1914, p. 2, survey of foreign affairs in 1913; 9/22 Jan.; 14/27 Jan.; 17/30 Jan.; 6/19 Mar. 1914, p. 4, Men'shikov article.

[39] *Rech'*, 1/14 Jan. 1914. The Slavophile paper *Svet* commented gloomily that nobody would regret the passing of 'the old fatal, ill-starred year', 31 Dec. 1913/13 Jan. 1914.

national character [of her economy], or else the further unconcern for national interests in government circles will lower Russia in time to the level of the Ottoman Empire or China'.[40]

The *Rech'* was also bewildered at the German press attacks. It admitted there was an excessive nationalist fervour in some of the press but this derived as much from fear as from strength. And it was ridiculous to accuse the government of aggressiveness: 'If it is at fault in anything, it is rather in the quality directly opposite to any striving for aggression: its panic fear before any shadow of international complications.' In Milyukov's view it was 'apparently not a question of what Germany has already got in the Near East but what she wants to get, by seizing the favourable moment'. Even he, the liberal leader most aware of the dangers of a conflict, advised: 'May our diplomacy not be too easily frightened.'[41]

This consciousness of political weakness was supplemented by awareness that Russia was economically not in the same league as her rivals on the international scene. She simply did not have the same weapons to hand and was incompetent in using them when she did. 'Russia has almost lost political influence in the Balkans,' a leader in the *Novoe Vremya* claimed in December 1913,

but even when we were influential our commerce could not take advantage. . . . All western Europe extends its commercial influence to the Balkans—but not Russia. . . . We cannot think in such conditions of economic conquests, which however are the guarantee of political success . . . our merchants and industrialists are not pioneers of economic success but harmful parasites.

[40] *Novoe Vremya*, 9/21 Jan. 1914, first leader, p. 5, 'The German Bosphorus'; 17/30 Jan. 1914 (Asia Minor); 18/31 Jan., first leader, p. 4, 'Germany and the Armenians; 19 Jan/1 Feb., p. 5, first leader, 'Germany in the Middle East'; 21 Jan./3 Feb., p. 4, first leader, 'German friendship'; 31 Jan./ 13 Feb., p. 4, 'Germans in Persia'; 19 Feb./4 Mar., p. 4, first leader, 'The German-Chinese Entente'; 20 Feb./5 Mar., leader (Commercial treaty); 21 Feb./6 Mar., first leader, 'The Russo-German Commercial Treaty'; 1/14 Mar., p. 4, first leader, 'German Hypnosis' and Men'shikov article.

[41] *Rech'* on Liman von Sanders 5/18 Jan. 1914 advised Russia should 'take "real" measures to protect the interests and rights of Russia' and not again be 'always too late'; 23 Feb./8 Mar., first leader; 26 Feb./11 Mar., first leader; 28 Feb/13 Mar., first leader and survey of press; 16/29 Mar., p. 3, survey of press ('Psychology of Fear').

And with the depressing news of the failure of Russian commerce in Mongolia despite the most favourable conditions, the *Rech'* exclaimed: 'Are we really now not even capable of beating the Chinese?'[42]

The requirements of Russia's economic development remained in 1914 a matter of heated debate in government and public. The commercial relationship with Germany in particular raised tension amongst business interests and in nationalistically sensitive circles. The Russo-German commercial treaty of 1904 was widely believed to have been wrenched from them to Germany's advantage when Russia was vulnerable in the Russo-Japanese War. Already in early 1912 Kokovtsov noted the emotional and partisan manner in which the question of revision of the treaty was being approached. Previously industrial circles had been sensitive about too little protection. But on the eve of the war the revelation of the export of grain from Germany to Russia's western provinces, and even re-export of Russian products, aroused agrarian circles also. To some extent it was a conflict between agrarian and industrial interests, each claiming priority for its own section of the economy in the renegotiation of the treaty. But the debate struck a deep chord in the Russian press and public.

The underlying consciousness of Russia's relative backwardness, of the limited dynamism of her economy, and the limited confidence of the public in the government's ability to manage it effectively, together with some of the indisputably disturbing facts revealed on the eve of the war, brought Germany into focus as the economic opponent just when the latter's political role as unequivocal supporter of Austria and even as a direct threat to Russian interests at the Straits was made evident. Germany's role in Russia's foreign trade had been increasing. There had been a flood of imports in 1913 and Germany took the largest share of this increase. In 1913 45 per cent of Russian exports and 50 per cent of her imports were with Germany. No other great power was so dependent on one market. For Russia the German market was far more significant in her total trade than was the Russian market for Germany. There had been efforts to encourage the British to compete more effectively in exports to

---

[42] *Novoe Vremya*, 24 Nov./7 Dec. 1913; *Rech'*, 1/13 Jan. 1914, p. 2.

Russia during the period of the Entente, but to no avail. The German predominance continued and intensified. It was not only the weight of trade with Germany which was disturbing, for that had an important impact on Russia's western provinces, strategically vital, but politically ill-integrated into the Russian Empire. The government, in agreement with the right-centre of the political spectrum in press and Duma, responded to this situation with measures to reduce Finnish trade with Germany, and at the end of 1913 a bill was introduced to impose tariffs on grain imported into Russia's western provinces. To this was added in April 1914 a limitation on government orders with German firms in the defence industries. With the resulting protests of the German press a further twist was added to the wave of publicly expressed hostility between Germany and Russia on the eve of the war.[43]

The danger from Germany was seen to lie not only in her internal role in the Russian economy through direct trade. German commercial dynamism in other parts of the world of political importance to Russia intensified Russian insecurity, since it was accepted as axiomatic that political influence followed economic. This was not so much the case in the Balkans, where Russian trade and economic interests were negligible, but in Asiatic Turkey, where with the progress of the Baghdad railway it was expected that Germany's economic role would spread towards the Caucasian frontiers. And in north Persia, where Russia had a dominant share of the market, it was the danger of German commerce, rather than British, that was feared, even

[43] Kokovtsov, op. cit. (above, n. 19), ii. 86–7, 126–7; Bonwetsch, op. cit. (above, n. 24), ch. 1, pp. 12–40; F. Fischer, *Krieg der Illusionen* (Düsseldorf, 1969), 527–41; *Rech'*, 10/23 Jan. 1914, p. 2; 25 Jan./7 Feb., p. 3; 12/25 Apr. press survey; 19 Apr./2 May, p. 2; 22 Apr./5 May, p. 2. *Novoe Vremya*, 31 Jan./13 Feb. 1914, p. 4 on the dismissal of Kokovtsov; 21 Feb./6 Mar., first leader; 4/17 Mar., p. 4; 6/19 Mar., leader, p. 4: 'In the past twenty years our western neighbour has actually held firmly in its teeth the very vital sources of our well-being and like a vampire has sucked the blood and sweat of the work of the Russian farmer'; 28 Mar./10 Apr., leader; 14/27 Apr., leader, p. 2: 'At the moment we are in the position of a defender, Germany economically is plundering us and politically strangling, threatening not only further economic destruction, but also military defeat'; and 15/27 June, leader. I. M. Goldstein, *Russko-germanskii torgovyi dogovor i sleduet li Rossii byt' koloniei' Germanii?* (Moscow, 1913); B. Monastyrev, 'Rossiya — koloniya Germanii', *Voennyi Sbornik*, Sept. 1914 (written before the war), no. 9, pp. 95–108. SOGD, sess. 2, pt. 4, 24 May/6 June 1914, debate on budget of Ministry of Trade and Industry, cc. 1475 ff.

though it formed as yet not much more than 5 per cent of Persian trade. Time was running out and increased the nervousness of government circles. Sazonov's curious agreement of 1911 with Germany to build the Khanaqin–Teheran link with the Baghdad railway would shortly have to be implemented as the Baghdad line progressed. And only a short delay could be obtained from the Turks and the French banks and entrepreneurs who were keen to go ahead with railways in eastern Anatolia. These would not only raise new strategic problems, but also deprive Russian commerce of the benefits of geographical isolation, which was considered essential to enable it to compete in the markets adjacent to her Asiatic frontiers.[44]

The relationship with France also aroused Russian sensitivity and the ever-ready suspicion of dependence on scheming foreigners. And with good reason. Kokovtsov had negotiated the last three major loans with France. In 1908 he had had to remind the French that Russia was not Turkey or China, and in 1913 he concluded that he would 'willingly change France for anyone else . . .' In 1914 rumours about the terms of the recent railway loan, the Peugeot affair, and the increasing role in the Russian economy of syndicates in which the French played an important role, increased the sensitivity of the public and of industry to Russia's possible economic dependence as the European situation became more tense. Yet the intensity of feeling against France on economic grounds was less than that against Germany, as it was not complemented by the political antagonism. France's economic role could be more easily seen as constructive, and as competing with Germany in encouraging the development of native Russian industry. Foreign capital invested in Russia, its supporters assured, would soon become Russian, whereas Germany's role as major commercial partner and exporter of industrial goods to Russia (although also as a substantial investor) provided the basis for an underlying apprehension expressed at its extreme in the conviction that Russia was in danger of becoming a 'colony' of Germany.[45]

---

[44] L. G. Istyagin, *Germanskoe proniknovenie v Iran i russko-germanskie protivorechiya nakanune pervoi mirovoi voiny* (Moscow, 1979), 168–204.

[45] R. Girault, *Emprunts et investissements français en Russie* . . . (Paris, 1973), 561 ff.; Kokovtsov to Neratov, 21 Sept./4 Oct. 1913, in Marchand (ed.) op. cit. (above, n. 6), ii. 448–50.

There was thus in 1914 a heightened awareness of the ties and limitations in the economic field which bound Russia in different ways to France and Germany. The resulting irritation was aggravated by the evidence of an incipient economic crisis in May and June— depression on the stock exchange requiring government intervention and causing the fall of the rouble. The St Petersburg Kadet F. A. Rodichev warned in the Duma: 'If you ask the question, what is the mood of trade and bourse circles what do you see and hear? Everywhere you feel the fear of something threatening; something dangerous and repulsive is imminent, a consciousness of an approaching catastrophe. All feel it, including those who are preparing it.'[46] It is not possible of course to establish a definite link between this crisis and the response of Russia on 24 July to the Serbian ultimatum. But given the premiss that the Russian government did not act in isolation and out of contact with significant sections of the public, its impact on the mood and atmosphere of society and government should not be discounted. And the organ of 'progressive' Moscow business men was not behindhand in its encouragement of a firm response to the ultimatum: 'It is time to put an end to these lusts for pillage', it noted on 25 July.[47]

As for the press in general, apart from Milyukov's *Rech'*, it welcomed the Russian government's response to the ultimatum. In fact, after all its recent experience and criticisms of Russian diplomacy it could hardly believe that a firm position was being taken. Before the Austrian declaration of war on Serbia most organs seemed to believe that Russia's firm stand was the very way to prevent a war. But they rejoiced in the unbelievable coincidence of view between government and 'public'. The *Birzhevyye Vedomosti* commented with amazement that not since the Serbian–Turkish war of 1876 had Russia been so decisive: 'However much various well-wishers abroad tried to intimidate Russia, her diplomats rested on the support of public opinion, and displayed absolutely no signs of retreat from the position she had first taken up—that the integrity and independence of Serbia must be completely protected.' Nevertheless, as late as 29 July

---

[46] SOGD, sess. 2, pt. 3, 1914, c. 1625; *Rech'*, 16/29 May 1914, p. 2, survey of the press; p. 2, article by Tugan-Baranovskii; 6/19 May; 21 June/4 July, p. 2, survey of the press.
[47] Discussion in Girault, op. cit. (above, n. 45), 573–5; *Birzhevyye Vedomosti*, 13/26 Jul. 1914, press survey quoting *Utro Rossii*, 12/25 July 1914.

this paper noted that Russian opinion remained calm and hoped that a war which would 'put back the life of Europe by fifty years', could still be avoided. Likewise the *Novoe Vremya* on 25 July: 'The government can be certain that the worthy language it has chosen is comprehensible to all Russian citizens.' And on 28 July it observed: 'In these disturbed and solemn days the firm voice of the government is indivisible from the hearty and courageous voice of Russia. The great country after some eclipse keenly feels its well-being. Instead of the usual oppressive depression there is a flood of cheerfulness and belief in our own strength.' Looking back on 1 August it seemed to the same newspaper that 'our enemies helped us to find ourselves: we did not know it and nor did they. Hardly had we heard one measure of the government with satisfaction than it was followed by another still more energetic, corresponding still more to the prestige of a great people.'[48]

[48] *Birzhevyye Vedomosti*, 15/28 July 1914 (quote), also for the whole of the crisis and in particular its extensive press survey; *Novoe Vremya*, dates given.

5

Germany and the Coming of War

HARTMUT POGGE VON STRANDMANN

> Had we not been prepared to risk this war, then we should never have bothered to found the Reich and should have continued to exist as a nation of small states.
>
> Max Weber, 22 October 1916

THE South Schools, a large lecture hall in the Examination Schools of Oxford University, is adorned with portraits of English, Swedish, and Prussian monarchs. Among them is the portrait of Wilhelm II, the last German Emperor, grandson of Queen Victoria. This large picture, the work of the Berlin painter Alfred Schwarz, was a present from the Kaiser to Oxford University in gratitude for being awarded in 1907 an honorary degree, the Doctorate of Civil Law.[1] The *Oxford Magazine*, a journal focusing on events in the university, commented on the announcement of the award in the *University Gazette*: 'The German Emperor is, on private grounds, a *persona grata* to England, and especially to Oxford, which he visited and, we believe, learned to like as a boy, and "on his public forum" he is one of the two or three most interesting personalities, perhaps the most interesting, now living.'[2] On 15 November 1907 a deputation headed by the Chancellor, Lord Curzon, and the Vice-chancellor, T. H. Warren, conferred the degree upon the Kaiser by Diploma at Windsor Castle during one of his many visits to England. The press in England,

---

[1] University of Oxford Archives, HC/M/3/23, p. 9, Hebdomadal Council Act, 19 Jan. 1909.
[2] *Oxford Magazine* (7 Nov. 1907), 54.

Germany, and even in France reported on the honour bestowed upon the Kaiser. In 1985, the British Prime Minister, Margaret Thatcher, was refused the same degree by a majority of Oxford dons, but no such opposition was voiced to the Kaiser in 1907. In fact the resolution to confer the degree upon the Emperor had been passed by Convocation *nemine contradicente* beforehand. Whatever the individual feelings in Oxford may have been the Kaiser's political stance had not yet created sufficient antagonism to deny him the honour.

The subsequent fate of the Kaiser's portrait accurately reflects the change in Anglo-German relations over the next fifty years. The portrait arrived in Oxford in 1909 and was eventually hung in Schools.[3] Soon after the outbreak of the First World War the picture was taken down when the building was converted into a military hospital. Thus the painting was saved and the dignity of the wounded British soldier preserved.

Whatever may have happened to the Kaiser's honorary degree after 1914 the fate of the portrait can be established with some accuracy. It simply sank into oblivion. In the inter-war years relations between Britain and Germany did not recover sufficiently for the portrait to reappear. During the Second World War it remained buried in the cellars of Schools. After 1945 it took a considerable time for the links between the United Kingdom and the Federal Republic to return to a normal footing. The re-emergence of the German Rhodes Scholarships in 1969, which had originally been introduced with the Kaiser's help, may illustrate this point. Thus there was no incentive to mount a search for the Kaiser's portrait either after 1918 or after 1945. However, when a request was made to the Clerk of the Schools to find another missing portrait, he was able to report to the Curators in November 1956 that the painting of the Kaiser had been discovered in the basement, rolled up and without a frame. The Curators, imbued with a sense of history which does not differentiate between enemies and allies, villains and tragic heroes, resolved to have it restored. A year later, on 31 October

---

[3] *Oxford Magazine* (21 Jan. 1909), 132. The portrait represents the Kaiser in his robe of a DCL and wearing the insignia of the Garter. See also private communication by the Assistant Archivist of the University of Oxford Archives, 9 Nov. 1984.

1957, they decided to hang the portrait, now back in full splendour and framed, in South Schools.[4]

The Kaiser's gift to Oxford and the fate of the portrait in 1914 could lend weight to Arno Mayer's emphasis on the continuing domination of the *ancien régime* and the utmost importance of the monarchs in Europe before the First World War.[5] If this were the case then the First World War could be interpreted as a squabble amongst the royal families which got out of hand. But the crowned heads of Europe did not significantly contribute to the outbreak of the war. For that the Austrian Emperor was too old, the Russian Tsar too weak, and the Kaiser too inconsistent and too erratic. Of course their approval was needed for important decisions, but they no longer initiated them. Instead they accepted the international constellations as they had developed and went along with the decisions which led to the war despite some misgivings. During the summer of 1914 the impression given was one of vacillation rather than of decisiveness and determination. Power lay in the hands of a relatively small number of political and military leaders whose concepts and designs were moulded or supported as the case might be by various social and political groups. The European kings and queens contributed in different ways and degrees to the prevailing atmosphere, but they were no longer in control of political affairs. They formed the last link in a chain of events and decisions which was dependent on the public as a whole. Consequently it does not make sense to burden *ancien régimes* with the responsibility for war. In the twentieth century the situation was far more complex and representatives of *ancien régimes* were only one factor which helped to create an atmosphere which made wars possible and acceptable.

Was the war mainly the result of rising Anglo-German antagonism as the fate of the Kaiser's portrait suggests?[6] Despite

---

[4] Private communication by Assistant Archivist of Univ. of Oxford Archives, 9 Nov. 1984. See also the minutes of the Curators of the Schools, 8 Nov. 1956 and 31 Oct. 1957. I am grateful to the Clerks of the Schools, W. H. Miller and his successor, G. A. Barnes, for providing me with this information and checking the relevant minutes.

[5] A. Mayer, *The Persistence of the Old Regime: Europe to the Great War* (London, 1981), 135 ff.

[6] In this context see G. Hollenberg, *Englisches Interesse am Kaiserreich* (Wiesbaden, 1974); P. Kennedy, *The Rise of the Anglo-German Antagonism 1860–1914* (London, 1980), 386–409.

the tensions between France, Britain, and Germany over Morocco in 1905 and 1911, the clash between Austria and Russia and the Balkan crises in 1912–13 were more instrumental in causing the war than the Anglo-German confrontation. Nevertheless there were groups in Germany which vied with Britain for the position of first world power. They saw in Britain the main antagonist to German ambitions and therefore believed that a future war in which the two countries would fight each other would become the War of the British Succession.[7] However, the presence of this underlying ambition in certain German circles should not deflect our attention from the fact that it was the ensuing crisis in the Balkans which triggered the major European confrontation in 1914.

Once the war had started between Germany and Austria on the one side and Russia, France, and Britain on the other more states soon became involved. The first power to do so was the Turkish Empire at the end of October 1914, an event which extended hostilities into the Middle East. So even before Italy and the United States joined the war, in 1915 and 1917 respectively, the conflict could be considered a world war because the British Empire came out in support of Britain, because Japan and Australia conquered the German possessions in the Far East, and because the Germans defended their colonies in Africa. In 1917 even China and Siam, under pressure from the Western Powers, joined their ranks in the struggle against the Central Powers. Closer to home, in the Middle East the Turkish Empire was fighting the Russians in the Caucasus and the British in Palestine. Yet the war in Europe dominated the stage.

The label 'world war' has been questioned by some non-European analysts who prefer to call the war a 'civil war within the European community of nations'.[8] This view opposed the Eurocentric view of modern history and reminds European historians that there were important regions outside Europe which were not directly involved in 1914. True, the war was fought mostly in Europe, but it affected the entire world, especially in economic matters. Generally speaking, in 1914,

---

[7] The historian Max Lenz coined the slogan about a future War of the English Succession in 1900.

[8] K. M. Panikkar, *Asia and Western Dominance, 1498–1945* (London, 1953), 259 ff.

Europe was still regarded as the hub of the world, not only economically but also politically. The fact that the Austrian-Hungarian government was already borrowing heavily on the American capital market before 1914 does not detract from the above statement.[9] Thus a major war in Europe was a world war.

The geographical closeness of the European states to one another may strengthen the view that in war they behaved like the feuding members of a family. But this is a superficial argument. Despite the existence of a general European culture and despite the broad similarities of political developments in the major states of Europe, in 1914 the dominant nationalist currents of opinion preferred to underline the differences between the various states. Chauvinism triumphed in 1914 and the war was, like so many other modern wars, a violent clash of national ambitions and national interests. Despite the existing tensions between the major European powers and despite the armaments race, war might well not have broken out in 1914 had it not been for the determination of one power to exploit the Balkan crisis to change the international status quo in its favour.

From 1914 onwards, the public in several countries was preoccupied with the origins and causes of the war as well as with the motivation and the war aims of the various powers. For obvious reasons historians took a prominent part in this discussion. One of the first books to appear was entitled: *Why We Are at War: Great Britain's Case*.[10] It was published by six Oxford historians in September 1914. With the help of the British and German *White Books* they analysed the causes of the war as they saw them. They blamed Germany's obsession with power and militarism for the war and held that England's intervention was based on the need to uphold international law. And they went

[9] S. R. Williamson, jun., 'Vienna and July 1914: The Origins of the Great War Once More', in P. Pastor and S. Williamson, jun., *Essays on World War I: Origins and Prisoners of War* (New York, 1983), 12–13.

[10] E. Barker (New College), H. W. C. Davis (Balliol College), C. R. L. Fletcher (Magdalen College), A. Hassall (Christ Church), L. G. Wickham Legg (New College), F. Morgan (Keble College), *Why We Are at War: Great Britain's Case* (Oxford, 1914).

on to say, convinced of their moral superiority, that 'if we have harped on England's interest, it must not for a moment be supposed that we have forgotten England's duty. But England stands today in this fortunate position, that her duty and her interest combine to impel her in the same direction.'[11] Duty was interpreted in this context as coming to the aid of smaller nations, i.e. Belgium and Serbia. Although the Oxford historians believed that the nations were guided by certain abstract principles during the diplomatic crisis preceding the outbreak of the war, no reference to opposing ideologies, of the kind common today, can be found. Ideas and principles which seemed to some to be worth fighting for were introduced mainly after hostilities had begun in order to justify the entry into the war and the war effort of the country concerned.

One principle which stood above all others was, however, already discernible hours before the outbreak of hostilities: all governments declared solemnly that they were about to be engaged in a defensive war. Most people accepted this type of legitimization. The clash of power interests was not referred to as the reason for war, and even most Germans and Austro-Hungarians were only too willing to endorse the official version that the war was merely defensive. Few people appreciated the paradox that in such a chauvinist political climate a defensive war should be fought on all sides.

While the propaganda campaign was heating up, readers of the *Oxford Magazine* must have followed with astonishment an episode in the journal.[12] In January 1915 the magazine published a letter by Kurt Hahn who, on his return from England in August 1914, worked for the Press and Information Department of the German Foreign Office. His letter was addressed to Lord Sandon, a friend of his from his time as an undergraduate at Christ Church. Hahn tried to show that it was not really the violation of Belgian neutrality which had caused Britain's entry into the war. He pointed instead to the assurances Sir Edward Grey was supposed

---

[11] Barker *et al.*, op. cit. (above, n. 10), 122.
[12] *Oxford Magazine* (22 Jan. 1915). Hahn's letter is dated Dec. 1914, but he writes as if the battle of the Masurian Lakes had happened a week ago. In fact the battle took place on 10 and 11 Sept. 1914. So it is possible that the letter was written in September, but delayed until December, perhaps by German Foreign Office officials.

to have given to Russia and France, soon after the delivery of the Austrian ultimatum, should war break out over Serbia. He accused Grey of being misinformed, incompetent, and deceitful, but he was unable to substantiate his claim. Hahn went on to state that it was France that had breached Belgian neutrality first, that Grey was unaware of Russia's and France's real intentions, and that he had underestimated Germany's love of peace. Moreover, he rejected the news about Russian advances into Germany and denied allegations about German brutality in Belgium and on the high seas. The editor of the *Oxford Magazine* defended the publication of the letter against strong criticism by using Hahn's appeal to one of Oxford's attributes, the 'strong sense of fair play which does not desert men, even if their self-interest is at stake'.[13] It is difficult to estimate what effect this letter had on its readers in Oxford. But it does not seem to have influenced the character of the continuing propaganda war.

The general belief in a defensive war may help to explain why there was such a confused and apologetic debate about the origins of the war after 1918–19. For the German government in 1914 it was crucial, even before the war had begun, that Germany should appear to have been 'forced into war'. Ever since, various German governments have been busy rejecting any charge that Germany might not have fought a defensive war. The German Foreign Office therefore went to extraordinary lengths in insisting on Germany's defensive role in order to forestall the suggestion that she had started the war. Instead imperial Russia was to be blamed.[14] Germany's entire official propaganda was directed against Russia. Even the six Oxford historians noted that 'German professors' agreed with the German *White Book*'s intention of fastening the blame for starting the war upon Russia. In the ensuing propaganda campaign the Oxford dons rejected their German colleagues' assertion that England had allied herself with 'Muscovite barbarism'.[15] In this context it may be of interest to

[13] Ibid. (29 Jan. 1915), 168.
[14] E. J. C. Hahn, 'The German Foreign Ministry and the Question of War Guilt in 1918–1919', in C. Fink, I. V. Hull and M. Knox (eds.), *German Nationalism and the European Response, 1890–1945* (Norman, Okla. and London, 1985), 46 ff. See also F. Fischer, *War of Illusions: German Policies from 1911 to 1914* (London, 1975), 370–88 and 463–7.
[15] Barker *et al.*, op. cit. (above, n. 10), 115.

point out that in the above-mentioned letter Kurt Hahn refrained from referring to the main thrust of German propaganda. But if the nations involved in the war generally believed that they were fighting a defensive war, this begs the obvious question. Who was the aggressor? For the powers of the Triple Entente, France, Britain, and Russia, it was clear that Germany and Austria had started the war whereas most Austrians and Germans clung to the official version that the other side had attacked the Dual Alliance first. Beyond the realm of claims and counter-claims nobody made a serious analysis of the reasons why each side believed that it fought a defensive war. Such a study would have demanded a knowledge of the political, military, and economic establishments, their plans, ambitions, and assumptions. Clearly this was beyond the inclination of diplomats and publicists as well as historians at the time. What is more, even critical observers in their own countries were mostly in the dark about the reasons for the claim that a defensive war was being fought. Therefore the Independent Socialist, Karl Kautsky, could write after the war: 'Since the outbreak of the World War, one question occupies all minds. Who brought this terrible disaster upon us? Which people and which institutions have caused all this?'[16] Kautsky published this question after the war. Had his book come out during the war it would have appeared to be unpatriotic especially when nationalism was running high and when those involved in the war effort needed the conviction that they were fighting for the right cause. The longer the conflict lasted and the greater the human sacrifice became, the more the chance of an objective assessment declined. At first only two authors examined critically the German case. Grelling's famous *J'accuse* and the writings of the former Krupp-director Muehlon appeared early in the war. Later Prince Lichnowsky's critical memorandum of 1916 was leaked and led to very strong defensive measures by the German government.[17] Even after the war very few critical assessments of Germany's pre-war role were published in Germany. Apologetic studies predominated. German post-war propaganda scored its major success when a revisionist current began to

---

[16] K. Kautsky, *Wie der Weltkrieg entstand* (Berlin 1919), 13.
[17] Hahn, op. cit. (above, n. 14), 46–7; J. C. G. Röhl, *Zwei deutsche Fürsten zur Kriegsschuldfrage: Lichnowsky und Eulenburg und der Ausbruch des Ersten Weltkriegs* (Düsseldorf, 1971), 19–24. Lichnowsky had drafted his memo in 1915.

emerge during the 1920s which questioned the victors' diktat with its claim of Germany's sole responsibility for the war. In the end Lloyd George's politically motivated dictum that 'the nations slithered over the brink into the boiling cauldron of war' came to be generally accepted.[18] On the German side this was interpreted as a vindication of the war-time belief that the Central Powers were fighting a defensive war.

German politicians, publicists, and historians were only too eager to use the myth of a defensive war to be rid of the notion of war guilt and to revise the Peace Treaty of Versailles. Even after the Second World War historians continued to reject German responsibility for the outbreak of war in 1914. Academics like Karl Dietrich Erdmann, who has recently acquired a dubious reputation because he did not reveal some major anomalies in his edition of the Diaries of Bethmann Hollweg's one-time assistant, Kurt Riezler, declared as late as the 1960s that no government had wanted war in 1914, but that no government had been able to prevent it.[19] His colleague, Egmont Zechlin, argued on similar lines when he pointed to the vicious circle in which all governments had found themselves. Only later did he modify his judgment by admitting that Germany had been prepared to risk a war.[20]

Erdmann's and Zechlin's interpretations are to some extent compatible with those views which try to emphasize how little room for manœuvre the statesmen of 1914 had. Given the polarization between the two alliance systems, it is argued, and the dependence of military planning upon the prevailing political constellations, the diplomats were left with little freedom to break out of an inflexible situation in 1914. But this supposed lack of freedom does not mean that the participants in the July Crisis

---

[18] D. Lloyd George, *War Memoirs*, i (London, 1924), 32. The rest of the paragraph was equally welcome: 'Not even the astutest and most far-seeing statesman foresaw in the early summer of 1914 that the autumn would find the nations of the world interlocked in the most terrible conflict that has ever been witnessed in the history of mankind.'

[19] A controversy about Erdmann's edition raged through the German newspapers and periodicals in 1983 and 1984. A polemical account of the controversy appeared in B. F. Schulte, *Die Verfälschung der Riezler Tagebücher: ein Beitrag zur Wissenschaftsgeschichte der 50er and 60er Jahre* (Frankfurt, 1985).

[20] See E. Zechlin's collection of essays, *Krieg und Kriegsrisiko: zur deutschen Politik im Ersten Weltkrieg* (Düsseldorf, 1979).

were prisoners of a situation, nor does it mean that they were incapable of handling an international crisis satisfactorily.[21] In fact most of them were unwilling to leave a framework of reference which they had accepted or even created for themselves. Thus the impression cannot be avoided that those German historians who prefer to believe that the 'men of 1914' had no room for manœuvre are largely motivated by apologetic tendencies.

It is only a small step from believing in the lack of political flexibility during the July Crisis to an acceptance of the strength of general causes of hostilities.[22] The analysis of the international system, of military planning, of the economic situation, and of the social problems in each country has tended to shift the emphasis away from the question of who caused the war and who had the greatest interest in starting it. Once we accept that the war was not foisted upon a reluctant Europe by an automaton and that it did not break out accidentally, the causes have to be established and that power identified which pushed more for war than the others. This is not to say that the net of investigation cannot be cast more widely to bring in a broader range of reasons and explanations for decisions and to expose some of the underlying assumptions. Both approaches are necessary to give a comprehensive explanation of why one power pushed for war and the others accepted the challenge, and why influential and vociferous sections of the population were willing to endure the war for so long.

One consequence of concentrating on international relations in 1914 and the arms race is the development of an analogy between the present and the years prior to the First World War. However, the analogy proves misleading when the international

[21] In a recent article D. E. Kaiser has argued that the German government's freedom of movement was severely restricted because of 'serious regional, religious, political, and class antagonisms'. This remark may apply to some political reforms, but during the July Crisis the political leaders in Berlin on the whole demonstrated a level of firmness and determination which left little room for any 'restrictions': D. E. Kaiser, 'Germany and the Origins of the First World War', in *Journal of Modern History*, 55 (1983), 473–4.

[22] See for an excellent general account and a critical examination of the general causes, J. Joll, *The Origins of the First World War* (London, 1984).

situation of 1914 is compared with that of today. Miles Kahler, for example, has played down the fact that there was one country in July 1914 which wanted war more than any other and which pushed Europe over the brink.[23] Nevertheless the analogy has attracted some political analysts of the present political situation who have only a vague knowledge of the complexities of 1914 and who are worried about the dangerous political atmosphere between East and West at present. They are concerned that a war could break out now on lines similar to those in 1914. Among them is Helmut Schmidt, the former Chancellor of the Federal Republic. To him the outbreak of the First World War was an accident, the result of escalating international tensions and the arms race. He makes no reference to the fact that Germany had started the war. George Kennan has also taken up this theme and elaborated it in his most recent book *The Fateful Alliance*.[24]

However, the analogy between the present and the pre-1914 situation is unconvincing because it is based on the false premiss that no one wanted war in 1914 and that no one could avoid it. Although this premiss is not borne out by recent research, it nevertheless could have dangerous implications for the present. It could, for instance, imply that in certain international circumstances wars are inevitable because there is no more room for political manœuvre. Against the fatalism of this outlook it has to be pointed out that decisions which lead to war are made deliberately, that no power slides into war, that in a complex international situation there is always at least one power which is inclined towards war: there is no automatic road to Armageddon.

In the present state of research, the evidence that Germany and Austria started the war and dragged the rest of the powers into it is even stronger than in the early 1960s when Fritz Fischer published his analysis of German war aims policies.[25] Now the demands of the 1960s for detailed analyses of the war aims of

[23] M. Kahler, 'Rumours of War: The 1914 Analogy', in *Foreign Affairs* (1979/80), no 2, 374–396.

[24] G. F. Kennan, *The Fateful Alliance. France, Russia, and the Coming of the First World War* (New York, 1984).

[25] Fischer's *Griff nach der Weltmacht* appeared in English under the title *Germany's Aims in the First World War* (London, 1967).

the other states have been largely fulfilled. Thorough studies for all the major European powers have been undertaken which are based on the extensive use of unpublished material.[26] The evidence gathered makes the view that Germany fought a defensive war untenable and the interpretation that all nations 'slithered over the brink into . . . war' unconvincing. It is clear that there was no general drift into war, although one was predicted for the none too distant future.

In the literature other general reasons for the inevitability of the war have been put forward. But the assumption that a general European war must have general European causes is not borne out by the evidence. The alliance system, the arms race, the highest stage of capitalism, the Anglo-German trade rivalry, the supposedly age-old clash between Teuton and Slav, or colonial rivalry, or the assumed hereditary animosity between France and Germany: all have been referred to in order to make the war appear as an event from which there was no escape. The analogy with the weather has been used by some authors to illustrate the inevitability of war and make its central outbreak seem like the workings of a fate beyond human control. Expressions like 'the darkening of the horizon', 'the gathering of clouds', 'the stifling atmosphere', 'the distant thunder', 'the first lightning', and finally 'the breaking of the storm' have been used to provide explanatory images for the outbreak of war in 1914. But the war was not a natural catastrophe.

---

[26] See for some of the recent (post-1976) work: A. Hayashima, *Die Illusion des Sonderfriedens. Deutsche Verständigungspolitik mit Japan im Ersten Weltkrieg* (Munich, 1982); R. Bosworth, *Italy and the Approach of the First World War* (London, 1983); D. French, *British Economic and Strategic Planning 1905–1915* (London, 1982); J. F. V. Keiger, *France and the Origins of the First World War* (London, 1983); G. Krumeich, *Aufrüstung und Innenpolitik in Frankreich vor dem Ersten Weltkrieg: die Einführung der dreijährigen Dienstpflicht 1913–1914* (Wiesbaden, 1980): an English trans. has been published by Berg in Leamington Spa (1984); D. C. B. Lieven, *Russia and the Origins of the First World War* (London, 1983); H. G. Linke, *Das zarische Rußland und der Erste Weltkrieg. Diplomatie und Kriegsziele 1914–1917* (Munich, 1982); Z. S. Steiner, *Britain and the Origins of the First World War* (London, 1977); D. Stevenson, *French War Aims against Germany 1914–1919* (Oxford, 1982). A recent East German account of the pre-war era tries to analyse the 'objective causes of the growing German expansionism and within that framework the concrete economic conditions which led to the political decisions for unleashing the First World War': W. Gutsche, *Monopole, Staat und Expansion vor 1914: zum Funktionsmechanismus zwischen Industriemonopolen, Großbanken und Staatsorganen in der Außenpolitik des Deutschen Reiches 1897 bis Sommer 1914* (Berlin, 1986).

If one were to follow some populist literature, general political analyses, and the press, the political climate would appear to have been laden with animosities which did not improve relations in Europe. However useful general atmospheric studies might be, they are no substitute for the search to find out which of the European states intended to pull the trigger first. Otherwise it remains unclear why the war broke out in August 1914 and not in 1915–16 or, for that matter earlier, in 1913. What is more, the emphasis on very general causes for the war tends to make the intention to start a war seem irrelevant. The stress A. J. P. Taylor has laid on 'war by timetable' makes the outbreak of war appear to be automatic.[27] However, what the mobilization demonstrated is how well prepared the military plans were and how quickly military actions could be started. But the historian who is interested in the question of why wars break out in particular situations has to go further and analyse the links between causes, motivations, aims, reasons, and actions.

The attraction of automatic causes of the war is also shown by the work of American scholars who tried to make use of the quantitative method.[28] They went through the great documentary editions which appeared after the First World War and through which each country tried to prove that it had not caused the war, and quantified certain terms and certain reactions. To their surprise the term 'war' was increasingly used during the crisis of July and to top it all even more in August 1914. Whatever the merits of the quantitative methodology, it does not seem sufficiently convincing in this context to be useful for historical analysis. Thus a survey of general causes may show why war was possible and even likely, but not why it broke out in the summer of 1914.

The First World War was, like any other war, the result of political and military decisions which exploited international constellations and in turn realized political aims and concepts.

---

[27] A. J. P. Taylor, *War by Time-Table. How the First World War Began* (London, 1969).
[28] See K. J. Gantzel, G. Kress and V. Rittberger (eds.), *Konflikt–Eskalation–Krise: sozialwissenschaftliche Studien zum Ausbruch des Ersten Weltkrieges* (Düsseldorf, 1972). See the work of the so-called Stanford group of quantifying perceptions: O. Holsti, 'The 1914 Case', in *American Political Science Review*, 59 (1965), 365–78; D. A. Zinnes, 'A Comparison of Hostile Behaviour of Decision-Makers in Simulated and Historical Data', in *World Politics*, 18 (1965), 474–502.

Obviously the decisions leading to war in 1914 were not taken in a vacuum, remote from public opinion, economic concerns, and domestic pressures. The interplay between the public at large and the political and military leadership was crucial for the years before the outbreak of war and the actual crisis in July 1914, regardless of whether we look at the different political systems of France, Britain, Germany, or Russia. Of course, it remains difficult to establish a direct link between public pressures and political actions, especially as the political and military leaders cannot be separated from the public at large. How strongly both sides were similarly affected can be seen in the mounting international crises in the first years of the century. The prospect of war escalating from crisis to crisis may have heightened the expectation of war, but it also had a numbing effect and the public in the European states became used to the fact that international crises did not result in the major war so often forecast. But while public opinion soon forgot the latest crisis, the political and military leaders often prepared new initiatives to cope with the effects that crisis had had on the international, domestic, and military scene. In this way Germany and Austria edged closer to war after 1912. The political and military leadership grew increasingly familiar with the idea that a major war was coming without knowing exactly when. Politicians and generals did not talk each other into war; they expected a major war to happen, although few had any clear vision of who would start it and when. In any case international crises were not good opportunities for starting a war because none of the major powers was sufficiently prepared, from a military point of view, to spring a surprise upon the enemy in such a crisis.

In fact, if we look at the international crises and if we bear in mind that before 1914 war was still regarded as an acceptable and legitimate extension of politics, then it is surprising that peace was preserved between the major European powers between 1871 and 1914. But if peace survived several earlier crises then war cannot have been inevitable in 1914. Despite the existing alliance systems each crisis had a different international constellation. The first and second Moroccan crises found France and Britain on one side and Germany on the other. If war had broken out then Germany would have been the aggressor and it is doubtful whether Austria-Hungary would have supported Germany. In addition a great number of Germans would not have fought for a stretch of land in North Africa.

The Bosnian crisis of 1908–9 provided a scenario which was similar to that of 1914, but during the Bosnian crisis Russia was unwilling to remain firm and France as well as Britain was unwilling to aid Russia militarily. The Balkan Wars of 1912–13 posed a more serious threat to peace, but the joint efforts of Britain and Germany in bringing about a settlement prevented the escalation of a side-issue — namely the Austro-Serbian clash over Serbia's access to the Adriatic — into war.

In 1914 the situation was different. This time the belief was widespread in Austria that the Dual Monarchy had been provoked directly by Serbia. With Russia backing Serbia, the Dual Monarchy asked Germany for assistance. Again there would have been no war if Austria, in pursuit of punishment, had been willing to guarantee Serbia's political integrity and if Russia had decided not to make a stand against Austria's intention to crush Serbia. So it seems that it was the escalation of the July Crisis at the end of the month which led to war. Popular opinion reacted correspondingly. In all belligerent countries there was a sharp increase in enthusiasm for war in certain sections of the population once the mobilization orders had been issued. Yet it was not a general craving for war which had pushed reluctant governments over the brink. On the contrary, most governments hoped to carry their populations with them. In Germany the government knew that it would have popular support on its side if Russia appeared as the aggressor and could be blamed for starting the war. The ensuing enthusiasm was obviously linked to the expectation of a victorious outcome which in all European countries overrode any pessimistic outlook. As far as we know, the so-called August enthusiasm was expressed mostly by groups on the political Right. Recent research by Becker in France and Ullrich in Germany has indicated that there were sizeable sections of the population which did not join the wave of enthusiasm sweeping through some urban centres in Europe.[29] Those who

[29] J. J. Becker, *The Great War and the French People* (Leamington Spa, 1985); V. Ullrich, *Kriegsalltag: Hamburg im Ersten Weltkrieg* (Cologne, 1982).

were opposed to the war felt increasingly isolated and finally ceased to speak up. In some industrial centres in Germany the anticipated increase in social hardship was the main reason for the lack of enthusiasm. There were, however, groups or individuals in each of the European countries who expected or even desired war. Generally speaking, political and military leaders were not following a current created by those who wished for war, but the general acceptance of war created an atmosphere which made it easier for decisions leading to war to be taken without many moral scruples. This was particularly so in Germany, whereas the governments of the states of the Triple Entente reacted rather than acted. The fact that none of these states made dramatic efforts to prevent the outbreak of war does not mean that they actually wanted war. To them war was acceptable, but without the initiative from Berlin and Vienna, Russia, France, and Britain would not have retaliated by war. The German Foreign Secretary, Gottlieb von Jagow, realized this when he told the journalist Theodor Wolff on 25 July 1914 that 'neither London, nor Paris nor St Petersburg wants war'.[30] Paul Kennedy is therefore right to criticize George Kennan for expressing the view that the Franco-Russian alliance of 1894 made war practically unavoidable.[31] There was a twenty-year gap between the conclusion of that 'fateful alliance' and the outbreak of the war, long enough to interpret the alliance more as a contribution to the stability of Europe than as a cause of war in 1914.

As there was no strong conflict of interests between Germany and Russia there is no particular reason why war should have broken out between the two countries despite the growing animosity in the national press. This was not the case in the relationship between Austria and Russia, which was marred by severe antagonism and a clash of interests in the Balkans. So the potential for hostilities had intensified steadily since the nineteenth century.

---

[30] B. Sösemann (ed.), *Theodor Wolff: Tagebücher 1914-1919. Der Erste Weltkrieg und die Entstehung der Weimarer Republik in Tagebüchern, Leitartikeln und Briefen des Chefredakteurs am 'Berliner Tageblatt' und Mitbegründers der 'Deutschen Demokratischen Partei'*, i (Boppard, 1984), 64. See also Fischer op. cit. (above, n. 14), 398 and Kaiser, op. cit. (above, n. 21), 472-3.

[31] P. Kennedy, 'The Domesday Machine of 1914', in *New York Times*, 21 Oct. 1984.

In contrast France and Britain were the powers least willing to enter a war. It is relatively easy to establish the case for France if we consider the French situation in July 1914. The French President, Poincaré, and his Prime Minister, Viviani, returned from their state visit to St Petersburg only on 29 July, too late to have any substantial influence on the crisis. In addition the Germans had managed to decode the telegraphic communications between Paris and the French delegation, and were also able to jam the frequency. The German accusation after 1918 that France and Russia plotted the war during Poincaré's state visit was mere propaganda. The delivery of the Austrian ultimatum to Serbia on 23 July was so timed that the French delegation would be on its return journey and too far away from St Petersburg to be called back for consultations. The visit was designed to cement the Franco-Russian alliance which after the second Moroccan crisis and the Balkan Wars was not in good shape. The visit succeeded in this respect, but, apart from mutual assurances, nothing definite was decided.

Back in France Paris was in the grip of the Caillaux scandal. Madame Caillaux had shot the editor of the *Figaro* who had published some of her husband's early love-letters. As late as 29 July *Le Temps* was still covering the Caillaux scandal, but had little to say about the worsening of the international situation. France followed events rather than leading them and until the very last days of July there was no sense of a crisis in Paris.[32]

When mobilization was declared on 1 August Frenchmen rallied to the cause of national defence in the face of German aggression. It was widely accepted that the French government had no hand in unleashing the war. In any case, Poincaré favoured a firm stand against Germany, but not a war. Recent research has established him as a politician who was keen on finding a *modus vivendi* with Germany rather than as a warmonger whose main aim in life was to regain the provinces of Alsace and Lorraine. The *Kölnische Zeitung*, a mouthpiece of the German Foreign Office, confirmed the generally peaceful attitude prevalent in France. On 1 August the Paris correspondent of the paper noticed that there was no enthusiasm for war or revanchism to be found. He even noted that some people in France regretted that there was no

---

[32] See for this Keiger, op. cit. (above, n. 26), 159 and 167.

alliance with Germany, because then the world would be safe. To them Germany was closer and meant more than Russia. And the London correspondent of the same paper reported that a general animosity against Germany was missing in England too.[33] However, the mood in London and Paris changed rapidly as the likelihood of war increased. In Britain it was hoped that war could be avoided, and some efforts at mediation were made which Germany turned down on 27 July. But Britain was deeply involved with the Irish situation and worried about a possible confrontation with Russia in Persia. Thus the Austro-Serbian clash was, to begin with, not of the greatest concern for British politicians. But once the prospect of a European conflagration began to loom, those groups which regarded India as the most important British preoccupation were not all that unhappy about a war between Germany and Russia, because a serious weakening of the latter would reduce, for some time, the potential for Anglo-Russian conflicts in Asia, even if Russia belonged to the ultimate victors. Britain's multi-dimensional concerns in foreign policy do not make it easy to detect consistency in her political line or to identify the dominant groups which influenced the politicians. Nevertheless the majority of the Liberal Cabinet followed a consistent line in its foreign policy when it decided to defend France against a German invasion.

In comparison with the two Western powers Russia had gone a step further. The situation in Belgrade and Vienna was being closely watched. On the day after the delivery of the Austrian ultimatum to Serbia it was decided at a meeting of the Russian Council of Ministers to make a stand against the diplomatic pressure from Austria and Germany. It was held that 'firmness rather than conciliation was likely to secure peace'.[34] Russia did not want to repeat her experience in the Bosnian crisis and preferred to present a much more resolute image. Her firmness was not solely dictated by her concern for Serbia. The forthcoming trade negotiations with Germany cast their shadow. The signal was that Germany should expect a much tougher Russian stance at the negotiating table when the trade treaty and the tariffs were at issue. Russia resented being at the mercy of Germany's industrial power.

[33] T. Goebel, *Deutsche Pressestimmen in der Julikrise* (Berlin, 1939), 178.
[34] Lieven, op. cit. (above, n. 26), 141 ff.

At the meeting of ministers it was also resolved to prepare for partial mobilization of some military districts, against Austria, should events require it. This would be in reaction to Austria's moves if she decided to escalate the crisis. But neither the anticipation of mobilization nor the possibility of ordering it was equated with causing the war, as Kennan would make us believe. Only when Austria had rejected Serbia's reply and when she finally declared war against Serbia on 28 July, did Russia order partial mobilization. Even then Russia did not want to fight a war. But as Austria was unwilling to guarantee Serbia's political integrity despite the general acceptance of some punitive measure, Russia was left with little choice.

At this stage a new situation emerged as Berlin tried to put pressure on Russia to stop her military preparations in the hope that Russia would refuse to comply with the German *démarche*. Berlin calculated correctly that St Petersburg would be unwilling to repeat the process of backing down as in 1909. As the Russian conviction grew that the Central Powers were bent on war, the Tsar ordered full mobilization on 29 July, after Austrian artillery had begun to shell Belgrade, the Serbian capital. However, the order for full mobilization was rescinded in response to a telegram from the Kaiser to the Tsar on that same day. This created a hopeless situation, and under pressure from his Foreign Minister and his Chief of Staff the Tsar was persuaded on 30 July of the need for general mobilization. It was argued that delay would destroy Russia's chances in any conflict before it had even begun. General mobilization was part of Russia's new firmness, but was not intended to mean war, although the Russian Foreign Minister, Sazonov, believed that Germany wanted it. The Chief of Staff, Yanushkevich, also had military reasons for ordering general mobilization. Partial mobilization against Austria was proving unworkable.[35] The French warning against Russian mobilization came too late. The French government feared that it would provide Germany with the pretext for mobilizing herself. In the event the French government proved to be right.

The German response to the Russian threat was swift, first by mobilization and then by her declaration of war against Russia

[35] F. Fischer, *Krieg der Illusionen: die deutsche Politik von 1911 bis 1914* (Düsseldorf, 1969), 709–13.

on 1 August, whilst the Austrians followed suit only five days later. It has often been pointed out that Russia's mobilization made a European conflict likely. Even Fritz Fischer has argued that Russia has to share some responsibility for the outbreak of the war because she was determined to defend the status quo in the Balkans against any Austrian expansion.[36] That is the reason, it is said, why she was the first power to order a general mobilization. However, this argument overlooks the fact that the German leadership was waiting for just this move. Before the Russian order for mobilization appeared, the Prussian War Minister had tried to declare 'the state of imminent danger of war', but was held back by Bethmann Hollweg and Moltke, the Chief of Staff.[37] The Chancellor resisted military pressure for action because he believed it was essential to wait until he could accuse Russia of being the aggressor and of having started the war. The evidence for his insistence on this sequence of events is overwhelming. Once Russian mobilization had been proclaimed it would be possible to issue a call to arms to defend the fatherland. This move was vital to enable the Social Democrats to join the war effort and so unite the German people.[38]

The German press in July 1914 indicated clearly that Russia would be held responsible if war broke out.[39] The officially inspired tenor was therefore anti-Russian and most papers accepted this line. Even before the Russian order for mobilization became known the German war mood was noticeable. The news from Russia fell on prepared ground. Thus we cannot avoid the impression that, by means of the Austrian action, a trap was laid for Russia into which she fell when she declared her mobilization. However, there is another argument as to why it is difficult to deduce from Russian actions in July any intention to start a war. A qualitative and technical difference existed between the

---

[36] Fischer, op. cit. (above, n. 35), 708.

[37] Joll, op. cit. (above, n. 22), 20.

[38] E. Zechlin, op. cit. (above, n. 20), 64–94. See here the reference to the German *White Book* which was published on 3 August 1914. The book aimed at removing any doubts among Germans that Russia might not be the aggressor. The book was especially successful with the SPD. See also the chapter about the SPD in W. Gutsche, *Der gewollte Krieg: der deutsche Imperialismus und der 1. Weltkrieg* (Cologne, 1984), 154–75.

[39] Goebel, op. cit. (above, n. 33), 177 and 180 ff.

Russian and the German mobilization.[40] The former was intended to prepare the Russian army for war and then to wait for the formal declaration of hostilities. It was still hoped in St Petersburg that war would be prevented and that Russia's firmness would stop the Austrians from crushing Serbia. German mobilization, on the other hand, meant the beginning of the planned military offensive into Belgium and France.

How was it possible that the term 'preventive war' came into use in order to describe the German actions? The term was necessary to substantiate the German claim that she was fighting a defensive war when she was launching a massive offensive in the west and not in the east. This leads to another, yet related question. Why did Germany declare war against Russia when mobilization had been ordered only two hours before and when the German army was not ready to strike at the Russian forces? The reason was France. France was obliged to come to Russia's aid once war had been declared upon Russia. But she could only help militarily if she launched an offensive herself against Germany. This the German army tried to prevent by speedy mobilization and an immediate offensive in the west. In this narrow technical sense it seems possible to use the term 'preventive war' for the planned early operations in the west, but if the war on the whole is meant then the term is misused. The German General Staff had already used the term years before when it was demanding another war against France after 1871 because it was feared that otherwise France would start a war against her eastern neighbour. However, France was never in a position to attack Germany and it is very doubtful whether she ever would have been. Some historians and a few politicians of the time emphasized the politically negative effects which increased Russian and French military strength would have on Germany in the future. In this situation when spending on armaments was growing the term 'preventive war' loses its precise meaning because it comes to be burdened with too many imponderable factors and as yet unknown developments. Bethmann Hollweg used the term in 1917 in an apologetic sense, although admitting that the initiative for war had come from Germany. Some historians have accepted this interpretation in

---

[40] Joll, op. cit. (above, n. 22), 78 ff; Fischer, op. cit. (above, n. 14), 499.

order to render the German action understandable and to hold
the other powers responsible for their own development of
military potential.[41] What is the upshot of analysing the use of
the term 'preventive war'? It makes it clear why Germany had
to let Russia appear as the aggressor and why it wanted to exploit
the Franco-Russian alliance in order to start a 'preventive war'
against France. The obvious deduction from these German
intentions and calculations is that it was Germany which pushed
for war. What were the reasons for Germany's desire for war?
To answer this question we have to go back into the nineteenth
century.

The victory over France in 1870–1 led to the foundation of the
Second German Reich. The dreams of earlier decades were
fulfilled. However, this unification was regarded as the first step
in the construction of a larger empire. The exclusion of Austria
at a time when free trade became dominant in Europe meant that
any economically motivated expansion would be directed
outwards, that is away from Central Europe. Overseas trade
would necessitate the building of a fleet and colonies would
become attractive as potentially secure markets for exports. The
direction outwards was underpinned by Bismarck's assertion in
1871 that Germany was a 'satiated' power. The Chancellor's
remarks were addressed to the other powers in order to quell
international concern over Germany's victories and the creation
of a powerful empire in the heart of Europe. However, there were
numerous Germans who did not share this cautious attitude
towards Europe and who demanded an overseas expansion of
the Empire. The Chancellor's more cautious approach to
international politics prevailed, at least for the time being.
Bismarck's outlook was aided by the onset of the world
depression in 1873, which hit Germany strongly and curtailed
the exuberance which had followed the foundation of the
Reich.

The demand for overseas expansion was intensified as soon
as the economic crisis of the 1870s was overcome. The social
and political groups which supported this pressure were even

---

[41] Fischer, op. cit. (above, n. 14), 468–70.

prepared to be rid of Bismarck at the end of his Chancellorship because it was felt that he stood in the way of a dynamic Germany. A few years later the editor of the critical magazine *Die Zukunft* was able to sum up the perception of an expansionist Germany in the following way:

But we are not 'satiated'. We need fertile land, large open areas which could buy our goods at decent prices. This has become necessary since large industrial complexes have developed in the heat of a greenhouse and since the standard of living of our nation has risen considerably compared with previous times. Otherwise we shall be so dwarfed that we shall become a second Belgium.[42]

The colonies Germany had acquired during the 1880s were regarded as insufficient. The launching of *Weltpolitik* in 1896 announcing Germany's interventionist intentions for the entire globe did not satisfy expansionist ambitions.[43] The German colony in China, Tsingtou, the South Sea island of Samoa, and the Caroline Islands were not sufficient substitutes for either a larger overseas empire or military expansion in Europe. Only the construction of a large battle-fleet would, it was felt, provide Germany with a lever for her *Weltpolitik*, but it would take twenty years until the so-called Tirpitz Plan was completed.[44] Waiting for the fleet required considerable patience and in the early years the supposed instrument of German expansionism looked like a hammer without a handle. The building of the battle-fleet increased considerably the financial burden of the military budget so that expenditure for the army had to be frozen. The army accepted, at least for the time being, the role of second fiddle in the apportionment of the military budget.

Possibly this was a way out of a strategic dilemma which the German army had faced since 1870. Should it prepare itself for an old-fashioned 'war of nations' in the future? This would mean that the next war would be decided by a few large battles. Or

[42] H. D. Hellige (ed.), *Walther Rathenau, Maximilian Harden: Briefwechsel 1897–1920* (Munich and Heidelberg, 1983), 139.

[43] Kaiser is mistaken when he assumes that *Weltpolitik* was adopted 'largely for domestic reasons'. There is not sufficient evidence for that. To see *Weltpolitik* as a means to appease the Kaiser in a crisis of political leadership misses the point about German imperialism: Kaiser, op. cit. (above, n. 21), 444–7.

[44] V. R. Berghahn, *Der Tirpitz-Plan: Genesis und Verfall einer innenpolitischen Krisenstrategie unter Wilhelm II* (Düsseldorf, 1971).

should it face up to a 'people's war' which would embroil entire
nations in a long-drawn-out war at the end of which one state
could establish its supremacy over the others? Both phases had
characterized the war against France in 1870–1, although the full
political consequences of the 'people's war' had not
been implemented. France was allowed to recover militarily
from its defeat within a short time. The elder Moltke regretted this development and was haunted thereafter by the
need to fight another, final war against France. As early as
1873, Moltke had pointed out that a war with France would
come soon and from a military point of view 'the sooner the
better'.

In this situation it looked as if the General Staff was left with
two options: the future war would be either a full-blown 'people's
war', or a short war which could be dressed up as 'preventive
war'. The requirements for manpower and armaments would
vary accordingly, and the horrors of the winter campaign in
France in 1870–1 made the second option preferable. Ever
since, the General Staff seems to have thought in terms of
a 'preventive war' against France in the knowledge that—
even though Russia was not yet France's ally—a war against
France would most likely be a war against Russia as well.
This strategy required a highly trained and mobile army,
backed by fast mobilization plans. In 1875 and in 1887
Moltke had called on Bismarck to start a 'preventive war'
against France and Russia, but on both occasions the Chancellor
had refused.

Moltke had assumed that a future war would have to be fought
against both France and Russia. Greater French speed and military
efficiency would provide Germany with another justification for
attacking France first. A preventive blow would stop the full
deployment of French military power before Germany had to turn
against Russia. Meanwhile the politicians would have to find a
solution for France in order to avoid a long-drawn-out 'people's
war'. However, at the end of his life Moltke warned against the
short-war illusion and the dangers of a 'preventive war' because
he believed now that the risks involved were too high. He
therefore advocated a high level of armaments and a large army
as a deterrent against any future major war. In this situation it
was understandable that the army was willing to hold back and

let the money go towards the construction of a large battle-fleet[45]

Only when the Tirpitz Plan had failed, when the naval race with Britain had challenged the financial constitution of the German Empire, and when ten years of *Weltpolitik* had yielded very little real gain, did army circles resume their campaign for an enlargement of the army. Against the warnings of the elder Moltke the belief gained ground that Germany, backed by the Schlieffen Plan, could win a short 'preventive war'. She needed to mobilize her resources more fully to make her first blow even faster and more powerful. In this way a 'people's war' with possible revolutionary consequences would be avoided. Consequently the dictum 'the sooner, the better' gained in weight. Only when the German army had been substantially strengthened could it continue to be the guarantor of the Second Reich and its further aspirations. But Germany could not, without a tax reform, afford a massive increase in the army and the navy at the same time. So the navy had to give way. Until the late 1890s army increases had been justified to the Reichstag by referring to the need to match the numerical strength of the French and Russian armies. The moment the Navy Bills had been passed this argument was replaced in the public mind by a need for further reorganizations of the army. By 1911–12 the General Staff was determined to revert to the old argument that further army increases were needed to catch up with a supposed French and Russian numerical superiority. Consequently this time the navy was pushed into the role of second fiddle.

Hand in hand with a change of priorities in armaments spending the aims of foreign policy underwent a corresponding change. Overseas expansion was now regarded as less important and Germany's hegemonial aspirations on the European continent were to be secured once and for all. In alluding to the old slogan that 'our future lies on the water', Harden was able to express the new sentiment early in 1913: 'Now our future lies on the continent. This awareness has returned to the German people.'[46]

[45] S. Förster, 'Optionen der Kriegführung im Zeitalter des "Volkskrieges". Versuch über Helmuth von Moltkes militärisch-politische Überlegungen nach den Erfahrungen der "Einigungskriege"', unpubl. MS. See also Förster's book, *Der doppelte Militarismus: die deutsche Heeresrüstungspolitik zwischen Status-Quo-Sicherung und Aggression 1890–1913* (Stuttgart, 1985).
[46] Fischer, op. cit. (above, n. 35), 278.

While this reorientation in German policies was taking place, war broke out in the Balkans in 1912. Compared with previous decades the German position was already different. Now the Minister of War was emphasizing the German interest in the Balkans. He pointed out, after the victory of the Balkan powers over Turkey, that a new strategic situation had emerged there. Russia's influence had been strengthened at the expense of Turkey, the power Germany was trying to win over. The relative unpreparedness of the German army, as had been revealed in 1905 and 1908, led to the planning of a new army bill and to the so-called War Council of 8 December 1912, where the Kaiser expressed his anger at Britain's determination to aid France should Germany try to destroy French military power. At the Council the younger Moltke repeated the military dictum that a war should be fought and 'the sooner the better'. In the aftermath of the meeting the navy lost its primary position and the Tirpitz Plan was given no new encouragement. Instead a massive new army bill was to be introduced which would increase the German army by 140,000 men.[47] The upshot of the meeting was that the inter-service rivalry was decided in favour of the army, that the military preparedness for war was to be stepped up, and finally that the Kaiser was forced to accept the primacy of the army and the corresponding change in foreign policy. Moreover, it had become very difficult for the Kaiser to shrink away from war should a favourable situation arise, as had happened on other occasions.

How did the General Staff convince the Chancellor of the need for a massive army bill with all the consequent acceleration of the arms race? Firstly, Bethmann was willing to accept any army bill at this stage if it would prevent a navy bill. Secondly, he was sufficiently impressed by the spectre of Russian military superiority to be ready to support the planned counter-measures in the form of a new army bill. Although war was not imminent

---

[47] For the so-called War Council see John Röhl's revised text, 'Der militär-politische Entscheidungsprozeß in Deutschland am Vorabend des Ersten Weltkrieges', in John C. G. Röhl, *Kaiser, Hof und Staat: Wilhelm II und die deutsche Politik* (Munich, 1987), 175–202. See for the growing military influence in politics H. Pogge von Strandmann, 'Nationale Verbände zwischen Weltpolitik und Kontinentalpolitik', in H. Schottelius and W. Deist (eds.), *Marine und Marinepolitik 1871–1914* (2nd. edn. Düsseldorf, 1980), 296–317; S. Förster, op. cit. (above, n. 45), 208 ff.

the pan-Germans were pleased with what they called a modest increase. They believed that Germany was now on the path to war because the bill had made war more likely. While national extremists braced themselves for war it is interesting to speculate as to when it was that the alliance of military 'hawks' and right-wing nationalists had been able to predispose Berlin towards war-willingness. It could be argued that this was unnecessary because a substantial consensus in this respect dominated the political scene in the German metropolis. However, the Chancellor gave the impression that he was vacillating between two principles: necessity and opportunity. After the Zabern Affair of 1913 he seemed to be ready to use the next suitable opportunity for an offensive war particularly as the implementation of the army reforms had provided Germany with a sizeable advantage over her potential enemies. However, the political situation abroad and at home had to be made favourable before Germany's military strength and economic weight could be activated. Therefore it is not surprising to learn that, in May 1914, after the German army had carried out its reforms, Moltke requested that Jagow, the German Foreign Secretary, start a 'preventive war'.[48] Moltke believed that Germany was now in a favourable position before the Russian and French armies carried out their own army reforms. In fact the French and Russian army reforms provided an insufficient justification for starting a war, since the Franco-Russian military build-up had been taking place ever since 1894. So Moltke had to dramatize the potential effects of these measures. He painted a gloomy picture of Germany's military future and urged the government to start a war before the other two powers would be, in his estimation, too strong for Germany's 'preventive war' to succeed. The message was clear: the German army was ready for an early war and the General Staff hoped the campaign would be decided in the first few battles. However, if the war did not take place very soon, then Germany would have to step up her military preparations even further. This could lead to political difficulties, especially with the Reichstag. Moltke discussed with the Kaiser in May 1914 how the army could increase its manpower by calling up more men

---

[48] Fischer, op. cit. (above, n. 14), 401–2. In early June Bethmann seemed to have been reluctant to go with Moltke's plea: Kaiser, op. cit. (above, n. 21), 469.

in each year and by reducing the number allowed to opt out. Obviously these measures would accelerate changes in the character of the army, but would, so it was believed, increase its efficiency. They would be the next politically convenient step towards enlarging the army should war not break out in the near future.

Let us picture the scenario which would enable Germany to take advantage of a situation in which she would not appear as the aggressor and in which she could unite the German people in one cause. The ideal situation for Germany was a conflict in the Balkans because she would not, to begin with, be directly involved. It was expected that the growing tensions between Austria and Serbia would soon reach crisis point. The German ambassador to Vienna had explained that if Austria was going to bring about a military solution to this conflict, then it was essential that Russia in her role as Serbia's ally must appear as the aggressor. Later the German Foreign Secretary supported this strategy by underlining that in a future war in the Balkans, Austria needed a hostile act from Serbia.[49] Then Germany could point to the local character of the crisis between Vienna and Belgrade and warn Russia against intervention on Serbia's side. If Russia were to intervene nevertheless, then it would become possible for Germany to appear as the provoked party.

The military and political plans dovetailed when Austria blamed Serbia for the hostile act of the Sarajevo murders. Austria claimed that she was morally justified in taking action against Serbia, but was not able to do so without German support. Austria's action was not the last fling of a disintegrating power. Over the six years immediately before 1914 Austria had pursued a much more expansive policy in the Balkans with the ultimate aim of achieving predominance.[50] Serbia's rising power threatened Austrian

[49] Fischer, op. cit. (above, n. 14), 295 and 298. See also F. Fischer, 'Die Neutralität Englands als Ziel deutscher Politik 1908/9–1914', in F. Esterbauer, H. Kalkbrenner, M. Mattmüller, and L. Roemheld (eds.), *Von der freien Gemeinde zum föderalistischen Europa: Festschrift für Adolf Gasser zum 80. Geburtstag* (Berlin, 1983), 281–2; Gutsche, op. cit. (above, n. 38), 46 ff, 50.

[50] See, for the following, F. Fellner, 'Die Mission Hoyos', in W. Alff (ed.), *Deutschlands Sonderung von Europa 1862–1945* (Frankfurt, 1984) 283–303. See also W. Gutsche, op. cit. (above, n. 38), 52–8.

policies and so, shortly after the assassination at Sarajevo, the Austrians opted for a military solution. Over the previous two years Austrian policy-makers had moved steadily towards a war with Serbia. Now in early July 1914, Count Hoyos, who belonged to the hawks in the Austrian Foreign Ministry and who was one of its leading figures, volunteered to go to Berlin and gain the assurances needed for Austria to attack Serbia. Backed by a consensus among the political leaders in Vienna, Hoyos's mission was the first move towards war. The assassination was to serve as a pretext for settling a power conflict.

It is worth noting that the initiative came from Vienna and it would be worth speculating what Berlin might have done, and how it would have pushed for war if the Austrians had not seized the initiative. Although a war against Serbia had been desired in Vienna for some time, in spring 1914 Austrian foreign policy in the Balkans had been subjected to a major review. A war against Serbia now fitted into the plan to win Bulgaria as an ally instead of relying on Roumania. A localized war against Serbia suited Austria's plans, but the Dual Monarchy seemed to be less interested in a major war. In Berlin, on the other hand, a different climate prevailed. Here intensive consultations had taken place between political and military leaders before Hoyos's arrival. Thus Hoyos's mission went well. The German side endorsed Austria's reorientation of her foreign policy and was willing to support a war against Serbia if Austria did not flinch from the consequences of such a policy. According to Hoyos both sides were fully aware of the fact that an Austrian war against Serbia could lead to a European one. In echoing military thinking Bethmann Hollweg added that if a general war became inevitable 'then the present moment would be more favourable than a later one'.[51] After Hoyos's return to Vienna the Austrian Ministerial Council resolved, on 7 July, to issue Serbia with an ultimatum containing demands which she could not possibly accept. Thus the war against Serbia was decided in the full knowledge of a possible European conflict. The Permanent Under-secretary in the German Foreign Office, Zimmermann, had told Hoyos that an Austrian attack on Serbia would lead 'with a probability of 90 per cent to a European war'.[52] The young hawks in the Austrian

[51] Fellner, op. cit. (above, n. 50), 295.
[52] Ibid. 296.

Foreign Ministry in co-operation with German diplomats in Vienna now began to press, being aware of the consequences, for the opening of hostilities against Serbia at the end of July.

Originally Hoyos may have hoped that Germany would help Austria without pursuing more far-reaching aims, but soon he and others realized that the German General Staff wanted more than a localized action in the Balkans. He noted in his memoirs that the German aim was to 'fight an imperialist war of conquest against the Western Powers via us and Serbia'.[53] This is not to say that Vienna assumed a secondary role in German strategic planning. Austria was still one of the Great European Powers and sufficiently independent to pursue its own expansionist aims which were not identical with those of Germany. But in terms of military planning Austria fulfilled a vital function which was agreed between the two staffs. Instead of merely supporting Austria in her destruction of Serbia, Germany needed Austria to bind the Russian forces while she carried out her massive offensive through Belgium and France. However, Austria was unable to exploit this particular aspect of military strategy because the German Foreign Office had issued warnings that Austria might lose her last ally if she did not adapt to German priorities. Consequently her existence might be in danger. The chances of finding another ally were remote because of the increasing animosity between Russia and Austria. Yet it did not suit Austria to declare war against Russia on 6 August when she had to yield to German pressure. Moreover, Austria was pushed into taking up an offensive in Galicia against Russia early in the war when she really wanted to defeat Serbia first. The Austrian reluctance to start a campaign against Russia nearly caused a panic in Berlin. As Moltke told Tirpitz on 5 August: 'If Austria had shied away we would have needed to search for peace at any price.'[54]

The two powers were dependent on each other for the pursuit of their ambitious imperialist aims, but Germany's greater military and economic power made Austria Germany's junior partner. Bearing in mind Austria's determination to increase her influence in the Balkans even at the risk of facing Russia, there was no alternative available to the alliance with Germany. The survival

[53] Fellner, op. cit. (above, n. 50), 298.
[54] A. v. Tirpitz, *Erinnerungen* (Leipzig, 1919), 243.

of the Dual Monarchy as an expansionist factor in the Balkans was wedded to the hegemonial aspirations of the German Empire. In spite of this, some historians have pointed to the German fear of losing her last major ally if the Kaiser had not issued the so-called blank cheque at the end of Hoyos's mission to Berlin. Germany, they argue, was forced to support the Dual Monarchy against her better interests. However, the new Austrian evidence makes this view untenable and sheds new light on the German reference to *Nibelungentreue*. What we have is part of Bethmann Hollweg's campaign to pin the role of the aggressor on Russia and to give the impression that Germany had been dragged unwillingly into the conflict. The moral value of the assassination in Sarajevo was that it supported the German position as an ally of the victim of 'murderers'. It is interesting to note that this official version was resented by some newspapers in Germany, notably the *Rheinisch-Westfälische Zeitung*.[55] The editor pursued an anti-Austrian line and opposed the idea that Germany should support Austrian expansion in the Balkans. To his mind Austria was doomed and therefore not worth any German support. He pleaded for a reorientation of German foreign policy and an alliance with Russia. He therefore rejected the reference to *Nibelungentreue*. When the Austrian ultimatum was issued to Serbia he was convinced that it was a pretext for Austria to declare war on Serbia. Although the editor may have got wind of the Austrian plans he seemed not to be aware of the ultimate German design; later, however, he supported the war against France and especially against Britain.

After the ultimatum had been delivered the German press discussed the likelihood of a localized war, while the German General Staff, from the middle of July onwards, began to push for the pursuit of German interests, that is for a European war. Even before the Serbian reply to the Austrian ultimatum had been handed over, the German General Staff had worked out the ultimatum for Belgium which was handed over to the German Foreign Office two days before the Austrian declaration of war against Serbia.[56] It is therefore not surprising to learn that

[55] Goebel, op. cit. (above, n. 33), 92 ff.
[56] K. Kautsky, Max Montgelas, Walter Schücking (eds.), *Die deutschen Dokumente zum Kriegsausbruch*, 2 (Berlin, 1919), doc. 376, fn. 1. See also F. Fellner, op. cit. (above, n. 50), 298. See below for the growing pressure the General Staff exerted in favour of war.

Germany did not have any interest in pursuing a peaceful solution of the Serbo-Austrian conflict, nor in localizing it.

The arguments the military used to justify a European war on strategic grounds referred to the growing military strength of Russia and France. By 1917 it was feared that the combined Franco-Russian forces would make it impossible for Germany to win a war. Ostensibly they also feared that in this situation France and Russia would attack Germany. This argument proved to be a trump card against any wavering politicians or a reluctant Kaiser. It was also very useful in lending a certain credibility to the claim that not only the offensive against France but the war in general was a 'preventive war'. Did the military really believe in their claim that by 1917 Germany would have become so vulnerable that she would become the victim of an offensive war launched by the Entente? There is very little evidence for this, but it was a useful argument to justify pushing for war sooner rather than later, and for starting the war in 1914. In addition, German military thinking followed the lines that if one power were to become militarily superior to another this power would seek to translate the superiority into reality at the next opportunity. Obviously in 1914 the German General Staff believed the German military strength to be superior to that of the Entente.

The General Staff did not have a high opinion of the Russian army.[57] It was known that the training of their soldiers had not been very good, that they were not well equipped, that a large section had to be kept at home to crush any revolutionary attempts, and that the maintenance and the manning of the fortresses absorbed a sizeable proportion of the army. It was believed that by 1917 this would not have substantially changed despite the portrayal of Russia as an ever-growing military giant.[58] By contrast, respect for the French forces was much greater. But the difficulties the French government faced in overcoming political opposition to the introduction of the three-year service law were well known in Berlin. It was also known that the extension of military service would be unlikely to last.

[57] Fischer, op. cit. (above, n. 14), 398, 475, 492–3.
[58] R. Ropponen, *Die Kraft Rußlands* (Helsinki, 1968), 280 ff. For further reference to the weakness of the Russian army see Kaiser, op. cit. (above, n. 21), 473.

So any prediction about military strength in 1917 was fraught with uncertainty. It was also very difficult to say anything about the possible international constellation in 1917. But whatever the assessment of the future might have been, the German position in 1917 could not have been worse than in 1914. On the contrary, it could have improved, especially if France and Russia had taken over the role of the aggressive power bloc. If France and Russia had become the powers which wanted to change the status quo in Europe, then Britain would have distanced herself from them. So why could Germany not wait until 1917? The official explanation was that the military and political situation would then have worsened for Germany. But this was by no means certain, especially as the European states were all entering a period of fundamental changes. The editor-in-chief of the *Berliner Tageblatt*, Theodor Wolff, rightly criticized in private discussions with members of the German Foreign Office the constant reference to a deteriorating situation by 1917.[59]

It thus seems likely that any reference to 1917 served as a pretext for action in 1914. It was the perception of favourable opportunities in 1914 which influenced the military and political decisions in the July Crisis. Where did Germany stand in the summer of 1914? She had increased the strength of her army in the two army bills of 1912 and 1913 and had carried out her army reforms. Should war break out then it would be ideal if it started with an Austrian attack against Serbia. Russia's anticipated alliance with Serbia would enable Germany to identify St Petersburg as the aggressor and there was consequently a chance that Britain might keep out of the war, at least at the beginning. Faced with this scenario, it was easy for Moltke to reassure Bethmann Hollweg when asked in July 1914 whether Germany could win a two-front war: 'We shall manage it' (*Wir werden es schaffen*).[60]

The Chief of the General Staff did not allude to any future superiority of the Russian forces. He knew that in 1914 Russia and France were carrying out their reforms and were therefore, from a military point of view, in a weak position. He felt sure

[59] B. Sösemann (ed.), op. cit. (above, n. 30), 167 (17 Feb. 1915).
[60] K. D. Erdmann (ed.), *Kurt Riezler: Tagebücher, Aufsätze, Dokumente* (Göttingen, 1972), 272 (25 May 1915).

that the Schlieffen Plan would succeed as Austria would hold back Russia. So it is not surprising to hear of the optimism in the General Staff at the end of July which both the Bavarian military attaché and the Bavarian envoy in Berlin described. The Kaiser's possible intervention on behalf of peace had been successfully staved off, the press had generally expressed a willingness to fight a European war even before news of the Russian mobilization became known, the German Social Democrats were ready to accept a war with Russia, anti-Russian feeling in Germany had risen steadily, and preparations for German mobilization had gone well. The optimism reached an even higher level when Russia mobilized first. The Bavarian military attaché noted in his diary: 'I run to the War Ministry. Beaming faces everywhere. Everyone is shaking hands in the corridors: people congratulate one another for being over the hurdle.'[61] Now Russia could be blamed for starting the war which the military circles had hoped for, and the German people could be assured that Germany was fighting a defensive war because Russia had forced war on her. The desire to believe in the defensive argument was stronger than any desire to prevent the war. The Bavarian ambassador reported back to Munich: 'Prussian General Staff looks ahead to war with France with great confidence, expects to defeat France within four weeks; poor spirit in the French army, few howitzers and poor quality guns.'[62] And Admiral von Müller noted in his diary: 'The mood is brilliant. The government has managed brilliantly to make us appear as the attacked.'[63]

In the wake of the war enthusiasm which gripped many Germans, there was relief that the period of waiting and tension was over. It was felt that a victorious Germany would achieve a hegemonial position which had not been sufficiently secured when the Reich was founded back in 1871. Nobody would have heeded Montesquieu's warning that an empire founded by war has to maintain itself by war. From this statement would follow the argument that if a war of further expansion were fought, then it would no longer be only a question of maintaining the Empire.

[61] B. F. Schulte, *Europäischer Krieg und Erster Weltkrieg: Beiträge zur Militärpolitik des Kaiserreichs, 1871–1914* (Frankfurt, 1983), 207.
[62] Fischer, op. cit. (above, n. 14), 503. Lerchenfeld to Hertling, 31 July 1914.
[63] J. C. G. Röhl, 'Admiral von Müller and the Approach of War, 1911–1914', in *Historical Journal*, 12 (1969), 670.

If the aim of the war was hegemony, then it could put at risk the very existence of the Empire once that war was lost.

All the available evidence suggests that it was mainly Germany which pushed for war and that without the German drive to extend her hegemony a major war would not have started in Europe in 1914. However, it must be stated that the German aspirations had existed for some time without resulting in war. If it had not been for the Austrian initiative in early July and the Russian decision to remain firm and call what was perceived as an Austrian bluff at the end of July, Berlin would have found it difficult to push for war in the summer of 1914. Yet Berlin had, before Hoyos's visit, anticipated the Austrian move. 'The military keep on urging for a war now while Russia is not yet ready', reported the Saxon envoy, and the Saxon military attaché wrote a day later: 'The General Staff thought that it would not be too bad if there was a war now.'[64] So Austrian determination and Russian firmness suited German intentions.

But why were Germany's rulers so keen on war? Did they leap forward into the dark as some historians would make us believe? Did the German policy-makers really see no way out, but to engage in a *Flucht nach vorn*? What gains would Germany make which she did not already have? Was Germany not the biggest power on the Continent? Was her economy not expanding? Germany regarded herself as bursting at the seams. There was a consensus among the non-Socialist parties, the military, and the business men that Germany needed to be a larger empire on the Continent as well as overseas. But this expansion was not intended to divert attention from a growing domestic crisis, though much depends on the definition of a crisis. None of the indicators pointed to a crisis situation. The economy was booming. A brief recession in 1913 had by the spring of 1914 come to an end. In the large business concerns there was little fear of trade-union power despite the recent wave of strikes. The Social Democrats were divided and had recently voted in favour of the taxes with which the army bill of 1913 was to be financed.

[64] Fischer, op. cit. (above, n. 14), 475.

In this situation the Conservatives found themselves isolated, threatened more by the rising power of the Reichstag than the Social Democrats on the one side and by nationalist populism on the other. The rallying of right-wing pressure groups in 1913 indicated a regrouping on the Right rather than an initiative to check a growing political crisis.

Similar developments took place on the military side. A growing 'militarism from below' put pressure on the older type of 'militarism from above'. The demand for a larger army which had gained ground through the foundation of the *Wehrverein* (Defence League) aimed at eliminating the privileges of those who were able to opt out of the principle of equal conscription for all. In the wake of the two army bills, the purpose of the enlarged army, the politics of militarism, and nationalist themes were much more widely discussed than ever before. In this climate the shift of the General Staff towards war as a method of advancing Germany's expansionism seems crucial. If the international constellation were right, then the army would become the most consistent factor in pressing for war. This is not to say that sole responsibility for the war rested with the General Staff. In his recent article, David Kaiser, the American historian, followed Fischer's line of argument that it was Bethmann Hollweg who influenced the decision for war because of his belief in the need for German expansion. The success of such a policy was ultimately based on military supremacy established by war against France and Russia.[65] So the Chancellor, Kaiser argues, made the decision for war in conjunction with the military even though he was later to blame 'the generals' for plunging Germany into war.[66] A division between military and civilian leaders in this respect did not exist. Even if it had been the other way round and it had been the political leaders who had pushed for war, it would not have made much difference to the exploitation of the situation in 1914. The strength of the Chancellor's position is also demonstrated by the fact that he was even able to influence

---

[65] Kaiser, op. cit. (above, n. 21), 445, 458, and 468. See also Fischer, op. cit. (above, n. 14), 442–6.

[66] Fischer, op. cit. (above, n. 14), 468: Conrad Haussmann's report about a conversation with Bethmann in 1917 in which he admitted that the war 'was in a sense a preventive war'.

some military decisions by delaying the proclamation of the 'state of imminent danger of war' in certain areas.

Although there was widespread support for the line the government took, some industrialists like Stinnes and Rathenau were convinced that Germany would achieve its economic predominance in Europe without a war.[67] However strongly the political and military leadership was influenced by the public and its political debates, the war was not started for domestic reasons nor to defend a social status quo. The concept of expansion based on a military victory found enough support to command a consensus among the military, political, and business leaders of Wilhelmine Germany. The drive to the east and to the west was underpinned by an imperialist culture which spread the virtues of Social Darwinism, the conquest of markets, the penetration of spheres of influence, competition between capitalist partners, the winning of living-space, and the rising power of the state. Buoyed up by an assumed military superiority, general economic strength and particular industrial vigour, widespread optimism and a mood of belligerence, the military and political leaders found, when they made the decision to push for war, that this was an acceptable option to many Germans, possibly even to the majority. The notion of 'cultural despair' is of limited value. There were no signs of panic and no indications that Wilhelmine Germany could not continue to muddle through politically for years to come. Confidence, determination, and the belief in victory were the ingredients of a willingness to fight an expansionist war, disguised as a defensive or preventive action, which was widely shared by political and military leaders, political groupings, as well as large sectors of the population. This consensus enabled Germany to sustain the war effort until the military defeats of August and September 1918.

---

[67] H. Claß, *Wider den Strom. Vom Werden und Wachsen der nationalen Opposition im alten Reich* (Leipzig, 1932), 217; H. Pogge von Strandmann (ed.), *Walther Rathenau, Industrialist, Banker, Intellectual, and Politician: Notes and Diaries 1907–1922* (Oxford, 1985), 183–4.

6

France and the Coming of War

RICHARD COBB

Il est clair désormais que nos camarades ne sont morts que
parce que l'histoire est souvent bête et criminelle, et ce
cinquantenaire ne peut être que la commémoration de la
sottise et du crime . . . Tout est absurde dans notre histoire
. . . chacun a voulu sauver son pays et a contribué à le détruire
en même temps que l'Europe tout entière.

Jean Guéhenno in 1964

Il faut l'embrasser [la guerre] dans toute sa sauvage poésie.
Quand l'homme se jette en elle, ce ne sont pas seulement
les instincts qu'il retrouve, mais des vertus qu'il reprend
. . . C'est dans la guerre que tout se refait.

Abel Bonnard in 1912

In his novel, *Love and Mr Lewisham*, first published in 1900,
H. G. Wells comes up with what may have been an unconsciously
telling phrase that has a certain bearing on the events of fourteen
years later. The young couple have leased two furnished rooms
in the wastes of Clapham. Their extortionate landlady is a German
called Madam Gadow. She overcharges for scuttles—she calls
them 'kettles'—of coal. The young husband takes the matter up
with her: 'She was very voluble, gesticulatory and lucid, but
unhappily bilingual, and, at all the crucial points, *German*. Mr
Lewisham's natural politeness restrained him from too close a
pursuit across the boundaries of the two imperial languages.'
Wells is, of course, being jokey; still, I like that phrase, suggesting
as it does a *dialogue*, albeit to the exclusion of all others. When
one considers the period 1904 to 1914, there often seems to have
existed a certain contradiction between the realities of the
prevailing social exchanges and educational links and the new
couplings provided by diplomacy and the emerging systems of

alliances, rather as if the former were having some difficulty in keeping up with the latter, or had taken absolutely no account of them.

At upper-class and middle-class levels at least, Anglo-German contacts were much commoner and apparently more generally acceptable than Anglo-French ones. In Ford Madox Ford's novel, written in 1913 and published two years later, under the apparently accidentally prophetic title, *The Good Soldier*, one is struck by a negative factor, the absence of any French characters, in this last cosmopolitan gathering of a summer Homburg: grand dukes, English cads and adventurers, Belgian barons, Austrian aristocrats, German professors and princelings, even a few Americans, but apparently no French at all, as if the citizens of a republic had managed to exclude themselves from such a monarchical assembly. There seems to be no place under the lime-trees or in the open-air restaurants or at the *Kursaal* for a nation of Tartarins in pince-nez, tussore coats, and panama hats, even though these would be the current international walking-out outfit of the June to August visitors come to take the waters, to flirt, to gamble, and to relax. Katherine Mansfield, one recalls, though she *loathed* it and wrote a pretty virulent book about the experience, had been sent by her well-to-do parents to a German pension. Marguerite Yourcenar, in her two studies of her childhood, *Archives du Nord* and *Souvenirs pieux*, reminds us that daughters of the Belgian provincial nobility were thought to be perfectly safe in similar establishments, but that there would have been no question of exposing them to the manifold dangers of a sinful and anticlerical Paris. Admiral Tirpitz, no great friend to this country, still sent his daughter to Cheltenham Ladies College, and my old friend Lise Rogge, the granddaughter of *Hofprädiger* Rogge, Court Chaplain to the Hohenzollerns from the 1860s to the Kaiser's abdication in 1918, was entrusted, I find it oddly, to the Convent of the Sacred Heart, in Royal Tunbridge Wells.

Professor Howard has already referred to the Germans— including Prince Lichnowsky and the Duke of Saxe-Coburg-Gotha—who were honoured in the Encaenia of June 1914; so I decided to follow up his very valuable suggestions, to look up both the honorands and the matriculands of Oxford University in the ten years leading up to the July Crisis. The University did indeed honour a few Frenchmen: Paul Cambon, at the behest of Viscount Goschen, on the occasion of the latter's installation as Chancellor, in 1904; the mathematician, Henri Poincaré, in the previous year; Saint-Saëns (a D.Mus.) in 1909; the classicist Bémont in 1910; the philosopher, Bergson, in 1911; and none after that. A university statute of 1903 had exempted from Responsions holders of the *Matura* from Germany, Russia, and Austria-Hungary; the *baccalauréat* had to wait for a similar exemption till 1907. I am not suggesting that this was a deliberate discrimination against French students; more likely the delay was due to the realization that there was very little demand (as is still the case) from that quarter, owing to the relentlessly competitive nature of the French educational system. This is certainly borne out by the figures: out of 1,032 matriculands admitted in the session 1911–12, there were only three Frenchmen, all non-collegiate; in the session 1913–14, the number had gone up to four, one each to Christ Church, Balliol, and Worcester, the fourth non-collegiate. Of the seven, two were from the fashionable and affluent *lycée* Janson-de-Sailly, rue de la Pompe, in the XV1me, one was from the Sorbonne, and one from the University of St Andrews; another came from the Ecole des Roches in Verneuil, the French public school that had been founded in imitation of Rugby—a bold effort indeed—by Baron de Courbatin, the close friend and admirer of Arnold, and the founder of the Olympic Games. In the same two academic years, there were seventy-four German matriculands, most of them no doubt Rhodes Scholars. I learnt recently, on a visit there, that Charterhouse had a number of German boys in the school before 1914; and, in recent years, the school has had two Bismarcks and a Bethmann Hollweg.

It would be interesting to pursue such matters further. Were Anglo-German marriages commoner than Anglo-French ones during this period? I suspect that they were, and that they were exclusively aristocratic (Elisabeth von Arnim, the creator of a famous garden in the unpropitious terrain of East Prussia, was certainly not the only Englishwoman married to a Junker at this time), upper-middle-class, or professional. There is, however, no doubt that a great many Scotswomen—including the mother of the unfortunate Louis Rossel—married French *pasteurs*, most of whom they would have met as theological students at Edinburgh. At working-class level, Mlle from Armentières would have to wait for her Thomas Atkins till 1918 or 1919, when several hundred British soldiers married French girls—and often attractive jobs— in the Nord, the Pas-de-Calais, and the Somme, accounting for the number of existing English surnames in places like Albert, Bapaume, Douai, Roubaix, Lille, Calais, Etaples, Valenciennes, Saint-Omer, Péronne, and Amiens. But we have now strayed to the far end of that terrible war.

From all accounts, the German presence in pre-1914 London, Manchester, and Liverpool was much more visible than that of the French, and people like myself, born in 1917, will have heard of the numerous German bands that, according to my mother, disappeared almost overnight, as if in response to some secret order, in the last days of July 1914. Certainly, in the type of English school story—girls' or boys'—so brilliantly analysed by Isabel Quigley, the French master or the French mistress is generally an object of ridicule, when not an outright figure of fun, and fair game for ragging: they wear funny clothes, go on about A E I O U, and the female ones have moustaches. Of course there must have been a *few* convinced Francophiles apart from those in high places like Sir Henry Wilson; but people like Kipling seem to have been pretty rare. There is the rather mysterious case of Sir Edward Spears (originally Spiers), born in Ireland and later holding a commission in an Irish regiment, but whose mother had been born in Thann, in Alsace. I suppose he could muster as a Francophile, though he has given us some wonderfully acid portraits of Weygand, Vuillemain, and the amazingly untidy Messimy.

A French friend of mine, Arthur Birembaut, who was a schoolboy from 1914 to 1916 in the mining locality of Hénin- Liétard and who was repatriated to France by the Spanish and Swiss Red Cross in the latter year, has commented on the strange fact that, while living under German occupation, he was still being taught history out of a textbook in which England was assigned the role of hereditary enemy and in which much was made of the incandescence of *la Pucelle*. It may, of course, have been a textbook that was a bit out of date, for, by 1914, the Malet (the earlier half of the celebrated Malet–Isaac, an early victim of Vichy's educational reforms) was already in use at least in Paris *lycées*. Malet himself, before teaching at Louis-le-Grand, had been private tutor to the Crown Prince of Serbia, Alexander, who later went on to Saint-Cyr, coming out *promotion Puebla*, and was assassinated on the Canebière in 1934. His tutor, aged fifty in 1914, volunteered for active service and was killed on the western front in September 1915. In this respect, the great Paris stores seem to have been well ahead of the slow-moving school textbooks; as early as 1908, the Bon Marché had included in its Christmas catalogues elaborate dolls in Russian uniform (dolls in British, Serbian, and Belgian uniforms were ready for the Christmas sales of 1914).

In 1913, Albert Simonin, attending school in the Parisian suburb of La Chapelle, won the school prize for reading and reciting. It was a handsome book, bound in red cloth, the pages gold-edged, entitled *Tu seras soldat*. A year or two earlier, in 1910 or 1911, as he was to recall later, his two elder brothers, Louis and André, began spending all their time off work in boxing and wrestling establishments, gyms, and the then very rare swimming-pool (*piscine Hébert*) in a conscious effort to improve their physique, as if, like other young men in their age-group—they would be twenty-one and twenty in 1914—in Paris, and, no doubt in London and in Berlin but maybe not in Vienna —they had been unconsciously, or perhaps deliberately, preparing themselves for what was to come in the summer of 1914. Fitness was already the thing, even or maybe especially, in this working-class suburb, young men of the middle class going more for fencing. Certainly, most of the gyms and boxing establishments were situated in the rue du Faubourg-Montmartre, within walking distance of the three north-eastern *arrondissements* and the outlying suburbs beyond. Simonin adds that in this quarter, La Chapelle, young men who had been found unfit for military service tended to be looked upon with pity and even contempt, and were liable to see their engagements broken off at the behest of the girls' parents.

It is time to leave the elusive subject of Anglo-French and Anglo-German social and educational contacts and that of the *décalage* between school history and the realities of alliances, and to take a closer look at French opinion as it evolved during the stiflingly hot days of the July Crisis. (Apart from a violent thunderstorm on the afternoon of Saturday 1 August, the peals of thunder competing with the urgent tone of the tocsin from a score of churches, it did not rain in Paris till 11 September.) The school holidays had begun as usual on 14 July after school prize-giving, so that most middle-class families had left Paris, going off to the seaside, the mountains, or their villas in the suburbs or in the country. Until about Monday the 27th Paris had retained its usual summer quiet, the western *arrondissements* on both banks seemed to be half-dead in the torpor of the heat, and there were hardly any prams in the Bois de Boulogne (though still plenty of less elaborate ones at the other end of the city, in the unfashionable Bois de Vincennes).

The newspapers and journals, even a fortnight after Sarajevo, concentrated on the usual holiday themes: *concours de plage*, prizes for the best sand-castles, and that sort of thing, and for those less privileged, who had stayed behind in the capital, there was the usual excitement about the last stage of the *Tour de France* and the forthcoming *traversée de Paris à la nage* from the bridge of Charenton to that of Sèvres. *L'Illustration* dated Saturday 18 July carried articles on the centenary of the entry of Geneva into the Swiss Confederation, on President Huerta of Mexico, and on the usual public rejoicings of 14 July. A week later, on Saturday 25 July, the same magazine had pieces on the trial of Mme Caillaux, the Carpentier–Smith match, and the visit of President Poincaré to Russia. Even as late as the 31st, a leading Paris paper was to carry the delightfully bucolic advertisement in the column devoted to *Petites Annonces*: 'Jeune ménage avec enfant désire louer pour trois mois petite maison tranquille, avec jardin, près rivière poissonneuse, de préférence Normandie ou Bourgogne. Ecrire 3,418, bureau du journal', a programme designed for some quiet *pêcheur à la ligne*, well away from it all, but that was likely to have been brutally overtaken by public events as far as the fisherman was concerned in the next two days or so.

The new Viviani government, formed in the middle of June, had itself been described as *un gouvernement de vacances*, in the sense of a government of transition, a stop-gap, until such time as Joseph Caillaux could decently be offered the post of premier, which he could not be while his wife was still on trial for the assassination of Calmette and unless she had been acquitted. The trial of Mme Caillaux remained the principal item of news in all the Paris papers throughout the first half of the week beginning on Monday 27 July. But it was a *gouvernement de vacances* in a more literal sense. Poincaré himself looked forward—or so he says after the event in *L'Union sacrée*—to joining his wife and his brother-in-law at the family home in the Meurthe as soon as he had returned from Russia and Scandinavia, as originally planned, on the 31st. While in St Petersburg, he was to be introduced to the doyen of the diplomatic corps, the German ambassador to Russia, the comte de Pourtalès, who told the President that he was looking forward to his forthcoming visit to Castellane, in the Basses-Alpes, to visit the French side of his family at their country seat. Both men agreed that the wooded slopes of Lorraine or the lavender foothills of the Alps would offer a welcome respite from the terrible heat of all of Europe's capital cities.

When we think of the summer of 1914, it is indeed the stifling heat that we are most likely to evoke, partly because it has a dramatic quality in its own right—the succession of days of that matchless summer which Harold Macmillan never failed to recall when referring to his Balliol contemporaries. Then, in old newsreels, we can see the men marching off in shirt-sleeves, the women waving to them in their summer dresses or pelting them with flowers from summer gardens. But a child's measurement of time, because it is so much less dramatic, is perhaps better adjusted to getting the succession of the seasons into a more banal proportion. And so, once more, back to Simonin. The first public event that had really caught the imagination of this *enfant du faubourg* had been the great floods of the Seine of February–March 1910, the level of which may still be seen marked on the quays of the Left Bank: *crue de 1910*. Then had followed three scorching summers: those of 1912, 1913, and 1914, much of which the child had spent at the *piscine Hébert*, situated most handily in La Chapelle. Perhaps then the years had been getting into training for the final conflagration.

Childhood memory is one thing, the imagination of a novelist is another. The three volumes, *L'Eté 1914*, of *Les Thibault*, a bad novel, dreadfully long-winded, but offering all the same valuable observations on the weekly and week-end scene of July–August, refer, under Sunday 19 July, to the usual working-class crowds— *métallos*, apprentices, hairdressers' assistants, butcher boys, shop-girls, and secretaries—in the *guinguettes* of the valley of the Marne, Antony, Robinson, Fontenay-aux-Roses, and Rosny-sous-Bois. On the Sunday following (the 26th), Jacques Thibault had encountered a score of young cyclists, *moustaches en guidon*, their saddle-bags loaded with long loaves, provisions, and bottles of wine, as they headed westwards for the woods between Saint-Germain and Saint-Nom. He noticed that they were wearing striped vests and cotton shorts.

Gallieni was having a holiday of rather a different kind. He had gone to Saint-Raphaël on the same Sunday, the 26th, to be with his wife, who was desperately ill in a nursing-home, and who died on the day after his arrival, Monday the 27th. The General did not get back to Paris till Thursday the 30th. There were even later departures and returns. On the morning of the 31st, Mme Weygand, the wife of the Lieutenant-Colonel of the *5me hussards*, took the train to Metz to meet her thirteen-year-old son who was on his way back from a holiday with school-friends in Germany. They must have just about made it back.

Indeed, until Friday the 31st, the private calendar at least seemed to continue on a relatively unhurried course. On Sunday the 26th, Jouhaux and Jaurès had gone off to attend the Socialist International in Brussels. They were to leave the Belgian capital on Thursday the 30th. Jaurès was in no great hurry, insisting on taking in the Musée de l'Art Ancien to have a look at the Flemish Primitives. By all accounts, he was in excellent spirits and in no great hurry to return to base. Even on his return to Paris the same evening, he was still sufficiently confident that there was plenty of time in hand—at least ten days, according to his calculation— to suggest that that there should be a special congress of the Socialist Party at Le Pré-Saint-Gervais on 9 August to discuss the international situation. It was only on Friday the 31st, that he, like many humbler observers, first had the impression that time was no longer on his side, and that he was being overtaken by the increasingly precipitant course of events. What he would in fact have done about them is still a matter of dispute among pious *jauressiens*.

It was on the same Friday morning, the 31st, that the wandering and increasingly desperate Jacques Thibault noticed for the first time that the main thoroughfares were thronged with people—many of them young couples—who were walking briskly, not dawdling, in this direction or that, as if with a sense of urgent purpose, and in an effort, conscious or instinctive, to find some consolation in the fraternal presence of others similarly exposed. It was, he noticed, a day on which people avoided the quiet leafy squares, small side-streets, and the parks, making for the boulevards. Something else quite unusual that he spotted was the odd appearance of the windows of shoe-shops—the Raoul chain among others—haberdashers' and clothes' shops. They all seemed to be displaying only *men's* gear, most of it quite unseasonal for late July and early August: thick woollen socks, thick underwear, coarse woollen vests, heavy winter pullovers, and scarves. But it was the boots that were the most revealing: some advertised themselves coyly as *souliers de chasse*, but others spoke out quite boldly, whether in the old slang word, *godillots*, or, in a few instances, going the whole hog, *brodequins militaires*.

There were many other indications on that Friday—the last of a month that had started out so innocently and that had indeed retained its innocence almost up to the 30th—and even more on the following day, Saturday 1 August, that things were decidedly out of joint. Complete strangers could be heard addressing one another in a bizarre fashion, as if Parisians had all at once become figures out of Alice: playing-cards, days of the week, or dates in a new sort of calendar. 'What day are you?' And, before the other could get in an answer, 'I am on the first' (as if to suggest: 'beat that'). 'I am the ninth' ('Bad luck, you'll miss all the fun, it'll all be over by then'). 'I am the third, so I won't have to wait *too* long.' 'I am the eleventh' ('You'll never make Berlin at that rate'). Well, that was one destination. Others, more official, would follow; there does not seem to have been the slightest concern for security in that respect: Verdun (said with pride), Maubeuge (another trump card to be brought out with panache), Nancy (also much sought after, as if, all at once, the East, so little favoured touristically, save perhaps by those suffering from kidney diseases and in need of Vittel or Contrexéville, had come into its own, as the right direction in which to be heading), Briançon (a very low priority), Mont-Louis (even lower, a Louis XIV fortress amidst the snows of the highest Pyrenees), Brest, or Toulon (*espadrilles*, not boots, for them). A Paris workman dressed as a plumber, carrying his tools, but clearly not going to make it to work on the Friday, says, with a shrug, that it is Angoulême for him: 'Looks as though I'll miss out on the whole thing', he complains; for him clearly a posting to Angoulême was about as bad as being sent to Limoges (or Roromantin).

Jacques Thibault could make little of these cryptic references to numbered days, as if he had been eavesdropping on a game of cards the rules of which were beyond him. But he would not have long to wait in order to discover the explanation, which would be provided in a form both dramatic and characteristically mean, round about four in the afternoon of 1 August, with the appearance, in the wide plate-glass window of the big Bureau de Poste that faced the Madeleine, on the corner of the rue Royale and the Place, of a small white rectangle of paper, banal in appearance, headed in neatly penned letters with generous loops—a small monument to the regime's obsession with literacy and with elegant handwriting—underlined by a ruled line in red ink, in a hand recognizable as both feminine and bureaucratic (indeed, that of a *buraliste*), which, stuck on the inside of the glass so that it could not be easily removed, soon drew a large and jostling crowd: *MOBILISATION GENERALE. Le premier jour de la mobilisation est le dimanche 2 août* was all it said. Those to the front had seen it being put up by an *employée des PTT* wearing an administrative black smock. The fact that it was in neat schoolgirl handwriting, without a blot or a blemish, seemed to make it even more sinister than the long printed notices, topped by crossed tricolor flags, the letters huge and thick, and very dark, in that unfeeling, heartless print—*didot* or *elzévir*—that is still favoured, even now, by the French State when it addresses itself to its *administrés*, now transformed into *mobilisés* (an impersonal and emblematic female Republic, the stone Marianne that gazed out with blind eyes on to the plane trees of countless southern squares—the Mariannes were thickest in the Midi—seems to have taken a rather cruel delight in thus reducing her male citizens to past participles). At exactly the same time, similar printed notices were being posted up on the notice boards of the *mairies* of the twenty *arrondissements* of Paris, as well as outside those of every town and village in France. The sticking-up of the notices would be accompanied everywhere by the urgent ringing of the tocsin from the church tower or from the bell-tower of the Protestant *temple*.

The combination of official notice and tocsin represented a symbolic, though unconscious, token of the temporary truce between Church and State as a result of *L'Union Sacrée*. Some people seem to have been anxious to take the matter further, one of Poincaré's correspondents writing to suggest that this would be a suitable moment to dedicate a sinning and sinful nation to the cult of the Sacred Heart. The Head of State failed to respond. But, in the following days, local authorities were to report a steady influx back to France of French monks and members of the religious orders that had been expelled in 1905, crossing the Spanish border in order to volunteer. An even more bizarre train-load was reported to have crossed back into France from Belgium at Jeumont, consisting of two or three hundred French deserters and *insoumis* who had escaped into the kingdom—like Marguerite Yourcenar's father, M. de Crayencour—during the previous ten years. Of course, as the famous government statement hastened to reassure its fellow citizens: 'La mobilisation n'est pas la guerre', a statement that was almost at once to become one of the sickest jokes in the French language. But few people, even at the time, seem to have been taken in by it. Such was the general conviction that mobilization *was* war that the actual declaration of war three days later came as something of an anticlimax, and, in many places, passed almost unnoticed.

The authorities seem to have been surprised and relieved by the smoothness with which the vast operation of mobilization was carried out right from the start. Most of the *mobilisés* might, it is true, still be only semi-soldiers, their red trousers only issued later, at their point of departure. But nearly all were to reach their assigned destinations on time. Plans had been prepared well in advance. In 1910, Joffre, himself an engineer officer, had been given the important, if unglamorous, post of *Directeur de l'Arrière*, a post that carried with it responsibility over the *4ᵐᵉ Bureau*

(Transport and Supply), and put him in direct contact with the heads and the chief engineers of the main-line railway companies: Nord, Est, Ouest, PLM, POM. Two years later, in May 1912, a detailed plan worked out by Chief Engineer Sartiaux provided for the availability, at short notice—a week to nine days—of the prodigious number of 7,000 trains; thoughtfully, he even set aside a further potential 345, in the event of England coming into the war, for the transport of the BEF from Le Havre and the other Channel ports.

Unusually heavy railway traffic is hard to conceal, especially during stifling summer nights when most people would be sleeping with their windows open. Inhabitants of the quarters to the north and south that bordered on the two *ceintures*, the lines that linked up the main-line stations, those like Simonin and his family who dwelt near the sidings of La Chapelle that supplied the Gare du Nord, the suburbanites whose windows overlooked the deep cutting of les Batignolles and those of Villeneuve-Saint-Georges: all must have stirred uneasily in their sleep or have been awakened during *les heures blanches*—three or four in the morning—by the steady rumble of slow-moving trains, a noise that went on right through the night from about the 26th or the 27th. Nor could such concentrations of carriages and goods trucks have remained unnoticed during the daylight hours. A subject of early morning conversations in the cafés near the main stations would concern the number of empty trains that had been spotted after dawn from Monday the 27th. Something, suburbanites would comment, must be up. Travellers coming in from Melun brought extraordinary accounts of empty, stationary trains, engineless, and often of mixed provenance, the carriages from different companies strung up together, passenger ones mixed up with goods trucks, many of them with chalk marks on their sides—what in fact looked like chalked numbers—and chalk marks were something that would always catch popular imagination, especially in the Paris area, there was something ominous and shameful about them—waiting on side-lines the whole way from the *chef-lieu* of the Seine-et-Marne to the approaches of the Gare de Lyon. Equally bizarre were the reports brought in by travellers to the Gare du Nord of the presence along the immense sidings of Creil of several hundred stationary locomotives, smokeless and passive.

The stealthy nightly train movements might have been taken as merely preventive. But the evidence provided by the street scene in Paris on the night of Saturday to Sunday, 1–2 August, indicated quite clearly the steady, irreversible slide from peace into war. The rather impossible Jacques Thibault, totally out of step with the popular mood, had spent much of the evening hanging round *L'Humanité*. On his way home, he had been surprised to see the doors of Notre-Dame-des-Victoires wide open at midnight, the interior brilliantly lit by hundreds of candles, and the dark figures of young men queueing up outside the confession boxes. When he reached the great clock on the corner of the Quai de l'Horloge and the Boulevard du Palais, it was 1.40 in the morning. The boulevard seemed to shake with a continuous rumble of noise: the sound of hundreds of marching feet, no *fleur au fusil*, no patriotic songs, just a steady shuffle, as regiment after regiment headed northwards in the direction of the Gare de l'Est and the Gare du Nord: Avenue de l'Observatoire, Boulevard Saint-Michel, Boulevard du Palais, Boulevard Sébastopol. Along with the silent men could be seen hundreds and hundreds of horses, most of them brought in by the old horse route from the Perche, via the Porte d'Orléans, and being led by their bridles by soldiers wearing cavalry caps and long boots. There were no mounted troops to be seen. Every now and then the steady tramp of men in full campaign equipment and the clip-clop of the patient horses, their heads down, would give way to the heavier rumble of lorries and waggons, of wheeled artillery, horse-drawn, and the sound of civilian cars driven very fast by young soldiers. The noise went on through the entire night, the whole of Monday, and all through the night following. The sound could be heard in the empty Luxembourg Gardens and from as far away as the rue de Tournon and the rue de Seine.

On the Monday morning, from Boulevard Saint-Michel, Place Maubert, and rue Monge, came a different sound: the shattering of glass, and shouts, as young men in caps with long peaks and wearing chokers, who looked very much as if they had come down from the Buttes-Chaumont or the rue de Lappe, set about smashing up the various local branches of the Laiteries Maggi and the plate-glass windows and chairs and tables of the Brasseries Viennoises. Conversations overheard on the tram going down the Boulevard Saint-Germain to the Gare de Lyon, on the Monday morning, related to the queues of young couples forming outside the *mairies* of the 6me, Place Saint-Sulpice, and the 5me, Place du Panthéon, and waiting to get married. In the 5me, so it was said, the queues spread right back as far as the Place de la Contrescarpe. Onlookers also noticed, from early that Monday, that at most of the main intersections between the Porte d'Orléans and the Gare de l'Est, and particularly at the approaches to the bridges across the Seine, the familiar *agents de ville* had been replaced by gendarmes in black uniforms and wearing red armbands marked 'P.M.' in white, and steel helmets. The police had never been particularly popular with most Parisians, but a few commented that they rather missed those whom they had come to recognize from day to day. It was as if some reassuring monument had all at once been removed without warning, and that another link with peace had been brutally snapped.

On Tuesday the 4th, a squadron of planes carrying tricolor rings on their wings flew very low down the course of the Seine, from the Pont d'Austerlitz to the Pont de Sèvres. It was only about ten days since the much-publicized, much-awaited *traversée de Paris à la nage*. To the crowds on the Pont-Neuf, the Pont des Arts, the Pont Royal, and the Pont de la Concorde, it must have seemed an age. One day later, on Wednesday 5 August, Joffre left his office, 4bis Boulevard des Invalides—the 4bis has such a reassuring civilian ring about it—for his wartime headquarters at Vitry-le-François. In order to emphasize the full significance of the move, Messimy, the Minister of War, insisted on accompanying the General part of the way. War had come to Paris and to France.

How did people take it? How did they react? In so far as one can judge, mostly from evidence derived from individual sources: memoirs, diaries, even novels, the general reaction often seems to have been one of actual relief, following the uncertainties, the anxieties, and the bewilderment of the 29th, the 30th, and the 31st. With the announcement of mobilization, there would be an end to doubt and hesitancy, and people, that is men of military age, would know where they stood, what they had to do, above all *with whom* they would have to go. What was written in each individual *livret militaire* would put an end to the speculations of the previous days; it would also provide the comfortable feeling of being *encadré*. This was a crisis one did not have to face alone, but with one's mates. I don't think this is just a matter of conformism, of going along with the majority; it is something more positive than that. The most repeated comment seems to have been: 'Ça y est', in other words: 'We know where we are now and we have to get on with it.'

One could safely make one other general comment: urban opinion was much more enthusiastic than that of the general mass of the peasantry, which is often described by prefects and sub-prefects, and, more dramatically, in the reports of village *instituteurs*, better placed to judge rural reactions, as one of 'morne résignation'. There is not a trace of excitement in Barthas's account of the departure of the contingent from his village in the Minervois; the women are in tears, the men are reserved, there is no singing. One can read between the lines of what the prefect of the Seine-Inférieure does *not* say in his report to the Minister of the Interior, Malvy: 'L'état d'esprit, *notamment des grandes villes*, est excellent.' But, in Normandy, even these seem to have been decidedly muted in their response to events. We are told that the troop-trains leaving Rouen, Le Havre, and Evreux, steamed off in complete silence. Madame Lucie, who was 18 in 1914, in her book, *Confessions of a Concierge*, gives a very happy, colourful account of the *fête nationale* in her native Caen, a town with a large garrison in which the army had always been popular with local tradesmen. But, just over a fortnight later, there is no flag-waving. She walks in a very subdued mood with her fiancé to the station. She promises to write to him every day, a promise she was to keep, from August to October, when she was told of his death. But then Normans are not emotional people, and such accounts, both official and intimate, may simply indicate their natural reserve.

Naturally we know a great deal about the grand gestures. Both the Duc de Guise and the Prince Napoléon write to Poincaré to ask if they can return to France in order to volunteer. And in virtue of the *Loi d'Expulsion*, he has to tell them that they can't, though the Duc does get landed with some thankless job: a diplomatic mission to Bulgaria. We learn that there were over 20,000 foreign volunteers in the first fortnight of the war. Most of them are Danes, followed by Norwegians, Brazilians, Argentinians, and citizens of Uruguay (no doubt due to the close links between Montevideo and the Pays Basque and the Hautes-Alpes). There are a number of volunteers who describe themselves as Garibaldians.

There seems to have been surprisingly little opposition to the government in the days leading up to the 31st. Opinion appears to have been convinced that the new government, one-third of the ministers of which had been opponents of the *Trois Ans*, was doing its very best to maintain peace and should be given the benefit of the doubt. The government preserved a cool, intelligent, and rather machiavellian approach, suggesting that it had full confidence in the common sense and loyalty of provincial opinion. On the afternoon of the 30th, Malvy telegraphed the prefects, informing them that they should make arrangements for anti-war meetings to go ahead, even out of doors, provided that they were orderly and that the local authorities had an opportunity of reporting on those attending. Sixty-seven street meetings, twenty-five in Paris (none in the 5me, 6me, 7me, 8me, 16me) and forty-two in the suburbs, had been planned for the 30th, the 31st, and the 1st, but most of them were to be stopped by mobilization. Again, on the 30th, Malvy decided that those whose names were on the *Carnet B* lists should *not* be arrested.

Previous governments had had long and not unjustified doubts on the subject of the reliability of southern regiments, and Messimy clearly feared that there would be massive anti-war demonstrations all over the Midi. Malvy did not share these fears; and he was to be proved right. There were no meetings at all in the Var and the Isère, though they had been authorized by the two prefects. Even more surprisingly, no meeting was called in Saint-Etienne, the old anarcho-syndicalist stronghold. Information about these meetings is at best very patchy, and, when it comes from prefects, plain silly. But from what one gathers, either from the local press, or from the reports of *instituteurs*, there were only a few well-attended meetings in the south and south-centre: Montluçon, a large turn-out, Limoges, and Lyons. There was some violence in Avignon and Nîmes. In the Gard, of which Nîmes was the *chef-lieu*, anti-war meetings in the small working-class towns of Alès, Anduze, La Grande-Combe, and Le Cailar, as well as in all of them with predominantly Protestant populations—are described as having been well-attended, those in the Catholic villages of the department are said to have been ill-attended. Perhaps one should not make very much of this, the Protestant *bourgs* being those in which the mines and light industries were concentrated. But the biggest meetings took place in the north-east, in places like Albert, Denain, Bapaume, Valenciennes, Péronne, Beauvais, and the railway town of Creil. Only one demonstration got, for a time, completely out of hand, causing both the military and the civil authorities momentary alarm; this was in the railway suburb of Sotteville-lès-Rouen, at the approaches, from the direction of Paris, to the main station: *Rouen Rive Droite*, an old socialist and syndicalist stronghold that contained the marshalling yards not only of the vital Paris–Rouen–Le Havre mainline, but also those providing the loop-line Rouen–Serqueux–Amiens, which, once the British were in the war, was to be a key link in British army transport between the Rouen base, the crucially important Amiens, and the war zone. It soon took the proportions of a riot, and the gendarmerie had to be brought in from Rouen. Not only the railwaymen, but their wives, were directly involved. There were a number of arrests, but all were released on the same evening.

All in all, from a map both incomplete and often informed only by the platitudinous comments of the prefects, it would appear that working-class opinion pretty well all over France accepted, if reluctantly, the inevitability of war, at least by the 31st. Of course events had moved too fast for it to have been possible to have organized a concerted national campaign; by the 31st, such a moment had passed. Middle-class and working-class opinion had by then become convinced that the war had been forced upon a peaceable Republic as a result of German aggression. During these crucial days, no one seems even to have been *aware* of Austria-Hungary. (Poincaré was to note, with mild astonishment, that the Austrian ambassador had still not asked for his passport by 4 August.)

Rural opinion eludes us almost entirely. We hear of peasant families standing silently by the railway-tracks, watching the troop-trains go by. Even Poincaré, so moved by the wave of enthusiasm that had greeted him on his disembarkation at Dunkirk on the 29th—tears came into his eyes, but, as he notes in

L'Union sacrée, a Head of State does not cry in public—notices the lugubrious expressions of the men in faded blue smocks as they watch the presidential train speed through the rolling cornfields of the Somme and the Pays de France. Prefects are not interested in rural reactions to mobilization; it is the towns that worry them. We do have the personal testimonies of Grenadou, a peasant from the Beauce, and of Barthas, whom I have already mentioned, a barrel-maker from a village in the Minervois, in the Aude, in the south-west of France. Grenadou goes off to Chartres, after taking leave of his wife, almost without a word. Barthas, who had been a militant pacifist in the 1910s, and was *mal noté* as such by the local gendarmerie, is deeply saddened by the plunge into war, seeing all his hopes of ten years' militancy dashed by the ambitions of governments. But he reports for duty, is posted first of all to the fortress of Mont-Louis, and even manages to spend a few days over the border, in Spain, in order to find out what it feels like to be neutral. Curiously, he finds it rather dull. Later, serving in Flanders, alongside the British, he sees no contradiction between his previous activities as a militant pacifist and his duties as a soldier. He proves a good soldier, provided his NCOs and his officers are from the Minervois, and a very bad soldier each time he comes under the orders of a Corsican *sous-off*. He becomes a sergeant, but loses his stripes, after an argument with a brutal and insensitive medical officer. He gets back to his village, where he is once more *mal noté* when he refuses to attend the ceremony for the inauguration of the *Monument aux Morts*, which faces the blind-eyed Marianne from the other side of the Place de l'Eglise.

Between August 1914 and the end of the year, there were 841 cases of attempted desertion or *insoumission*—that is, failure to report for duty—brought before courts-martial: a figure surprisingly low. We hear of a smallholder from a Protestant village in the Gard who actually gets away to Switzerland (where, presumably, he has relatives). The prefect of the Basses-Pyrénées speaks of a few hundred young men caught while attempting to cross into Spain. The traditional Belgian route of desertion was now closed and under new management. At the time of mobilization, a small group of anarchists from Saint-Etienne take to the woods in the Monts du Forez; spotted by villagers, they are tracked down by the local gamekeeper, and arrested on

9 August. None is condemned to death; one of them is mentioned in dispatches (*cité à l'ordre de l'Armée*) for outstanding courage while under fire in December 1916. There is only one man from the Paris area—a metal-worker from Saint-Denis—among those tried. Most of those who actually come before *Conseils de Guerre* are Bretons and Normans. The Nantes court—which was thought to be severe, the town having had the highest casualties of any locality in the course of the first month of the war—tended to take a surprisingly lenient view with regard to the former. Most seem to have been peasants from the Breton-speaking areas of the Finistère and the Morbihan who, unable to read or understand any French, had simply failed to report, not knowing what could have been the purpose of these meaningless pieces of paper or what they were supposed to have done.

Most of the Normans were either drunks or tramps, or both, who, having no fixed addresses and moving from barn to barn, sometimes taking up casual work, had passed the first week of mobilization among the hedgerows and orchards and the lush meadows of the Pays de Caux and the Pays d'Auge in an alcoholic stupor, and in blessed ignorance of the great events in which they were supposed to have been included. Again, the court of the military district of Rouen seems not to have judged them too severely. Perhaps the judges were themselves Normans. Most of these vagrants had long since lost their *livrets militaires*, if they had ever been issued with them in the first place. Sent to the barracks at Rouen-Bon-secours, and temporarily cleaned up, they were soon to resume an existence mainly out in the open and in all seasons, reassuringly filthy and unshaven, once more safely removed from the dangers of washing, clad in sheepskins, the hides of animals, and vague woollen coverings of several thicknesses and with eiderdowns tied around the lot, but farther to the east, in more open country, and at several more removes from the consoling sources of 90-proof calvados and *cidre bouché*. I find the thought of a man who had simply *missed* the Coming of the War because he had been dead drunk throughout the crisis singularly heartening. It seems to put things back into the right proportions, and it provides a vaguely reassuring note on which to conclude.

Bibliographical Note

For this chapter I have drawn heavily on literary and auto-biographical sources. I have found the three volumes, *L'Été 1914*, of *Les Thibault*, by Roger Martin du Gard, an excellent source on day-to-day, even hour-to-hour, events in Paris. I have also made much use of Albert Simonin, *Confessions d'un enfant de la Chapelle*, of the *Carnets de Guerre* of Louis Barthas, and the recollections of Grenadou, in *Grenadou paysan français*. Bonnie Smith's *Confessions of a Concierge: Madame Lucie's History of Twentieth-Century France* has been useful. I have found Jean-Jacques Becker's *L'Opinion française devant la guerre de 14* indispensable and I have derived much useful information from Contamine's *La Bataille de la Marne*. The appropriate vol. 4, *L'Union sacrée* (Paris, 1927), of Poincaré's memoirs, *Au Service de la France*, i–x (Paris, 1926–33) is useful on public events. Fred Kupferman, *Pierre Laval, 1883–1945*, is informative on the subject of the threat to the *zoniers* of Aubervilliers provided by Gallieni's plans to make Paris into a military fortress, a threat that was removed by the outcome of the Battle of the Marne.

Edouard Bled, in his delightful recollections of his childhood spent in the eastern Paris suburb of Saint-Maur, on the far side of the Bois de Vincennes, *J'avais un an en 1900*, provides a sensitive and wonderfully wide-eyed complement to Simonin's more knowing account of growing up in La Chapelle during the same period. Bled combines a very acute sense of *period* with an equally alert awareness of *place*. Simonin and Bled are populists; Marguerite Yourcenar comes from a highly privileged and cosmopolitan background. Her posthumous (and uncompleted) book: *Quoi? L'Éternité* covers very much the same years (she was born in 1903).

The new edition of *La Grande Guerre, 1914–1918* by Marc Ferro provides a useful summary of the diplomatic lead-up to the July Crisis. Personal informants have been acknowledged in the text. Finally, I have relied on my own imagination and have also made some further use of my own book *French and Germans* (Hanover, NH, 1983; French translation, *Vivre avec l'Ennemi*, Paris, 1985).

7

Britain Enters The War[1]

MICHAEL BROCK

On 24 July 1914, when the news of the Austrian ultimatum reached London, the Prime Minister, H. H. Asquith, told Venetia Stanley that war between Germany and Austria-Hungary, on the one side, and France and Russia on the other, was now quite likely. 'So . . . we are within measurable, or imaginable, distance', he wrote, 'of a real Armageddon. Happily there seems . . . no reason why we should be more than spectators.'[2] Why did Asquith think that Britain could remain a spectator while the continental powers made war? And how did he come to adopt the opposite view?

Ten days later, on 2 August, Asquith set down for Venetia the six principles by which he was guided. These were:

1. We have no obligation of any kind either to France or Russia to give them military or naval help.
2. The despatch of the Expeditionary Force to help France at this moment is out of the question and wd. serve no object.
3. We mustn't forget the ties created by our long-standing and intimate friendship with France.
4. It is against British interests that France should be wiped out as a Great Power.
5. We cannot allow Germany to use the Channel as a hostile base.

[1] For permission to quote from, or cite, unpublished copyright documents the author thanks Lord Bonham Carter and the Rt. Hon. the Earl of Selborne. For access to manuscript collections he thanks the Curators of the Bodleian Library (Asquith Papers), the Master and Fellows of Churchill College (Chandos Papers), the House of Lords Record Office (Samuel Papers), the Imperial War Museum (Henry Wilson Diary), the Fellows of Nuffield College (Mottistone Papers), and the University of Sussex Library (Kipling Papers).
[2] *Letters to Venetia Stanley*, ed. M. and E. Brock (Oxford, 1982), 123. At Armageddon 'the kings of . . . the whole world' were 'to gather them to the battle of that great day': Rev. 16: 14, 16.

6. We have obligations to Belgium to prevent her being utilized and absorbed by Germany.[3]

The Prime Minister would have had most of that in mind when he wrote on 24 July. The puzzle is why none of it struck him then as entailing Britain's involvement should the Great Powers go to war.

Let us start by noting how intricate a pattern Asquith's six principles made. It is convenient to distinguish those principles which enshrined Britain's obligations (using that word in its wider sense) from those which defined her interests; but the distinction is no more than a convenience. To Asquith and his colleagues the one consideration shaded into the other, since they believed it to be extremely dangerous for Britain to neglect her obligations in a world ever ready to talk of perfidious Albion.[4] It would be equally mistaken to try to separate the Cabinet's attitude to Britain's Entente partners, France and Russia, from its attitude to Belgium, where Britain had a treaty obligation. Every well-informed observer knew that a German attack on France would involve the invasion of Belgium.[5] The French frontier defences were judged to be very strong; and the German General Staff would not contemplate confining their attack to the Franco-German frontier. British resistance in arms to a German attack on Belgium was thus bound to help the French, and, correspondingly, any attempt to help the French on land was likely to entail military operations in Belgium.

The agreement defining Britain's obligations in both cases may be briefly summarized. The Anglo-French Entente had facilitated an arrangement whereby French naval strength was concentrated in the Mediterranean, while the British fleet guarded France's

---

[3] Brock (eds.), op. cit. (above, n. 2), 146. Asquith reproduced the same points with some differences of phrasing when writing on 2 Aug. to Bonar Law: R. Blake, *The Unknown Prime Minister* (London, 1955), 223–4.

[4] Phrase used originally in a French poem, 1793. For an analysis of this question see Trevor Wilson, *History*, 64 (1979), 380–90.

[5] See *Nineteenth Century*, 59 (1906), 867 (Earl of Erroll); 70 (1911), 798–803 (A. W. A. Pollock); *United Service Magazine*, 33 (1906), 531 (Bannerman-Phillips); *National Review*, 52 (1909), 937–8 (Schlieffen's *Deutsche Revue* article); 54 (1909), 46–7; 55 (1910), 743–60; 57 (1911), 958, 962–7 (Lord Alan Percy, from Dec. 1909 Earl Percy); *The Times*, 23 Jan., 20 Feb. 1911 (unsigned: C. à Court Repington); *Fortnightly Review*, 96 (1911), 463–71 (anon.); *London Magazine*, 27 (1912), 279–90 (Hilaire Belloc); *Round Table*, iii. 418–24 (June 1913).

Channel and Atlantic coasts. A few months after this arrangement was made the Liberal Cabinet had defined its implications in a secret exchange of letters with the French ambassador. It put on record in November 1912 that, while the two countries should consult together if either was threatened with attack, the disposition of the fleets was 'not based upon an engagement to co-operate in war'.[6] Towards Belgium the British had treaty-based obligations of a rather different kind. Under the terms of two treaties of 1839 Britain was a guarantor of the neutrality of Belgium. If any of the guarantor states infringed that neutrality each of the others could claim a right, and would perhaps in some circumstances have a duty, to resist the infringement.[7] Exercising that right, as will be explained, might be a matter of some difficulty.

For the British to decide in their own interests to help France on land, two conditions would have to be fulfilled. The British government would need to be satisfied, first, that failing such help France might be crushed, and second, that the British help available would be effective in preventing a French defeat. On 24 July Asquith had no reason to think that either of these conditions would be met. In British Liberal circles France and Russia were commonly thought to be the equals of Germany and Austria-Hungary. 'The four nations now at war', the Liberal *Daily Chronicle* pronounced on 3 August, 'are pretty equally matched.'[8] Russia's military recovery from the disasters of the Russo-Japanese War was apt to be exaggerated in Britain as elsewhere.[9] Even if France were assumed to be in danger of

---

[6] The text of the letter to Cambon (22 Nov. 1912), including this phrase, formed part of Grey's speech, 3 Aug. 1914. He was interrupted while reading and inadvertently omitted the last sentence of the letter. For full text see H. H. Asquith, *Genesis of the War* (London, 1923), 267–8.

[7] See Christopher Howard, *Splendid Isolation* (London, 1967), 64–8; *Britain and the Casus Belli* (London, 1974), 27–32.

[8] R. C. K. Ensor was the paper's chief leader-writer. See also John, Viscount Morley, *Memorandum on Resignation* (London, 1928), 6. Nicolson, the Permanent Under-Secretary of State, Foreign Office, wanted intervention to prevent a Franco-Russian victory won independently of Britain. Most of the other officials feared that Germany would win and dominate Europe: A. J. P. Taylor, *The Struggle for Mastery in Europe* (London, 1954), 525.

[9] See, for instance, Brock (eds.), op. cit. (above, n. 2), 177. As early as Sept. 1908 Asquith had complained to Grey that, in seeking more British help, Clemenceau 'completely ignores the existence — from a military point of view — of his Russian ally': S. R. Williamson, *Politics of Grand Strategy* (London, 1969), 103.

defeat, it was thought that British intervention could do nothing to save her. The British army was, as the Kaiser soon announced, contemptibly small by continental standards.[10] 'To send . . . two or even four divisions abroad at the beginning of a war', Edward Grey told the French ambassador on 2 August, 'would entail the maximum of risk . . . and produce the minimum of effect.'[11] Any British obligation to France would be exclusively naval. It amounted to a duty either to give the French timely warning of British neutrality so that they could adjust their fleet dispositions,[12] or, alternatively, to protect the Channel and Atlantic coasts of France from attack.

Britain's interest in preventing the Belgian coast and the mouth of the Schelde from falling into the hands of a hostile power had been recognized for centuries. If the Belgian government either lost control of the country, or departed from neutrality by offering no protest or resistance when it was infringed, Britain would be entitled as a guarantor state to protect British interests by military action in north Belgium.[13] On the other hand, if the Brussels government fulfilled its duty as a treaty-bound neutral and remained in effective control of Belgium, even a British naval intervention off Antwerp could scarcely be made without a Belgian invitation. Failing such an invitation it could be held to constitute, not an attempt to uphold Belgium's status under the treaties, but a further infringement of her neutrality.[14] The British navy also faced the complication that the mouth of the Schelde lay in Dutch waters.[15]

Warlike intervention in Belgium in defence of their vital interests would thus present the British with considerable problems. It was equally predictable that they might be reluctant to interpret their duty under the treaties very actively. They would not be obliged to intervene unless invited to do so from Brussels on acceptable conditions.[16] Even such an invitation

---

[10] The Kaiser issued the order which gave the 'Old Contemptibles' their name on 19 Aug. 1914. The German term is perhaps closer to 'insignificant' than to 'contemptible'.

[11] *Brit. Docs. War*, 11 (1926), 275.

[12] See J. W. Headlam-Morley to Asquith, 3 Jan. 1923: Bonham Carter MSS.

[13] *Brit. Docs. War*, 8 (1932), 392 (Crowe), 397–8 (Haldane).

[14] See J. E. Helmreich, *Journal of Modern Hist.*, 36 (1964), 420–1.

[15] The Dutch built forts at Flushing shortly before 1914.

[16] The draft convention which a guarantor coming to Belgium's aid was to be invited to sign is outlined in Helmreich, op. cit. (above, n. 14), 423.

might not impose an obligation on the guarantor to give military, as opposed to diplomatic, support; and it might not have binding force should Britain be the only power which had received it and was able to comply. In effect, the Brussels government could do much to prevent a British intervention in arms in Belgium: what was far less clear was whether, if things were to swing the other way, it could do anything to ensure one.

The British government's decision in the war crisis would thus depend on the actions of the two main belligerents in the west, Germany and France, and on those of neutral Belgium which lay between them. We should look first, therefore, at what Asquith knew on 24 July about the German plan for an attack in the west, known to history as the Schlieffen Plan.[17] The title is misleading, not only because Schlieffen had embellished his strategic concept with so many variations that there had been something like a series of Schlieffen Plans, but still more because at least one crucial feature of the 1914 battle-plan had been devised, not by Schlieffen, but by his successor as Chief of the German General Staff, Helmuth von Moltke. It was thought unlikely that the invading German army would march through central Belgium. On the basis of the assessments made by the British and French staffs in 1911, Henry Wilson, the Director of Military Operations, had concluded that the right wing of the German invasion force would take the Ardennes route through south Belgium, remaining south of the Sambre–Meuse river line.[18] It was argued that

---

[17] See G. Ritter, *The Schlieffen Plan*, trans. A. and E. Wilson (London, 1958).
[18] See Lord Edward Gleichen, *A Guardsman Remembers* (London, 1932), 340–2; Williamson, op. cit. (above, n. 9), 169. Wilson's exposition to the CID, 23 Aug. 1911, is recorded in the minutes of the 114th Meeting (available, apart from PRO copy, in Asquith Papers, Bodleian Library, vol. 132, fos. 104–14: extract in *Brit. Docs. War*, 8 (1932), 381–2). See also C. Hazlehurst, *Politicians at War* (London, 1971), 315 (Wilson, Sept. 1911), 322 (Ollivant, 1 Aug. 1914). Some of the authors of the published articles mentioned in n. 5 reached the same conclusion as Wilson. For Wilson's continuing doubts see his diary, 7 Apr. 1912 (Imperial War Museum). Some of the statements written after the war on this issue should be treated with reserve. Cf. Repington's *Times* article cited in n. 5 above with his account in *Vestigia* (London, 1919), 304–5. Sir John French claimed in *1914* (1919), 10–11, that he had foreseen a sweep through the whole of Belgium: in view of his strategy with the BEF this is hard to believe. A film-script by Churchill (Jan. 1935) depicted Henry Wilson as telling the CID in 1911 that, if the Germans were to attack 'in three years' time', they would move north of

Moltke could not accept the weakening of his centre and left which sending the right wing through central and north Belgium would necessarily entail.[19] Moreover, the German government would be reluctant to invade the Netherlands as well as Belgium, since Germany relied on receiving supplies through the Dutch ports and these would remain open to world trade only if the Netherlands stayed neutral.

Between north Belgium and Germany lies a wedge of Dutch territory, the Maastricht Appendix (see Map). The existence of this Appendix made it very difficult to invade central and north Belgium while leaving the Netherlands inviolate. Any such operation would involve the capture of Liège, with its great fortresses, at the outset of the campaign. 'It seems certain', Wilson argued, 'that unless Germany is prepared to violate Dutch neutrality, or unless Belgium, through cowardice or neglect, allows the fortresses of Liège and Namur to fall into German hands, the advance of the German armies will be confined to the country south of the Meuse.'

These views were not peculiar to Henry Wilson and his immediate circle. Something similar to them had appeared, for instance, in the *National Review* in 1910;[20] and they had been largely accepted by the cabinet ministers who attended the Committee of Imperial Defence. On 29 July, when Asquith told Venetia Stanley of the first cabinet discussion about Belgian neutrality, he described an advance through Belgium as Germany's 'shortest route' into France.[21] If he was describing a German march through the Ardennes, this phrasing was correct. He would have been uncharacteristically inaccurate if he had used it about a sweep through central and north Belgium. Lloyd George would demonstrate with a map that the invaders would cross 'only . . . the furthest southern corner' of Belgium, while Charles Masterman recorded Churchill as saying: 'I don't see why we need

the Meuse: M. Gilbert (ed.), *Churchill, Companion Documents, 1929-35* (London, 1981), 998. In fact Wilson was reported in the minutes as saying this of an attack 'in ten years' time'.

[19] Wilson noted in his diary, 20 Aug. 1914: 'Immense German movement over the Meuse . . . The more the better, as it will weaken their centre': C. E. Callwell, *Wilson* (1927), i. 165. See also n. 99 below.

[20] See n. 5 above: *National Review*, 55 (1910), 753 (Percy).

[21] Brock (eds.), op. cit. (above, n. 2), 132.

FRANCE AND THE LOW COUNTRIES, 1914

come in if they only go a little way into Belgium.'[22] The same view was predominant, not only in the Cabinet, but among other Liberal MPs, as soon as the latter were obliged to admit that the German army would not leave Belgium inviolate. Charles Trevelyan, a junior minister who was to resign with Morley and Burns, wrote to Runciman: 'I draw a great distinction between (a) Germany marching through Belgium for military purposes to get at France; and (b) Germany seizing Antwerp and the whole of Belgium.'[23] Philip Morrell, another Liberal non-interventionist, told the Commons on 3 August: 'If Germany threatened to annex Belgium, or to occupy Belgium . . . we might be bound under our Treaty obligation to go to war to protect Belgium. But . . . what is it we are asked to do? We are asked to go to war because there may be a few German regiments in a corner of Belgian territory.'[24]

France's war plans were virtually unknown to Asquith on 24 July. During the first phase of the crisis, like all his colleagues, he assumed the French to be far too intent on defending themselves to bother about respecting Belgian neutrality. Some British commentators suspected that, whenever the intention of the German army to invade Belgium became clear, the French would at once invade from their side, and that French forces might easily end by being the first to cross the Belgian frontier. There was indeed some suspicion that the Germans' widely publicized intention of invading Belgium might be the prelude to an elaborate feint, designed to tempt the French into being the first to violate Belgium's rights under the Treaty.[25] Provided that the French were not actually the first into Belgium, they would hardly be blamed by world opinion for doing everything possible to defend their own soil.

---

[22] Lord Beaverbrook, *Politicians and the War, 1914-1916*, i (London, 1928), 29; L. Masterman, *C. F. G. Masterman* (London, 1938), 265. See also Lloyd George's remarks to C. P. Scott: Trevor Wilson (ed.), *Political Diaries of C. P. Scott* (London, 1970), 96-7, 104.

[23] C. Hazlehurst, op. cit. (above, n. 18), 70.

[24] 65 HC Deb. 5s. col. 1835. See also H. W. Massingham's letter, *The Times*, 4 Aug., 2b.

[25] *Brit. Docs. War*, 8 (1932), 380; B. Tuchman, *Guns of August* (London, 1962), 34, 64, 127; J. W. Headlam, *History of Twelve Days* (London, 1915), 377. See also Poincaré's cable to Paul Cambon, Mar. 1912, in D. J. Godspeed, *The German Wars* (London, 1977), 93.

The Belgians' attitude to their neutrality had been a recurrent worry for the Committee of Imperial Defence since the Agadir crisis of 1911.[26] The British had been too prominent in protesting about the Belgian Congo to be at all popular in Belgium. The Belgians disliked the prospect of the German army traversing their country; but the prospect of being rescued from that army, and of resuming Belgium's historic role as the cockpit of Europe, seemed still more unacceptable. As Asquith and those round him well knew, this Belgian distaste for British help against a German invasion had been greatly increased by the Anglo-French Entente.[27] By 1914 the Belgian government had ceased to think of Britain as a reliable and disinterested protector. The British were now seen as aligned with one of the warlike combinations which cared everything for victory and nothing for Belgium. In 1912 a British attempt at a resumption of Anglo-Belgian staff talks had been rebuffed.[28] The Belgian army was deployed, not against a German invasion, but to resist incursions into central and north Belgium from any direction.

Serious resistance by the Belgian army was therefore judged unlikely. 'I thought,' Churchill wrote, 'and Lord Kitchener who lunched with me [on 28 July] agreed, that Belgium would make some formal protest and submit. A few shots might be fired outside Liège or Namur; and then this unfortunate state would bow its head before overwhelming might.'[29] If the German advance through Belgium should be limited to the Ardennes it seemed in the last degree unlikely that the Belgian forces would do much to check it. They would stay on the northern flank of the German columns, guarding the line of the Meuse, or, as a German diplomat put it in 1911, 'lining . . . up along the road taken by the German forces'.[30] An advance by the German army

---

[26] See *Brit. Docs. War*, (8 (1932), 381–412; minutes of 120th CID Meeting (6 Dec. 1912); French to Seely, 20 Jan. 1913 (Mottistone MSS 12, Nuffield College); K. M. Wilson, *Bulletin of the Institute of Historical Research*, 50 (1977), 218–28. Dr Wilson gives a controversial interpretation of British strategy in *The Policy of the Entente* (London, 1985), 121–34.

[27] See Villiers to Nicolson, 11 Jan. 1913: H. Nicolson, *Carnock* (London, 1930), 399–400.

[28] *Brit. Docs. War*, 8 (1932), 401–3; Tom Bridges, *Alarms and Excursions* (London, 1938), 62–3.

[29] W. S. Churchill, *World Crisis*, i (London, 1923), 202.

[30] E. Cammaerts, *Albert* (London, 1935), 149.

south of the Sambre–Meuse line would disturb only about one-third of the area of Belgium and much less than a third of its population. It was hard to believe that in this case the Belgian government would take the terrible risks entailed in serious resistance. It was still more unlikely that it would call on a guarantor power for military help.

Belgium [Henry Wilson reported in September 1911] seems to contemplate . . . treating that part of her country . . . which lies south of the Sambre and Meuse as being in a different category to that part which lies to the north of those rivers. . . . It seems to be likely that the Belgians will not treat a German advance across her [*sic*] country as a violation of her territory, so long as such an advance is restricted to the country south of the Sambre and Meuse.[31]

The two conditions mentioned earlier—loss of control or acceptance of invasion by the Belgian government—were the only ones under which there would be a clear legal right to act without this invitation; and it was apparent that neither was likely to be fulfilled. A German occupation of Belgian Luxemburg would not create a situation in which the Brussels government could be said to have lost control of its territories; and, as far as form went, King Albert and his ministers clearly meant to treat a German march through the Ardennes as a 'violation of Belgian territory'. Their policy was to protest against that march, or even to resist it, just enough to establish that it was a violation and that they had not 'permitted' it. A report by the First Secretary of the Brussels Legation, sent in that same month, September 1911, had made this as clear as the conventions of diplomatic language could make it. He wrote, after a conversation with the Belgian Foreign Minister:

I observed that it would appear possible for German or French troops to pass through . . . that portion of Belgian territory which lies to the south . . . of Liège . . . without coming within range of the Belgian lines of fortifications, and I asked M. Davignon what the Belgian Government would do supposing such an attempt were made by either of the belligerents. He replied . . . most positively that the Belgian Government were absolutely determined to resist invasion from whatever direction it might proceed and in whatever portion of the kingdom it might be

---

[31] Hazlehurst, op. cit. (above, n. 18), p. 309.

attempted. 'I do not say', he added, 'that if the invasion took place in that corner of the kingdom . . . we should make our last stand there or that we should die there to the last man. We should probably fall back under the pressure of overwhelming forces on the lines of our fortifications . . . We are determined to remain absolutely loyal to our treaty obligations.'[32]

Even if the right to intervene without an invitation could be established beyond doubt, the political difficulty of doing this would be immense. 'We cannot', Harcourt told J. A. Spender on 2 August, 'be more Belgian than the Belgians.'[33]

By 29 July it was clear that Grey's mediation proposal had broken down; and on that day the Cabinet discussed British policy in the event of a Great Power war. Asquith said, according to Jack Pease, that, if France were attacked, the German army 'would go through Belgium and hesitate [to] attack in any other way'.[34] Britain's rights and duties under the 1839 Treaties were reviewed in the light of the Law Officers' opinion in 1870.[35] It was assumed that French military moves would leave Britain as the only guarantor power in a position to uphold the treaty provisions. Asquith's report to the King on 30 July did not contravene the non-interventionist prediction which he had originally made to Venetia. 'It is a doubtful point', he wrote, 'how far a single guaranteeing State is bound under the Treaty of 1839 to maintain Belgian neutrality if the remainder abstain or refuse. The Cabinet consider that the matter if it arises will be rather one of policy than of legal obligation.'[36]

By Sunday 2 August, while it was still possible for back-benchers to hold these comforting, non-interventionist views, it had become much harder for cabinet ministers to do so. The crisis

---

[32] *Brit. Docs. War*, 8 (1932), 386. The views of Count de Manneville, the French Chargé d'Affaires, recorded by the First Secretary, do not run counter to this (387).

[33] See Spender's comment on Temperley's Question 6: HLRO, Historical Collection 128, Samuel Papers, A/45, fos. 29 *et seq.*

[34] K. M. Wilson (ed.), *Cabinet Diary of J. A. Pease, 24 July–5 Aug. 1914:* *Proc. Leeds Phil. and Lit. Soc.* 19 (1983), 6.

[35] *Brit. Docs. War*, 8 (1932), 378–9.

[36] J. A. Spender and C. Asquith, *Asquith* (London, 1932), ii. 81.

was not developing as Asquith had expected. In the first place the British public, or, at least, the more articulate part of it, had begun to swing towards intervention. For the first few days the sequel to the assassinations at Sarajevo had looked like yet another Balkan quarrel. When it first became clear that Austria-Hungary would not be the only Great Power involved, attention was concentrated on Russia.[37] By 2 August that had changed. The British now saw the war as one in which France might be crushed. This change of focus greatly strengthened the interventionists. Russia was an unpopular power, especially in Liberal circles. To many British people the Russian government was an oppressive, backward autocracy stained by a record of anti-Jewish pogroms. When Grey made his interventionist speech to the Commons on 3 August he never mentioned Russia.[38]

As Foreign Secretary Grey was sensitive to this movement of opinion. Looking back, some months later, on the war crisis, he ridiculed 'the idea that one individual . . . in the Foreign Office could pledge a great democracy . . . in advance, either to take part in a great war or to abstain'. 'One of his strongest feelings' had been, he said, 'that he himself had no power to decide policy and was only the mouthpiece of England.'[39] Even apart from the swing of popular opinion he was under pressure from his Foreign Office officials and from the French ambassador to give France some help. Events had moved much too fast to allow any redeployment of the French navy. In any case the French government would have been unwilling, by ordering such a redeployment, to show that it despaired of British intervention; nor could it have matched German naval strength in the North Sea and the Channel whatever fleet rearrangements it might have made. Unless the Cabinet meant to allow the German fleet to bombard the Channel coast of France almost within sight of the British shore, it had therefore to envisage the possibility of using its naval strength to protect the French. After the first of that Sunday's cabinet meetings Grey was authorized to tell the French

[37] See D. C. Watt, 'British Reactions to the Assassination at Sarajevo', *European Studies Review*, 3 (1971), 233–47.

[38] For Ramsay MacDonald's comment on this omission see 65 HC Deb. 5s. col. 1830.

[39] G. M. Trevelyan, *Grey* (London, 1937), 250; Hazlehurst, op. cit. (above, n. 18), 52.

ambassador 'that if the German fleet comes into the Channel or through the North Sea to undertake hostile operations against the French coasts or shipping, the British fleet will give all the protection in its power.' Grey added, when speaking in the House of Commons the next day, that this was intended 'not as a declaration of war on our part, not as entailing immediate aggressive action on our part, but as binding us to take aggressive action should that contingency arise'.[40]

By the afternoon of Sunday 2 August the ministry was close to breaking up. Burns had resigned and Morley was to follow that evening. For the moment several considerations, apart from a natural liking for office, just sufficed to hold the other isolationists to their posts. They knew that a break-up would almost certainly lead to a warlike coalition. Asquith had read a letter from Bonar Law to the morning Cabinet.[41] The Conservatives were by now prepared to defy their more timid and isolationist supporters in the City of London.[42] Their shadow cabinet held, Bonar wrote, that 'it would be fatal to the honour and security of the United Kingdom to hesitate in supporting France and Russia at the present juncture; and we offer our unhesitating support to the Government in any measures they may consider necessary for that object.'[43] The peace demonstration in Trafalgar Square on the Sunday afternoon was a failure; and Asquith had let it be known that he meant to stand by Grey.[44] He had thus contrived to make clear by the time the Cabinet reassembled on the Sunday evening that if the isolationists insisted on asserting their principles they could do so only at the cost of bringing Britain closer to war: a government more pacific than the existing one was no longer a political possibility.

[40] 65 HC Deb. 5s. col. 1818. See also n. 51 below.

[41] K. M. Wilson, 'The Cabinet's Decision for War, 1914', in *The Policy of the Entente* (London, 1985), 135–47, provides an interesting account of this episode.

[42] For Conservative hesitations during the preceding week see Viscount Grey of Fallodon, *Twenty-Five Years* (London, 1925), i. 337; F. S. Oliver, *Anvil of War* (London, 1936), 79–80; W. R. Inge, *Diary of a Dean* (London, 1951), 97.

[43] Blake, op. cit. (above, n. 2), 222. A Conservative meeting was told of this letter, 14 Dec. 1914 and in August 1918 the *National Review* claimed that it had been highly effective. For Asquith's denial of this claim see S. Koss, *Asquith* (London, 1976), 158.

[44] H. Samuel to his wife, 2 Aug.; HLRO, S/157/697. See also Brock (eds.), op. cit. (above, n. 2), 146. According to Morley op. cit. (above, n. 8), 25, Asquith mentioned the possibility of a coalition at the morning cabinet on 3 Aug.

The more isolationist Ministers also knew, in the words of Pease's diary two days earlier, that 'a violation of Belgium might alter public opinion'.[45] Here too each new piece of information made an isolationist stance more difficult. Asquith had learned that all French forward units were forbidden to go within ten kilometres of the frontier with Germany.[46] A government which had given that order was not going to allow any rash incursion into Belgium. The prospect that no one would quite know which side had been the first to invade Belgian territory had faded. On 31 July Grey asked the French and German governments to give assurances that they would respect Belgian neutrality. While the French complied, the German government declined to do so.[47] Sunday 2 August brought news that German troops had occupied the Grand Duchy of Luxemburg. 'As regards Belgium', Crewe reported to the King after the Sunday evening Cabinet, 'it was agreed, without any attempts to state a formula, that it should be made evident that a substantial violation of the neutrality of that country would place us in the situation contemplated as possible by Mr Gladstone in 1870, when interference with Belgian independence was held to compel us to take action.'[48] When replying to the Conservative leaders on 2 August Asquith employed still more guarded phrasing about Belgium. 'It is right', he wrote, 'before deciding whether any and what action on our part is necessary to know what are the circumstances and conditions of any German interference with Belgian territory.'

When the Cabinet dispersed after the second Sunday meeting Asquith needed all his imperturbability. He had listed with his customary lucidity the six factors which would tell on the decision. The problem lay, not in listing, but in weighing them. How great was the risk that France would be defeated, and 'wiped out as a Great Power', before the Russian 'steamroller' could be brought into action? Was it true that the dispatch of the Expeditionary Force would do nothing substantial to help the French? How would the Belgian government react to the arrival

---

[45] K. M. Wilson (ed.), op. cit. (above, n. 34), 7.

[46] *Brit. Docs. War*, 11 (1926), 224; Tuchman, op. cit. (above, n. 25), 90–2, 95.

[47] *Brit. Docs. War*, 11 (1926), 218, 234–5, 240; Grey, op. cit. (above, n. 42), i. 329–30.

[48] Spender and Asquith, op. cit. (above, n. 36), ii. 82.

of German troops on its soil? How would the Belgians'
reaction affect that of the British public? The Prime Minister
was not crushed by these problems. He 'loathed the levity'
of the London crowds cheering for war; but buoyed up
by Venetia Stanley's letters, and by having shelved the Ulster
problem, he was in his best form. At his Sunday lunch
he had seemed to Jack Pease 'the most self-possessed and
natural' person in the room: he and his guests had discussed
'the soundness of Dryden's English'. He now went off with
three of his children and Edwin Montagu to dine with the
McKennas.[49]

Everything looked uncertain that evening, including the
continued existence of a government capable of taking decisions.
John Simon composed his resignation letter over supper.[50]
When J. A. Spender was starting on his Life of Asquith in
1928 he put various questions to the surviving members of
the 1914 Cabinet. It seems from the answers that, in the
case of most Ministers at least, support for the Channel
pledge was not regarded as entailing naval war with Germany.
Grey said in his reply that the pledge had been 'suggested
originally by an anti-war member of the Cabinet. . . . It
did not pledge us to war,' he added, '[and] was not thought
of as so doing.'[51] It was hoped that, if the pledge should
involve intervening in the war, Britain's part in the fighting
could be confined to naval operations.[52] Much uncertainty
prevailed over the Belgian Treaty. Would either the Belgian
government or the British Cabinet regard a German march
through the Ardennes as a 'substantial' violation of neutrality,
such as had to be resisted in more than a formal fashion?
Herbert Samuel, who had played an important part in the
Sunday discussions, was optimistic about both of the Cabinet's
decisions.

[49] Blake, op. cit. (above, n. 3), 224; K. M. Wilson (ed.), op. cit. (above, n. 34),
9; Brock (eds.), op. cit. (above, n. 2), 148.
[50] G. A. Riddell, *War Diary* (London, 1933), 3–5; Maurice Hankey, The
Supreme Command, 1914–18, 2 vols. (London, 1961), i. 161.
[51] Br. Library, Add. MSS 46, 386, fos. 64, 75, 77, 81–2 (answers to Q. 9);
Grey, op. cit. (above, n. 42), ii. 2; Churchill, op. cit. (above, n. 29), i. 202.
[52] Churchill to Lloyd George, 31 July: R. Churchill (ed.), *Churchill,
Companion Documents, 1901–14* (London, 1969), 1119.

I still have hopes [he wrote to his wife that evening] that Germany will neither send her fleet down the Channel nor invade Belgium, and that we shall be able to keep England at peace while rendering France the greatest of all services—the protection of her northern coasts from the sea and the protection of her 150 miles of frontier with Belgium. If we can achieve this, without firing a shot, we shall have accomplished a brilliant stroke of policy.[53]

The distance between a pacific Liberal such as Samuel and the Conservative leaders with their cry for outright support of France and Russia was considerable. The Cabinet was still adamant against sending even the smallest part of the Expeditionary Force across the Channel.[54] Little could be predicted except that the Cabinet's stance, and any warlike moves which might be made, were liable to be intensely controversial.[55]

The German government now produced the solution to the British Prime Minister's problems. At 7 p.m. on that Sunday 2 August the German ambassador delivered an ultimatum to the Brussels government with a twelve-hour time-limit. It had been drafted by Moltke, the Commander-in-Chief, on 26 July and sent to the ambassador three days later.[56] Unimpeded passage for the German army was demanded through the whole of Belgium, on the demonstrably false pretext that French troops were planning to cross the Belgian frontier. News of the ultimatum reached Asquith on the morning of 3 August.[57] This was quickly followed by reports of Belgium's refusal of its terms and of King Albert's appeal to George V for diplomatic support.

As this news spread in London and beyond the whole tempo changed. Previous hesitations disappeared: the limits to

[53] See n. 44 above.
[54] *Brit. Docs. War*, 11 (1926), 253, 275; Taylor, op. cit. (above, n. 8), 526 n. 3 (Benckendorff); 65 HC Deb. 5s. col. 1824. On 3 Aug. both the Liberal paper with the largest circulation (*Daily Chronicle*) and the one nearest to the government (*Westminster Gazette*) pronounced against sending the BEF abroad. As an example of Liberal caution on this see 14 HL Deb. 5s. cols. 136–7 (Crewe, Apr. 1913): for Foreign Office caution see J. Gooch, *Plans of War* (London, 1974), 295 (Nicolson, Apr. 1914).
[55] For the intense partisanship which characterized views on foreign policy in the pre-war years see P. Gibbs, *Adventures in Journalism* (London, 1923), 204–10.
[56] S. B. Fay, *The Origins of the World War* (2nd edn. New York, 1947), 502.
[57] Asquith told Bonar Law and Lansdowne when they saw him that morning: A. Chamberlain, *Down the Years* (London, 1935), 103.

involvement were forgotten; the pending resignations were withdrawn. Asquith's laconic comments in his daily letters to Venetia Stanley show how the news struck him:

3 August. 'The Germans, with almost Austrian crassness, have delivered an ultimatum to Belgium.'

4 August. 'We had an interesting cabinet, as we got the news that the Germans had entered Belgium . . . This simplifies matters.'[58]

Once Grey had secured the support of the Commons on the afternoon of 3 August the decision to confront Berlin with an ultimatum was taken for granted. It was simply assumed that, if the German government would not abandon its plan to overrun the whole of Belgium, the British would join France and Russia in war by sea and land. The terms of this British ultimatum do not seem to have been the subject of formal cabinet discussion.[59] The decision to send it was made before the Belgians had appealed for military, as opposed to diplomatic, support, and before there was confirmation that the German forces were actually in Belgium in any numbers.[60] The time-limit was put as late as 11 p.m., 4 August, London time, solely because it was doubted whether all British naval units could be ready until then.[61] On 6 August the Cabinet decided, with 'much less demur' than the Premier had expected, to send an Expeditionary Force of four divisions and a cavalry division to France.[62] These were the men who a mere four days earlier had agonized over whether they ought to restrict the German fleet from operating in the Straits of Dover.

It would be a mistake to see this pressure on the government

---

[58] Brock (eds.), op. cit. (above, n. 2), 148, 150.

[59] See Churchill, op. cit. (above, n. 29), 220.

[60] *Daily Telegraph*, 3 Aug., reported sighting of German motor-cycle detachments in eastern Belgium. See also *Brit. Docs. War*, 11 (1926), 286. For discussion of these reports see *Times*, 1 June 1915, 6c. German troops did not enter Belgium in force until morning of 4 Aug. For Albert's determination not to call on guarantors for military help until then see E. J. Galet, *Albert* (London, 1931, trans. E. Swinton), 62–3; *Brit. Docs. War*, 11 (1926), 298, 309, 338, 339. When the call was made, the Belgian Crown Council resolved by a majority against imposing conditions on Belgium's 'rescuers'; the minority included the Foreign Minister: Helmreich, op. cit. (above, n. 14), 427.

[61] Williamson, op. cit. (above, n. 9), 360–1; Wilson (ed.), op. cit. (above, n. 34), 10–11. Grey's telegrams to the ambassador at Berlin required that a satisfactory answer 'be received here by twelve o'clock tonight'. This was taken to mean midnight by Central European Time; and the ultimatum was held to expire as Big Ben struck 11 p.m.   [62] Brock (eds.), op. cit. (above, n. 2), 158.

for outright intervention solely in terms of generous emotion. It was inspired, not only by a wish to rescue 'poor little Belgium', but by a sudden realization that Britain was in danger. Christopher Addison, a Liberal who belonged to the isolationist Foreign Affairs group, noted after Grey's speech:

It . . . satisfied, I think, all the House, with perhaps three or four exceptions, that we were compelled to participate; that the Kaiser meant to ride roughshod over Belgium and get onto the Channel coast; and that unless we were prepared to see both France and Belgium wiped out, with no guarantee that we ourselves would not be the next victims, we must join with France and Belgium — apart altogether from the fact that we were pledged, as much as a nation could be, to defend Belgium.[63]

There was hardly any criticism of the rapidity with which the German ultimatum to Brussels was answered by a British one to Berlin. 'It is a mistake', a journalist wrote in 1920, 'to say that Mr Asquith carried England into the war. England carried Mr Asquith into the war . . . A House of Commons that had hesitated an hour after the invasion of Belgium would have been swept out of existence by the wrath and indignation of the people.'[64]

How did Asquith's mind move during the twelve days of the war crisis? What was the basis of his notion that Britain could remain as a spectator of a continental war? What were the unexpected factors which proved him wrong? Asquith expected, reasonably enough, that the German government would wage war along lines which would not force Britain to join Germany's enemies. The invasion of Belgium could have been mounted along such lines. If the German advance had been confined to the Ardennes, the Belgians would probably have submitted to it after no more than formal resistance, and would not have called for military help from any of their guarantors. Early in 1914 what purported to be a version of the Schlieffen Plan, in which the advance was restricted in this manner, found its way into a French

[63] C. Addison, *Four and a Half Years* (London, 1934), i. 32. This diary passage was dictated at the end of August.

[64] *The Mirrors of Downing Street* (London, 1920), 43–4. The anonymous author was Harold Begbie. See also H. B. Needham's interview with Lloyd George, *Pearson's Magazine*, Mar. 1915, p. 264; Lloyd George's Savoy Hotel speech, 12 Apr. 1917.

military journal: it was said to have been taken from German staff papers mislaid in a railway carriage. This naturally attracted the attention of the Belgian Foreign Ministry, and the Ministry's archives contain an unsigned minute on the matter in the hand of Baron Gaiffier, its Political Director. Gaiffier wrote that, if the German forces took the Ardennes route, the best course for the Belgians would be to enter a formal protest, to withdraw their forces north of the Meuse, and to stay quiet.[65] After the war, when it was almost treasonable to represent Belgian policy as less than heroic, one person still disclaimed all poses. In response to an expression of admiration for his noble conduct King Albert said: 'We were cornered into it.'[66]

In one area the German high command proved to have no intention of provoking Britain. There was to be no immediate challenge to the British fleet. How far Asquith foresaw this on 24 July, or indeed on 2 August when the Channel pledge was given, is not clear. Grey's remarks after the war, already quoted,[67] are suggestive, however. Some ministers must have appreciated that the German high command would need to put a very high value on bombarding the French coasts if they were to insist on this operation at the cost of adding Britain to their opponents. Trying to interrupt the passage of the British Expeditionary Force would be a good deal less effective than ensuring that it never sailed. Churchill recorded that he had been one of those holding this view about the Channel pledge. The Prime Minister may well have been another.

There were weighty reasons for judging that the attack on France would be left wholly to the German army. Even if it were assumed (as was indeed true) that Moltke and his colleagues did not shrink from provoking the British, there were technical reasons why bombarding the French coasts and trying to sink the BEF's transports would be unprofitable operations. The German high seas fleet had a short range of action. Its battleships had been built on the assumption of a British descent on the Heligoland Bight.[68] Everyone knew that the submarine and the mine were altering the terms of naval warfare. The obvious course for the

[65] See Helmreich, op. cit. (above, n. 14), 425.
[66] Tuchman, op. cit. (above, n. 25), 179.
[67] Br. Library, Add. MSS 46, 386, fos. 81–2.
[68] H. H. Herwig, *Luxury Fleet* (London, 1980), 147–9.

German Admiralty would be to delay any challenge to Jellicoe's larger fleet until these new weapons had whittled away Britain's superiority.[69] Despite its prominence in Grey's speech in the Commons the exchange of letters of November 1912 did not do much to bring Britain into the war; nor, in the event, did the reorganization of the British and French fleets which had preceded that exchange.[70]

Herbert Samuel clearly thought that the German high command, whatever their plans, would keep out of the Channel in order to keep Britain out of the war. The reverse was the case. The German fleet was kept out of the Channel because the high command had no fear of British intervention. No ships were to be risked even in the attempt to stop the BEF from crossing to France. If the British should throw their contemptible little army into the struggle, those six or seven divisions were to be caught by the great wheel of the German right wing and put into the bag with their French allies. An assurance that the German fleet would not operate in the Channel, provided that Britain would agree not to intervene, was duly issued by the German Embassy in London and appeared in the *Westminster Gazette* on the afternoon of 3 August.[71]

Asquith's initial assumptions were not unreasonable; yet for all his enormous ability he was not notably percipient. His prediction to Venetia on 24 July enshrined two large illusions. He assumed the British public to be as pacific as it seemed, and the German statesmen to be in control of their generals. In neither instance was the true situation easy to discern.

When Asquith wrote to Venetia it was difficult to imagine the British cheering for war against Germany. It had been the general impression in London during the spring and summer that relations between the two countries were better than for years past. On 14 May 1914 the Committee of Imperial Defence decided to 'act

[69] See, for instance, C. à Court Repington, *Blackwood's Magazine*, 187 (June 1910), 893-900, on 'the submarine menace'.

[70] Churchill had wanted in 1912 to take precautions against a misinterpretation by the French of the Admiralty's new dispositions. He wrote to Asquith, Aug. 1912: 'If France did not exist, we should make no other disposition of our forces': Asquith, op. cit. (above, n. 6), 83.

[71] See *Brit. Docs. War*, 11 (1926), 293. On 3 Aug. Grey told the Commons that this was 'too narrow an engagement'. By that time the ultimatum to Belgium had made the offer irrelevant.

on the assumption that the present international situation is likely to continue for the next three to four years'.[72] On 27 May the British press entertained a party of visiting German journalists to a luncheon in London at which a Conservative MP, giving the toast of the German press, 'affirmed the unbreakable ties of friendship between [the] two peoples'.[73] In June Conservative papers hailed the Kaiser as Britain's friend,[74] Conservative spokesmen having long made clear that the Ulster Protestants would rather be ruled by the Kaiser than by Roman Catholics from Dublin.[75] In the same month— June 1914—the Foreign Secretary thought: 'The German government are in a peaceful mood and . . . are very anxious to be on good terms with England.'[76] On the very day of the Austrian ultimatum to Serbia—23 July—Lloyd George, the Chancellor of the Exchequer, told the Commons that relations with Germany were 'very much better' than they had been 'a few years ago'.[77]

This British euphoria in 1914 was in contrast not only with the fears which prevailed on the Continent, but with warnings published in Britain only a little earlier. In 1912 the Russian military agent in Berlin had reported that the German leaders would see 1914 as giving them their best, and perhaps their last,

---

[72] S. Roskill, *Hankey, 1877-1918* (London, 1970), 135.

[73] P. Gibbs, op. cit. (above, n. 55), 214. The speaker was the Hon. Harry Lawson (who succeeded, 1916, as 2nd Lord Burnham). Gibbs gives date as 'June 1914', but 27 May seems correct (*Times*, 28 May, 6c).

[74] 23 June, when the British Fleet was visiting Kiel: *Daily Graphic*, 4b; *Morning Post*, 8e.

[75] For Ulster's attitude to Germany see Bonar Law, 1 Jan. 1913 (46 HC Deb. 5s. cols. 464, 471): *Morning Post*, 19 Dec. 1910, 9 Jan. 1911 (Andrews, Craig); A. T. Q. Stewart, *The Ulster Crisis* (London, 1967), 226. The Ulster Covenanters were not popular in Germany: F. Prill, *Ireland, Britain, and Germany, 1871-1914* (London, 1975), 134.

[76] K. Robbins, *Grey* (London, 1971), 287. On 5 May Nicolson told Goschen: 'Since I have been at the Foreign Office I have not seen such calm waters': Z. S. Steiner, *Britain and the Origins of the First World War* (London, 1977), 215. On 6 July Nicolson 'trusted' that Sarajevo would have 'no serious political consequences . . . outside of Austria-Hungary': *Brit. Docs. War*, 11 (1926), 25. See also B. J. Hendrick, *W. H. Page* (London, 1923), i. 288-9 for Col. House's reactions in June 1914 (though the impression of complacency given by the leading Liberals may have owed something to their determination not to alarm the French by adopting House's suggestions).

[77] 65 HC Deb. 5s. col. 727. He had spoken similarly at the Mansion House, 17 July.

chance of victory.[78] A report in *The Times* in August 1913 pointed to much the same conclusion.[79] The German military chiefs would want to strike, it was argued, as soon as their own army increases had become effective, and before French three-year military service and Russian railway improvements had tipped the balance against them. It seems odd that the British did not draw more alarming conclusions from the once-for-all capital levy for military purposes just collected by the German government;[80] but the strangest aspect of the euphoria concerns the area in which the British had usually been over-sensitive, namely naval affairs. The widening of the Kiel Canal to allow the passage of the newest German Dreadnoughts had begun in 1908. Ever since then the completion year for the widening had been foreseen as the likely date for Armageddon.[81] In 1908, during one of the Carnot debates held at Stanford University, a speaker expressed the fear that war would break out in 1914 when Germany would at last be able to deploy her fleet handily.[82] In 1911 Lord Fisher, the father of the Dreadnoughts, had been sure that Armageddon would start late in 1914.[83] Yet when the

---

[78] I. V. Bestuzhev, *Journal of Contemporary History*, 1/3 (July 1966), 96. See also A. Chamberlain, *Politics from Inside* (London, 1936), 123 (Dutch naval officers, 1908), 528 (M. Le Bon, Mar. 1913). These reports were largely correct: see Bethmann Hollweg's remark (1917): '[In 1914] the soldiers were saying that now it can still be fought without a defeat but not in two years from now': quoted F. Fischer, *War of Illusions*, trans. M. Jackson (London, 1975), 468.

[79] 20 Aug., 5d (by Repington).

[80] See the comments on British disregard of German war preparations in R. C. K. Ensor, *England, 1870–1914* (London, 1936), 469–71, 481–2. For Ensor's role in 1914 see above, n. 8. For Conan Doyle's comment in 1917 see 'Baron von Herling's' remarks in *His Last Bow: The Annotated Sherlock Holmes* (London, 1968), ii. 794.

[81] The significance of the widening was perceived by several British observers in 1908. See S. Gwynn (ed.), *Letters and Friendships of Sir Cecil Spring Rice* (London, 1929), ii. 115. Sir Charles Hardinge and other Foreign Office officials had seen the start of the canal works when on their way to Reval in the Royal Yacht in June 1908. Hardinge had even been told the completion date by an indiscreet German officer. He 'warned the Foreign Office that in five years time the Germans would be ready': Countess of Antrim's diary (Lord Bicester's MSS).

[82] I am grateful to Professor Emeritus Robert N. Boyd, New York University, for this information. The speaker was his father, De Estraye Cassell Boyd.

[83] R. H. Bacon, *Fisher* (London, 1929), ii. 139. Fisher put the date at October because he expected the Germans to complete harvesting before they marched. See also Roskill, op. cit. (above, n. 72), i. 119. Churchill, when briefing the Canadian ministers in a CID meeting, 11 July 1912, had stressed the significance of the Kiel Canal operations: Asquith, op. cit. (above, n. 6), 80.

widening was actually completed in the summer of 1914 little or no alarm was expressed in Britain.

Some of the optimism should be attributed to the willingness of the German government to compose long-standing differences. The Portuguese colonies question had been settled, though the agreement was still unsigned; and in June a settlement was achieved over the Baghdad railway.[84] The dominant reason why the warnings went unheeded was, however, of another kind. In 1914 the British not merely misjudged the continental scene: they neglected it. Everyone was thinking of what might soon happen, not on the Continent, but across the Irish Channel. It would be hard to exaggerate the degree to which Home Rule and the problem of Ulster were engrossing the attention of British people in 1914. A single example of this immense preoccupation must suffice. If one English writer had preached military preparedness for European war, it was Rudyard Kipling. Yet when, in December 1913, he was reminded by his friend, the editor of the *Morning Post*, of the German danger, Kipling replied entirely in terms of Home Rule. 'Does it occur to you', he wrote, 'that a betrayed Ulster will repeat 1688 in the shape of a direct appeal to Germany?'[85] Earlier in 1913 the Conservative leaders had been denouncing the Territorial Army as a sham and asserting that, once the expeditionary force was across the Channel, the country would be vulnerable to invasion. By the spring of 1914 all this had apparently been forgotten. The party leadership seemed ready to promote military disruption. It discussed whether the Conservative peers should amend the annual Army Act, and went on to exploit what was virtually a mutiny by cavalry officers at the Curragh. Earl Roberts, who had been the foremost advocate of compulsory national service, was now giving all his energies to organizing Ulster's private army.

Even in 1914 there were, however, some differences between Liberals and Conservatives in matters of war and defence. When faced with the prospect of a European war neither A. J. Balfour nor Austen Chamberlain would have predicted that the British

[84] Taylor, op. cit. (above, n. 8), 504, 518.
[85] C. Carrington, *Kipling* (London, 1955), 419. See also other letters from Kipling to Gwynne in Kipling Papers, Sussex University, 15/15/101, 104.

could remain as 'spectators'.[86] Coming as he did from the Liberal Imperialist wing of his party, Asquith was more alert to foreign dangers than most Liberals. Moreover, unlike his followers, he had not been wholly unprepared for the news which reached him on 24 July.[87] But his slight defect in percipience made him liable to be unduly impressed by the views of those nearest to him. He could predict the reactions of the Liberal back-benchers better than those of the public at large. The part of the electorate which he knew best was the most pacific and isolationist section of all. For many stalwart Liberals it was an article of faith that Tories were jingoes, bent on enslaving the working class through military conscription and then on embroiling Britain needlessly in war.[88] From this it might be inferred that appeals for Britain to intervene in support of France and Russia represented, at best the Tories bowing down to what John Bright had called 'this foul idol', the balance of power, at worst an attempt by Northcliffe and the other Conservative press lords once again to use a war scare to boost the circulations of their deplorable newspapers.[89] It was not easy for the Premier or his whips, operating, as they did, among Liberal stalwarts, to judge how opinion would move outside the National Liberal Club.

[86] For Balfour see *The Times*, 20 Nov. 1908 (Cardiff speech); 41 HC Deb. 5s., 22 July 1912, col. 866. It was Austen Chamberlain who insisted, 2 Aug., on the opposition's letter to Asquith.

[87] Grey's account, 6 July, of Lichnowsky's warnings (*Brit. Docs. War*, 11 (1926), 24–5) went to King and Cabinet: see Brock (eds.), op. cit. (above n. 2), 93.

[88] A. J. A. Morris, *The Scaremongers* (London, 1984), gives many instances of these beliefs and of the grounds for them. See, for instance, the quotation (p. 342) from C. P. Trevelyan, *Democracy and the Public Service* (London, 1913). For H. W. Massingham's view of the conscription campaign as 'a covert conspiracy to militarise the country and to undermine civil liberties', see A. F. Havighurst, *Massingham* (London, 1974), 221. Curzon and the editor of *The Times* were among those whose advocacy of conscription did not relate solely to national defence: Lord (Laurence) Ronaldshay, *The Life of Lord Curzon*, i–iii (London, 1928), iii. 118; *The Times*, 10 Dec. 1912, 9d. George Wyndham thought in 1907 that 'terror of Germany' might help to save 'the gentry of England': J. W. Mackail and Guy Wyndham, *Life and Letters of George Wyndham*, ii. 586.

[89] See, for instance, A. G. Gardiner's reply to Northcliffe's *Scaremongerings* pamphlet: *Daily News*, 5 Dec. 1914, 6d, e. For the suppression in the *Daily Chronicle* of items on German militarism see P. Gibbs, op. cit. (above, n. 55), 204–16; R. C. K. Ensor, op. cit. (above, n. 80), 484 n. 1. For Bright's phrase see J. E. Thorold Rogers (ed.), *Bright's Speeches* (London, 1869), 332 (Birmingham, 18 Jan. 1865).

Judging the movement even of Liberal opinion was difficult enough, since it involved assessing how a group of people, not all of whom were noted for realism, would react when their illusions had been stripped from them. Some Liberal back-benchers would not even recognize that a German attack on France was bound to come via Belgium. It was another article of faith in the party that militarist Germany was not as black as it was painted. 'Germany', the Liberal *Nation* had pronounced in March 1913, 'would not violate the neutrality of Belgium for the sake of some small military advantage if she might otherwise reckon on our neutrality.' On 29 July or thereabouts Grey was accosted in the lobby by a very active Liberal back-bencher who said, 'in a dictatorial tone', that Britain must not, under any circumstances whatever, intervene in the war. 'Suppose Germany violates the neutrality of Belgium?' the Foreign Secretary asked. 'For a moment,' Grey recorded, the MP 'paused, like one who, running at speed, finds himself confronted with an obstacle, unexpected and unforeseen. Then he said with emphasis "She won't do it." "I don't say she will, but supposing she does." "She won't do it," he repeated confidently.'[90]

Asquith was right to suppose that not merely fervent Liberals, but the British people as a whole, were pacifically inclined, and would want to stay out of the war. But we can see more clearly than he could that very few of them had any idea of what miseries and sacrifices intervention in the struggle might entail. Some barely realized that it might mean sending large British armies abroad. Nearly all of the recent fictional accounts of the 'coming war' had been stories about an invasion of Britain:[91] these invasion stories were indeed of so well recognized a pattern by 1914 that P. G. Wodehouse had published a skit on them.[92] Haldane's Territorial Army was meant to help in defending Britain. His Territorials had no obligation to serve overseas.[93]

---

[90] Grey, op. cit. (above, n. 42), i. 338.

[91] See I. F. Clarke, *Voices Prophesying War* (London, 1966), 131–61.

[92] *The Swoop, or How Clarence Saved England* (London, 1909).

[93] Even those who were devising Britain's war strategy did not suppose that the British would contribute an army of continental size in war: Roskill, op. cit. (above, n. 72), i. 134. Until Kitchener's call for recruits in Aug. 1914 there had been no notion of training a great army during a war. See, for instance, F. E. Smith, *Unionist Policy and Other Essays* (London, 1913), 77–8.

Again, Norman Angell had achieved an enormous sale for his book, *The Great Illusion*, first published with that title in 1910. Angell's thesis was that, as between advanced states, successful armed aggression would not bring any economic benefits to the aggressor. That certainly might have inculcated the view that the fear of Germany dominating Europe rested on outmoded preconceptions; and Angell's huge British readership showed the British to be anything but warmongers. Yet Angell denounced aggressive war, not defensive resistance; and some of what he wrote made intervention in war seem less frightening, for he had been eloquent on the economic impossibility of a long war.[94]

Angell wrote for the well-educated and articulate. These were not the circles about which Asquith was least perceptive. He found difficulty, as a highly trained intellectual, in seeing into the minds of simpler people; and there were a great many in the Britain of 1914 who had no more than primary education. The reaction of these people became important as the threat to France emerged. They lived, or tried intermittently to live, by a few simple rules. One of these was that you stood by your friends when they were in trouble. The Entente with France was ten years old. Asquith failed to foresee that, now the French ranked as friends, the man in the street would want to help them when they were in great danger.

Asquith could not have supposed that the British would want to remain as spectators of the war if, on an appeal from the Belgian government, they judged it to be both their duty and their interest to intervene. His prediction on 24 July thus hinged on the expectation that the German advance through Belgium would be confined to the Ardennes. The British and French experts did not know that the German commanders had overcome the two greatest problems entailed by an invasion of central and north Belgium. To prolong their right wing without denuding the centre and left they had devised ways of using reserve divisions to maximum effect in the front line by 'corseting' them between

[94] See J. D. B. Miller, *Norman Angell and the Futility of War* (London, 1986), 4–10, for an account of the growth of 'Angellism' between 1910 and 1914.

'active service' divisions.[95] To batter the Liège forts into quick submission Krupps had produced an artillery piece of unprecedented power, the 420-mm. howitzer. Only seven of these monstrous weapons were available when the invasion of Belgium began.[96] That proved to be enough. Henry Wilson's assessment was wrong. Apart from the very dubious evidence of those staff papers found in the railway carriage, there seems to be no reason for supposing that the German General Staff ever meant to confine the invasion of Belgium to the Ardennes.

Wilson may have had an ulterior motive in 1911 for assessing the position as he did. He had been faced at that stage with Liberal politicians who were hesitant about the whole idea of sending a British army to the Continent. It is hard to avoid the suspicion that he had wanted to depict a German deployment in the west in which the BEF would make the crucial difference to the numerical balance between the opposing armies. Suggesting that the German right wing would not be extended north of the Meuse helped him to give this account of the BEF's role. If the Germans stayed south of the Sambre–Meuse line, the French would be able to meet their enemy on level terms in the crucial sector, since the force marching westward through the Ardennes would have to be limited to what could be deployed and supplied along the roads of that region.[97]

If Wilson's assessment owed something to political calculation, the outcome held some irony. By July 1914 his analysis was producing the reverse effects to the ones he wanted, since it enabled the Cabinet's isolationists, on the assumption that Brussels would not call for help, to descant on the absurdity of

[95] The French Deuxième Bureau had known for some months before August 1914 that the German reserves would be used in the offensive; but they did not discover the full extent of this use until 24 Aug.: Tuchman, op. cit. (above, n. 25), 53, 282. See also C. E. Callwell, *Dug Out* (London, 1920), 16–17.

[96] Five of the rail, two of the road, model. See Tuchman, op. cit. (above, n. 25), ch. 11. The Škoda 305-mm. howitzer was also effective against the forts which Brialmont had designed in the 1880s. Krupp was large enough to finance construction of the first 420-mm. weapons; and the absence of any published financial allocation had helped to keep them secret. I am grateful to Dr H. J. O. Pogge von Strandmann for this information.

[97] Wilson calculated that each of the thirteen roads to the Verdun–Maubeuge sector could accommodate three German divisions, and that against this force the French could probably place 37 to 39 divisions; CID, 114th Meeting, 23 Aug. 1911: see n. 18 above.

being 'more Belgian than the Belgians'. In justice to Wilson we should keep in mind that the French staff agreed with his prediction.[98] Unlike the British, however, the French generals did not greatly mind whether it proved to be right or wrong. They were confident that if the German army made the wide sweep through central Belgium, they could cut it in half.[99] Churchill and others had questioned Wilson's view, and Wilson himself retained some doubts about it; but he seems never to have been asked the crucial question. Granted that the Schlieffen Plan depended on a very strong right wing, were the German General Staff likely to assent to a route which put a sharp physical limit on the strength of that wing?

A good deal can be said, however, in defence of Henry Wilson and his colleagues. They cannot be blamed for misinterpreting the preparations on the Belgian border. Those were entirely compatible either with an advance through the Ardennes or with an irruption into central and north Belgium via the capture of Liège. This was an age when an army, once beyond its railheads, moved at no more than three and a half miles an hour. Wilson was right to point to the almost insuperable problems of speed and supply which a wheel right through Belgium would impose.[100] What he failed to stress was that the Ardennes route represented no solution for the German General Staff: it would merely have entailed weakening Schlieffen's concept to the point of ineffectiveness.

Henry Wilson was dealing with political leaders of considerable stature. Asquith and Churchill were not liable to be overborne in judgment by his plausible presentations. The expectation in the British Cabinet that the Ardennes route would be chosen was not merely the lazy and wishful thinking of dedicated isolationists. Much as he hated war, Asquith did not rule out siding with France, whatever happened in Belgium and whatever the reaction of the Belgian government. In so far as he misjudged the event he did so because of the second of his illusions. When he looked towards Bethmann Hollweg he assumed that Bethmann would decide a

---

[98] As Gleichen makes clear, op. cit. (above, n. 18), 340–2.
[99] Tuchman, op. cit. (above, n. 25), 39 (de Castelnau).
[100] See L. F. C. Turner on 'the fatuous blunder of trying to maintain more than 600,000 men through the narrow aperture of Liège': P. M. Kennedy (ed.), *The War Plans of the Great Powers* (London, 1979), 213.

question as he would have decided it himself. He did not know how little control the Kaiser and Bethmann exercised. A country where the Chancellor hardly dared to ask the General Staff what they were doing was outside his comprehension. He assumed that, when it came to the moment of decision, the German government would be likely to choose an invasion route which would not force Belgium to call for British military help.

We do not know everything about what happened during the last days of July in Berlin and Potsdam; but we can be sure that events there belied Asquith's assumptions. The General Staff had concealed from the political leaders the worst political horror in their war plans, namely that their first objective was the capture of Liège and its forts. They needed a head start in the war in order to mount a surprise attack there; and they might decide to follow that with a massive bombardment. Bethmann does not seem to have been told this until 31 July.[101] The General Staff were in charge. Their mastery of organization, and their new 420-mm. howitzers, tempted them to keep to the bold course; but by 1914 the plans of Schlieffen and Moltke, devised and altered over the years, had become impossible to fulfil.

When Schlieffen went to work in the 1890s Russian mobilization was agonizingly slow. By 1914 it had been greatly accelerated: the railways were much improved, a strategic railway system being far advanced.[102] The German objective of destroying the French army before the Russian divisions were ready to advance had always been ambitious: it now seemed almost unattainable. Moltke dared not reinforce Germany's

---

[101] G. Ritter *The Sword and the Sceptre*, trans. H. Norden (London, 1972), ii. 266–7. The decision to start operations with the surprise attack on Liège had been taken by the General Staff in April 1913. After the war Bethmann Hollweg laid stress on how little he had known about the details of the General Staff's plans (Ritter, op. cit. (above, n. 17), 96).

[102] See N. Stone, *Europe Transformed, 1878–1919* (London, 1983), 335–6. Professor Stone has pointed out that Russia's Plan 20, which was due to come into effect in Sept. 1914, was intended to reduce the Russian mobilization period from thirty to eighteen days. The improvements in the Russian railways were widely noted in diplomatic circles. See Robbins, op. cit. (above, n. 76), 289 (Bertie's account of Grey's views, 16 July 1914). German spies had reported to Berlin that the Russians would not be 'ready' until 1916: A. von Tirpitz, *My Memoirs* (London, 1919), i. 343. On 26 July the Belgian Minister in Berlin reported that such factors as the remaining defects in the Russian railway system gave Germany a chance of waging a successful war which was unlikely to recur: J. B. Scott (ed.), *Carnegie Dipl. Docs.* (London, 1916), i. 429.

eastern defences against the expected Russian advance. France's military resurgence had induced him to strengthen his forces on the Franco-German frontier by shifting some of his weight on the western front from right to centre: he had to rule out any further weakening of the right wing.[103] As he could not slow down 'the Russian steamroller', an extremely rapid advance through Belgium had become all-important in his strategy. There could be no gingerly treatment of Belgian neutrality. Halts in the hope that the Belgian commanders would receive their 'cease fire' orders were out of the question. The decision to leave the Netherlands inviolate ruled out any initial advance on a broad front, with the German troops flooding over the Belgian frontier at many points like water over a dam. By the third week after mobilization, Liège and its forts had to be in German hands.[104]. Half measures had never been favoured by the German high command: by 1914 they seemed out of the question. Guarding against any delay had to take priority over what looked like a foredoomed effort to ensure that the British did not make their futile intervention. An ultimatum demanding full facilities must accordingly be presented to the Belgian government. Should this be accepted, the way would be clear.[105] Should it not be, ruthless methods, for which the Belgians would bear the responsibility, could be applied at once to safeguard the advance.

Asquith would never have referred to the 1839 Treaties as a 'scrap of paper';[106] but when he wrote to Venetia on 24 July 1914 he thought of them as documents which would leave him considerable freedom of action. It would have been one thing

---

[103] Schlieffen had made the German right wing six times as strong as the left: Moltke had reduced this preponderance to two to one: J. Terraine, *Mons* (London, 1960), 14.

[104] Ritter, op. cit. (above, n. 17), 166–7.

[105] Moltke's political obtuseness is shown by his hope that he could 'come to an understanding' with the Belgian government when they 'realized the seriousness of the situation': B. E. Schmitt, *Coming of the War* (New York, 1930), ii. 390 n. A last attempt to secure the Belgian government's submission was initiated on 9 Aug. The proposal reached King Albert via the Dutch government on 12 Aug. It was refused. Moltke also hoped that the ultimatum to Brussels would enrage the French into entering Belgium before the German army had done so: Fischer, op. cit. (above, n. 78), 510.

[106] Whether Bethmann Hollweg actually used this phrase to the British ambassador on 4 Aug. is discussed in Christopher Howard (ed.), *Diary of Edward Goschen, 1900–1914* (London, 1980), 298–302.

to be able to weigh up Gladstone's words of 1870, in light of a report that some German troops had crossed the Belgian frontier. To receive an appeal from King Albert when Brussels had been subjected to a brutal ultimatum was totally different. Lichnowsky, the German ambassador in London, was an Anglophile; yet, like Bethmann Hollweg, he could not quite comprehend what had happened. 'So it is all over,' he said reproachfully to Margot Asquith on 4 August, 'and you knew we *must* go through Belgium—there is no other way. We never counted that old, old treaty.'[107]

It is still extremely hard to analyse the twelve-day process by which Asquith was convinced that the British could not remain as 'spectators' of the war. Professor Arno Mayer suggested some years ago that the Liberal government indulged in excessive military preparedness and in 'diplomatic obduracy as part of their efforts to maintain a precarious domestic status quo'.[108] This theory does not square with the Ministers' actions and remarks during the war crisis. If Asquith had been pushing Britain towards war in order to be free of his Ulster troubles, he would have kept quiet about this sinister motive for promoting British intervention. His behaviour was not in the least like that. He mentioned casually and openly to every Liberal friend he met that there was one consolation in the whole ghastly business: it would put Carson and company in the shade.[109] The British government, like some others, expected war to generate disorder, rather than stave it off. Asquith held back two divisions of the BEF on 6 August because 'the domestic situation might be grave; and colonial troops and territorials could not be called on to aid the civil power'.[110]

[107] Diary, 1912–1914, 637: Bonham Carter Papers.
[108] 'Domestic Causes of the First World War' in L. Krieger and F. Stern (eds.), *The Responsibility of Power* (New York, 1969), 313.
[109] Brock (eds.), op. cit. (above, n. 2), 123, 126; R. Gathorne-Hardy (ed.), *Ottoline* (London, 1963), 258; Wilson (ed.), op. cit. (above, n. 34), 11. Asquith was not the only Liberal to express this view: see L. Masterman (ed.), *Mary Gladstone* (London, 1930), 477; H. Samuel to his wife, 29 July: HLRO, Samuel Papers, A/157/691.
[110] See 'War Council' minutes, meeting of 6 Aug.: PRO CAB 22/1/2. Kitchener seems to have hinted later that he had wanted to send all six infantry divisions; but the minutes show that this was not so: E. David (ed.), *Inside Asquith's Cabinet: Charles Hobhouse's Diaries* (London, 1977), 188–9. For Morley's fears of 'violence and tumult' see Morley, op. cit. (above, n. 8), 5–6.

It is arguable, and indeed highly probable, that, even if the German invasion of Belgium had been such as to provoke no serious resistance and no appeal to the guarantor powers, the British would soon have been fighting beside the French armies. That does not make the ultimatum to Belgium unimportant. A British decision to support France on land would have been very different from the decision to give Belgium all aid in resisting the German invasion. The second decision was taken quickly and supported by nearly the whole nation. The first would have been taken by a nation sharply divided, after much delay. It would almost certainly have been preceded by an acute governmental crisis. It might not have been taken in time for the British divisions to help in saving Paris.

The phrase, 'a decision to support France on land', represents a slight over-simplification, since Asquith and Grey, as was made clear above, had never envisaged a European war in which Belgium would be left inviolate. If the German army had simply marched through the Ardennes, and the Belgian government had decided neither to offer serious resistance nor to call on the guarantor powers even for diplomatic help, the German government would still have violated the 1839 treaty. The fears that this treaty-breaking power might achieve European dominance, and the calls to stand by France, would have been undiminished. On the other hand, traditional British alarms about Antwerp and the mouth of the Schelde falling into hostile hands would have been lessened; and many Liberals would have remained resolutely opposed to British intervention. In summary, Asquith and Grey would have had by 4 August reasons for intervening, and perhaps an inclination to intervene, almost as strong as those which they actually had in the event.[111] They would not have had the same overwhelming support for intervention from Parliament and people. There would have been doubts and hesitations about a British intervention against

---

[111] Both maintained afterwards, in Grey's words (Robbins, op. cit. (above, n. 76), 297), 'but for Belgium we should have kept out of it'. If this meant merely 'but for the infraction of Belgian neutrality', it was probably true. In so far as it connoted 'but for a Belgian appeal for our intervention', it was extremely dubious. As Lloyd George told C. P. Scott (T. Wilson (ed.), op. cit. (above, n. 22), 104), Grey's agreement not to 'insist on supporting France', provided 'Germany respected Belgian neutrality', meant little. Grey knew that the condition would not be fulfilled.

Germany on land. We should therefore be chary of suggesting that Asquith and Grey used the German ultimatum to Belgium simply as an excuse for intervention, simply as an explanation for a course on which they had already decided.[112] It probably did not alter what they wanted to do; but almost certainly it altered their judgment of what they could do, and of the speed at which this could be done. They used the ultimatum as an excuse; but, as that journalist wrote in 1920, it was also a propellant.[113]

We must concentrate not on the might-have-beens, but on what actually happened. As things turned out the ultimatum to Belgium was the climacteric point in the crisis. The world of 1914 is distant from ours and an effort of historical imagination is needed to understand it. We are looking at a generation of British people brought up in peaceful times. Their ignorance of war and its horrors allowed free play to their firm notions of what could not be tolerated. In the governing and professional classes there was a conviction that, if a Great Power were allowed to break an international agreement and to invade a small neighbour with impunity, European civilization would sustain a blow from which it might not recover. This was believed to be a risk even greater than that of intervening in the war. There was still much deference in British society: that view in a simplified form was accepted right down the social scale.

Once the Belgians had been faced with the German ultimatum, and had decided to fight and to call for help, most British people were convinced that their country must join in the struggle against Germany. Here is the testimony of Lord Loreburn, one of Grey's fiercest Liberal critics, an isolationist and Little Englander *par excellence*. He told C. P. Scott in September 1914 that he had decided to abstain from any further criticism of the government's foreign policy because 'if [Germany] persisted in attacking Belgium there was a just cause for us to defend Belgium'.[114]

---

[112] The view that the ultimatum provided no more than an excuse for decisions already made has, however, been ably argued by Wilson: op. cit. (above, n. 41).

[113] For the post-war controversies on this see F. Eyck, *G. P. Gooch* (London, 1982), 327; *Manchester Guardian*, 25 Oct. 1928.

[114] Wilson (ed.), op. cit. (above, n. 22), 106.

Here, from the other side, is a comment from one of the more pacific Conservative leaders. On 2 August Selborne wrote to a friend: 'Is not this war cloud awful? Any sympathies I have are with Austria, and for us to be involved in this Armageddon seems as indefensible as intolerable. . . . If Belgium or Holland summoned us, then my conscience would be clear because that would be a *casus foederis*.'[115]

Here, finally, is the sovereign whom Asquith regarded as the archetypal 'man in the street' of 1914 Britain. 'My God, Mr Page,' George V exclaimed to the American Ambassador, 'what else could we do?'[116]

The German ultimatum to Brussels gave the concept of the invasion of Belgium a new connotation. On 29 July the Cabinet had decided that the decision whether to resist such an invasion would be 'rather one of policy than of legal obligation'. On 6 August Asquith told the Commons: 'We are fighting . . . in the first place to fulfil a solemn international obligation which, if it had been entered into between private persons in the ordinary concerns of life, would have been regarded as an obligation not only of law but of honour, which no self-respecting man could possibly have repudiated.'[117]

For the three years preceding the war Churchill had never doubted that the German army would march through Belgium. This would hardly be guessed from the passage in *The World Crisis* where the decision to invade Belgium is coupled with the later one to wage unrestricted submarine warfare:

On two supreme occasions the German Imperial Government, quenching compunction, outfacing conscience, deliberately, with calculation, with sinister resolve, severed the underlying bonds which sustained the civilization of the world and which united, even in their quarrels, the human family. The invasion of Belgium and the unlimited U-boat war were both resorted to on expert dictation as the only means of victory. They proved the direct cause of ruin. They drew into the struggle against Germany mighty and intangible powers by which her strength was remorselessly borne down. Nothing could have deprived Germany of victory in the first year of the war except the invasion of Belgium; nothing could have denied it to her in its last year except her unlimited submarine

[115] To Edith Lyttelton: Chandos Papers, Churchill College, i: 5/19.
[116] Hendrick, op. cit. (above, n. 76), i. 309.
[117] 65 HC Deb. 5s. col. 2079.

campaign. Not to the number of her enemies, nor to their resources or wisdom; not to the mistakes of her Admirals and Generals in open battle; not to the weakness of her allies; not assuredly to any fault in the valour of her population or her armies; but only to those two grand crimes and blunders of history, were her undoing and our salvation due.'[118]

It would be mistaken to attribute these passages to the insincerity which is so often a part of war-making or its aftermath. In them Asquith and Churchill were simply expressing, not so much their own reactions to the German ultimatum to Brussels, as that of their countrymen. In 1986, on British television's Channel Four, an elderly Scotsman recounted his experiences in the Somme Battle. He was asked why he had volunteered for service. The passage of seventy years had not led him to alter or qualify his answer. He had been 'convinced', he said, 'of the rightness of the cause'; and he added: 'We knew that Germany had broken her treaty with Belgium.'

[118] Churchill, op. cit. (above, n. 29), 335–6.

INDEX